ARTHUR G. PATZIA

THE MAKING OF THE NEW TESTAMENT

ORIGIN, COLLECTION,
TEXT & CANON

FOREWORD BY
GEORGE R. BEASLEY-MURRAY

InterVarsity Press
Downers Grove, Illinois

InterVarsity Press® is the book-publishing division of InterVarsity Christian Fellowship®, a student movement active on campus at hundreds of universities, colleges and schools of nursing in the United States of America, and a member movement of the International Fellowship of Evangelical Students. For information about local and regional activities, write Public Relations Dept., InterVarsity Christian Fellowship, 6400 Schroeder Rd., P.O. Box 7895, Madison, WI 53707-7895.

Cover illustration: Foto Marburg/Art Resource, NY. The Evangelist Matthew from Gospel Book of Bishop Ebbo of Reims (816-834), Bibliotheque Municipale, Epernay, France.

ISBN 0-8308-1859-6

Printed in the United States of America

Library of Congress Cataloging-in-Publication Data

Patzia, Arthur G.
  The making of the New Testament: origin, collection, text and
canon/by Arthur Gerald Patzia.
     p.   cm.
  Includes bibliographical references and indexes.
  ISBN 0-8308-1859-6
  1. Bible.   N.T.—Introductions.   2. Bible.   N.T.—Canon.
  I. Title.
  BS2330.2.P37   1995
  225.1—dc20
                                                              94-45403
                                                                  CIP

23 22 21 20 19 18 17 16 15 14 13 12 11 10 9 8 7 6 5 4 3 2 1

14 13 12 11 10 09 08 07 06 05 04 03 02 01 00 99 98 97 96 95

Dedicated to my parents,
William (1903-   ) and Elsie (1908-1994) Patzia,
who first introduced me to the New Testament

Foreword

In a universe where the footprints of God can be discerned in the heavens above and on the earth beneath, in human history and in personal experience, the most transparent testimony to God remains the Bible, the heart of which is the revelation of God in Jesus Christ our Lord. This witness reaches its clearest expression in the varied writings of the New Testament—the four Gospels, a history of the earliest church, letters to churches and to individuals within them, and an exposition of God's purpose in history written to a group of churches under pressure.

To grasp the word of God made known through these very different works calls for effort on the part of modern readers. To this end many have set their hand to write books of "introduction to the New Testament." Following the example of Luke, who recorded that since many had undertaken to draw up an account of "the things that have been fulfilled among us," after careful investigation he himself also drew up "an orderly account" for his friend Theophilus and for the churches, so Arthur Patzia, after like diligent study, has believed it right to draw up his own account of the origin and nature of the New Testament writings for the guidance of all who would gain a clearer knowledge of them. His unfolding of the story of the making of the New Testament is unusually comprehensive, as a perusal of its contents will show. The telling of it is achieved in a readily understood manner, doubtless benefiting from years of experience in expounding it to student groups. It is good that the publication of such clear teaching is now available to a wider readership, and I warmly commend it to such.

George R. Beasley-Murray

Preface

Students of the New Testament have many questions about the text. The most important one probably centers on interpretation: What does the text mean? How can we understand the Word of God correctly and apply it to our life? The concern to assist readers of the New Testament in understanding its meaning has led to the production of a vast array of books on interpretation, commentaries, and various kinds of Bible dictionaries and study aids.

The Making of the New Testament is not a book that explains the meaning of the text. Rather, it seeks to answer other questions that are raised—questions such as: How did we get this text? Why are there only twenty-seven books? Why are the books arranged the way they are? Who are the authors, and why did some write Gospels and others letters? How was the text preserved throughout the centuries?

These—and other—questions and interests have led to this discussion of the literary world of the early church, the origin, collection and transmission of the text, and its canonical status by the end of the fourth century after Christ. The primary goal is to provide the reader with a single volume that combines the insights of several New Testament disciplines.

One such discipline is the historical-critical method, which deals with the topics of the authorship, occasion, purpose and content of each New Testament book. This type of information is included in most introductory courses on the New Testament. The focus in this book, however, is not with the "who," "why" and "what" questions, but rather with the issues that inform us *how* the sayings of Jesus, the traditions of the early church and the thoughts of certain writers eventually culminated in the New Testament.

An extension of this discipline leads into the second century, where we are able to observe how the various books of the New Testament were *used* and *collected* by the church. Here our study will include a brief examination of some early church fathers and the significant role they played in the formation of the New Testament.

Textual criticism, which deals with the transmission of the text, is the second discipline essential for understanding the composition of the New Testament. From it we are able to appreciate how the New Testament originally was written in manuscript form and how these manuscripts were copied and circulated throughout the churches of the Roman Empire. The study of textual criticism both gives us insight into the fascinating history of scribal activity and enables us to appreciate the nature and quality of the New Testament text that we possess.

A third discipline is the history of the New Testament canon. Here we discover the criteria that the early church used to determine which books were to be regarded as authoritative Scripture. The fact that this process extended over four centuries indicates that there were many important and controversial issues which contributed to finalizing the New Testament in its present form. The focus in this section will be on the historical factors rather than a theological discussion on the meaning of such concepts as revelation, inspiration and prophecy.

In many ways, this book is a *summary* of current and relevant New Testament scholarship. It is written primarily for nonspecialists—students and laypersons who desire to know how the New Testament came into being but who do not have the time, opportunities or resources to research this type of material.

Some information that is quite technical in nature has been placed in the footnotes. By doing this I have attempted to keep the body of the text as lucid as possible while still providing the reader with some additional ideas and resources for further study. College and seminary students should benefit from this text as a handbook or supplementary text to their classes in New Testament studies. Everyone is encouraged to consult more specialized sources for additional information.

A few Greek terms—with transliteration—have been used because of their significance for the subject matter being discussed. The brief glossary at the end is intended to serve as a handy reference for the technical terms that appear throughout the book and relate to the study of the New Testament. Students often encounter these terms but may have no handy reference work to consult. Unless specified, all quotations are from the NRSV (New Revised Standard Version).

Writing a book on this subject can be a risky undertaking because each one of us has certain presuppositions that affect the way we understand God's Word. In this regard each reader needs to remember that a book of this nature deals with a number of hypotheses. As much as we desire certainty when it comes to matters of the New Testament, we have to admit that we do not possess all the information about the writing, collection and canonicity of the New Testament that took place over a period of four centuries. In some cases, therefore, theories are constructed on hypotheses that seem the most plausible. Critical readers may wish to disagree with certain conclusions. This reality will be obvious from the text itself, because I have utilized ideas and materials from a number of different theological perspectives and provided bibliographical information that will enable the reader to pursue literary, compositional and textual matters in more detail.

I owe a special word of gratitude to several New Testament scholars whose ideas have enriched my understanding of the New Testament. Professor Bruce Metzger's classes at Princeton Theological Seminary, as well as many of his books and articles, helped me to appreciate and articulate the nature and value of the text and transmission of the New Testament. While I was doing doctoral studies under E. P. Sanders, he opened my mind to new possibilities within Paul's letters and theology. A hearty thank-you also goes to Professor George R. Beasley-Murray, whose scholarship enriched my life immensely when he was serving as a visiting professor on our campus. A final tribute belongs to the late Professor Robert A. Guelich (1939-1991), a beloved friend and colleague at Fuller Theological Seminary. Bob's insatiable search for truth, love for the church and concern for his students modeled for me the highest virtues of Christian integrity and scholarship.

Additional thanks go to my students in seminary and church study groups, whose questions over the years about the making of the New Testament have led me to read and research items that otherwise might have gone unnoticed; to my capable administrative assistant, June Hipschen, who assumed a significant share of my responsibilities while protecting my sabbatical time for writing and research; to several colleagues, including John Koeker, Bob Ross and Lincoln Hurst; to students Carol Chalberg, Judith Joy and Beverly Spellman for their helpful suggestions and corrections; to the editorial staff at InterVarsity Press, especially Daniel G. Reid; and finally, to my wife Dorothy and our children, whose understanding and sacrifices made additional time for this research possible.

Abbreviations

ABD	*Anchor Bible Dictionary*. Edited by David Noel Freedman. 6 vols. New York: Doubleday, 1992.
BibRev	*Bible Review*
BJRL	*Bulletin of the John Rylands Library*
CBQ	*Catholic Biblical Quarterly*
CBQMS	*Catholic Biblical Quarterly* Monograph Series
CHB	*Cambridge History of the Bible*. Edited by P. R. Ackroyd and C. F. Evans. 3 vols. Cambridge: Cambridge University Press, 1963-1970.
DJG	*Dictionary of Jesus and the Gospels*. Edited by Joel B. Green, Scot McKnight and I. Howard Marshall. Downers Grove, Ill.: InterVarsity Press, 1992.
DNTT	*Dictionary of New Testament Theology*. Edited by Colin Brown. 4 vols. Grand Rapids, Mich.: Zondervan, 1986.
DPL	*Dictionary of Paul and His Letters*. Edited by Gerald F. Hawthorne, Ralph P. Martin and Daniel G. Reid. Downers Grove, Ill.: InterVarsity Press, 1993.
EvQ	*Evangelical Quarterly*
ExpTim	*Expository Times*
GNT[4]	*The Greek New Testament*. 4th ed. United Bible Societies.
HE	Eusebius, *Ecclesiastical History*
HTR	*Harvard Theological Review*
IDB	*Interpreter's Dictionary of the Bible*. Edited by George A. Buttrick. 4 vols. Nashville: Abingdon, 1962.
IDBSup	*Interpreter's Dictionary of the Bible Supplementary Volume*. Edited by Keith Crim. Nashville: Abingdon, 1982.
Int	*Interpretation*
ISBE	*International Standard Bible Encyclopedia*. Edited by Geoffrey Bromiley. 4 vols. Grand Rapids, Mich.: Eerdmans, 1979-1989.

JAAR	*Journal of the American Academy of Religion*
JBL	*Journal of Biblical Literature*
JETS	*Journal of the Evangelical Theological Society*
JSNT	*Journal for the Study of the New Testament*
JTS	*Journal of Theological Studies*
LXX	Septuagint
NA^{26}	Novum Testamentum Graece, Nestlé-Aland, 26th ed.
NDNTS	*New Dimensions in New Testament Study.* Edited by Richard N. Longenecker and Merrill C. Tenney. Grand Rapids, Mich.: Zondervan, 1974.
NIBC	New International Bible Commentary
NovT	*Novum Testamentum*
NovTSup	Supplement to *Novum Testamentum*
NTCI	*New Testament Criticism and Interpretation.* Edited by David A. Black and David S. Dockery. Grand Rapids, Mich.: Zondervan, 1991.
NTI	*New Testament Interpretation.* Edited by I. Howard Marshall. Grand Rapids, Mich.: Eerdmans, 1977.
NTMI	*The New Testament and Its Modern Interpreters.* Edited by Eldon J. Epp and George W. MacRae. Atlanta: Scholars Press, 1989.
NTS	*New Testament Studies*
SBLDS	Society of Biblical Literature Dissertation Series
SBLMS	Society of Biblical Literature Monograph Series
TDNT	*Theological Dictionary of the New Testament.* Edited by Gerhard Kittel and Gerhard Friedrich. 10 vols. Grand Rapids, Mich.: Eerdmans, 1964-1976.
VT	*Vetus Testamentum*
WBC	Word Biblical Commentary
WTJ	*Westminster Theological Journal*
ZNW	*Zeitschrift für die neutestamentliche Wissenschaft*

PART I

THE LITERARY
WORLD OF
THE NEW
TESTAMENT

1. General Considerations

Imagine living in a world without such modern inventions as printing presses, typewriters, photocopiers, fax machines, personal computers and cataloged and computerized libraries. This is how it was during the centuries the Scriptures were being written and collected. Writing instruments and materials were primitive and crude; authors survived and wrote under difficult circumstances; but although many valuable works were lost or destroyed because they could not be duplicated or safely stored, an amazing number of them survived.

The literary world into which Christianity came was quite sophisticated and productive. We possess literature that goes back as far as the fourth millennium before Christ, to the ancient Near Eastern civilizations of Mesopotamia, Egypt, Assyria, Babylon and Canaan. Texts from these areas include mythic, epic, legal, historical and ritual material and are helpful for understanding biblical history and literature.[1]

The Old Testament comes from this general geographical region. It recounts Israel's beginnings from the patriarchal age (c. 2000-1300 B.C.), the reigns of David (1000-962 B.C.) and Solomon (962-922 B.C.), and the Major Prophets from the eighth to sixth century B.C.[2] This body of literature spans over one thousand years of history and involves at least thirty different authors. It is an indispensable source for understanding the New Testament and the emergence of the early church because of the historical and theological background it provides.

The Greco-Roman world also left behind a rich legacy of literary materials. From Greece, for example, we have the poems of Homer (the *Iliad* and *Odyssey* are attributed to him, c. 800 B.C.), and Hesiod (c. 633 B.C.), as well as materials from such famous philosophers as Plato (429-347 B.C.), Aristotle (384-322 B.C.) and Epicurus (341-270 B.C.). Great Roman writers include Cicero (106-43 B.C.), Ovid (43 B.C.-A.D. 17), Seneca (4 B.C.-A.D. 65), Pliny the Elder (A.D. 23/4-79) and his nephew, Pliny the Younger (A.D. 61-112).

Many writings from these authors have disappeared. Epicurus, for example, has three hundred rolls of writing attributed to him but all his main works are lost. About forty-eight of Cicero's orations and many of his letters have similarly disappeared. Some extant works of other classical authors have been judged to be forgeries. However, many ancient documents of literary value have been well preserved by the careful efforts of collectors, editors and publishers. These include partial collections of the letters of Aristotle, Epicurus, Cicero and Pliny. Approximately eight hundred copies of some of Paul's letters have survived in ancient manuscripts—in comparison with most ancient works, an amazingly large number.

The ancient world also possessed a number of significant libraries. The texts from the ancient Near East were discovered among the ruins of archives and libraries of such great cities as Nineveh, Babylon and Thebes. Athens, and Alexandria in Egypt, were great literary centers for the Greeks. Josephus, a Jewish historian (c. A.D. 38-110), records that Demetrius Phalerius, the royal librarian in Alexandria around 297 B.C., planned to get copies of all the books in the world for his library (*Antiquities* 12.2.1). We are not sure how well he succeeded, but later estimates of the collection run as high as 700,000 volumes by the middle of the second century B.C.[3] Pergamum in western Asia Minor had a library second only to that of Alexandria. Ancient sources estimate that it contained about 200,000 volumes.

A number of cities stand out for their literary importance at the beginning of the Christian era. Rome "was a city of writers, publishers, booksellers and bookstores" during the first century A.D.[4] Paul wrote one of his great letters to the Roman church. It is from Rome that Mark wrote his Gospel and Clement his letter to the church at Corinth (often referred to as *1 Clement*). Josephus, the Jewish historian, came to Rome and composed some of his later works there under the patronage of the Roman general, later emperor, Vespasian.

Ephesus, likewise, was an important center of learning. Acts 19:19 refers to a large number of valuable books that were collected and burned in response to Paul's preaching. ("A number of those who practiced magic collected their books and burned them publicly; when the value of these books was calculated, it was found to come to fifty thousand silver coins.") Most of Paul's correspondence to Corinth originated from Ephesus, and it is the most likely site where his letters were first collected, edited and published. The Johannine literature also emanated from Ephesus, The famous "Library of Celsus" was established in Ephesus around A.D. 125. Thanks to the careful restoration of Austrian and German craftsmen, it is the best preserved library of the ancient world.

The most famous library for early Christianity was founded in A.D. 253 in Caesarea after the death of Origen by Pamphilus, one of his disciples. It was in Caesarea that Origen completed his *Hexapla,* an elaborate edition of the Old Testament in six parallel columns. One column contained the Old Testament in Hebrew, one a Greek transliteration, and the others each contained different Greek translations of the Hebrew Scriptures. Jerome later consulted this *Hexapla* in the Caesarean library when he was working on the revision of the Latin Bible that eventually resulted in the Vulgate around A.D. 400. Eusebius (c. 260-340) became the bishop of Caesarea, and as the result of his writings, particularly his *Ecclesiastical History,* he became known as "the father of church history."

Several other archaeological discoveries illustrate the extent of literary activity during the formative years of Christianity. The discoveries in the caves near Qumran in Palestine produced a rich treasury of religious and community literature now referred to as the Dead Sea Scrolls. The Nag Hammadi Library, a collection of fifty-two tractates of Gnostic and other writings dating from the fourth century A.D., was discovered in 1945 along the Nile approximately forty miles northwest of Luxor, Egypt. In 1897, B. P. Grenfell and A. S. Hunt discovered a valuable cache of papyri among the ruins of Oxyrhynchus (approximately 120 miles south of Cairo, near modern Behnesa), an important center of Christian culture in the fourth century A.D. These materials, known as the Oxyrhynchus Papyri, include fragments of contracts, wills, business and love letters, receipts, tax lists and so on.[5]

In addition to the public and imperial libraries connected with major civilizations and cities, there were many private collections. Most large Roman houses had libraries. "Cicero," writes Goodspeed, "is said to have had a library in each of his eighteen villas."[6] Given the ravages of war during the Greco-Roman period, when many public libraries were destroyed by fire, it is likely that the preservation and reproduction of manuscripts was due to private rather than imperial ownership. However, Diocletian's persecution of Christians and his purge of books in A.D. 303 included private collections.[7]

Since the early Christians met in homes during the first three centuries, it is likely that the larger ones included libraries where manuscripts would be kept. Some house churches may have had a copy of the LXX—or at least parts of it, since it encompassed forty rolls—for study and worship. Other documents would have included letters from church leaders. Such was the case at Dionysius's church. He was bishop of Corinth around A.D. 150 and wrote to Soter, bishop of Rome:

> Today . . . we have passed the Lord's holy day, in which we have read your epistle. In reading which we shall always have our minds stored with admonition, as we shall, also, from that written to us before by Clement. (*HE* 4.23.11)

No doubt there were similar collections in other church libraries. We will learn more about this later, when we discuss how Paul's letters were used by the churches to which he wrote and how, with the passing of time, they were collected, edited and distributed.[8] Let us now turn to examine some of the ancient literature that specifically forms a background to the nature and composition of the New Testament.

2. The Hebrew Scriptures

At the time of Jesus, the Jewish people in Palestine and in the Diaspora had a body of authoritative religious literature known as "the Scriptures." Manuscripts of the Hebrew Bible were used in the synagogues for worship and instruction and for intense study by such religious leaders as the scribes and Pharisees.

Many passages in the Gospels show Jesus' great reverence for these Scriptures. As a Jew he would have been brought up to appreciate their significance for his people as well as for himself. From the Scriptures Jesus repudiates the devil during his temptation by appealing to "what is written" (Mt 4:4-10 and parallels); he inaugurates his public ministry in the synagogue of Nazareth (Lk 4:16-21) by claiming that he fulfills what is written in the prophet Isaiah (58:6; 61:1-2). And in his disputations with the religious leaders of his day, he often takes issue with their interpretation and application of the "scriptures" (Mt 22:29; Jn 10:35; 19:36), "the law" (Jn 10:34; 12:34; 15:25), "the law and the prophets" (Mt 5:17; 7:12; 22:40; Lk 16:16) and "the law of Moses, the prophets, and the psalms" (Lk 24:44). Jesus was in no way against the Scriptures, but only against misinterpretations. Matthew in particular takes care to explain to the Jews of his day that Jesus did not come to abolish the Law and the Prophets but "to fulfill" them (Mt 5:17).

Since the early church consisted mainly of Jewish believers, it should not surprise us that they had great respect for the Jewish Scriptures. By their confession of Jesus as the Messiah *(Christos)*, they believed that God had indeed inaugurated the kingdom of God and that they were living in the new age. What God had promised in the Scriptures had now been fulfilled in the person of Jesus and in the sending of his Spirit (Acts 2). They were the "true" Israel.

The early believers continued to use the Hebrew Scriptures in their worship and study, but these took on fresh significance and meaning for their faith as they began to study them in order to see how they bore witness to Christ. Peter used several texts to demonstrate to the crowd gathered in Jerusalem for the celebration of Pentecost that what was happening was a fulfillment of Scripture (Acts 2:16-21, 25-36). Paul, after his conversion, became a prime interpreter of the fact that the Hebrew Scriptures—the Law and the Prophets—had been fulfilled in Christ (e.g., Rom 1:2; 10:4; 1 Cor 15:3-4). In a sense, Paul and others were simply doing what the resurrected Lord had done on the Emmaus road to two bewildered disciples: "Then beginning with Moses and all the prophets, he interpreted to them the things about himself in all the scriptures" (Lk 24:27). This new center of reference for interpreting the Hebrew Scriptures led to increasing conflicts between believing and nonbelieving Jews. Although both could agree on the authority of the ancient Scriptures and their place in the religious life of God's people, they differed significantly on matters of interpretation.

The book of Acts records how the early apostles such as Peter and John were persecuted because they now claimed a new authority in the person of Jesus and used passages from the Old Testament to justify their beliefs and actions (Acts 2—6). Stephen, the first Christian martyr, was stoned because he used the Scriptures to condemn the Jews for their obduracy throughout history and for their role in the death of Jesus (Acts 6:8—7:60).

Paul attempted to demonstrate the true meaning of Scripture to the Jews but made very little progress with them. When he traveled throughout the Greco-Roman world and visited the synagogues to explain the Scriptures to his people, he often was rejected and persecuted (Acts 13:44-46; 14:1-7; 17:1-9; 18:1-11; 19:8-10). Many Jews continued to oppose him throughout his ministry up until his final arrest in Jerusalem (Acts 21—23). While he was able to win many Gentiles to the faith, Paul essentially was unsuccessful in convincing his own people of the true nature and purpose of the Law. Small wonder that he agonized so passionately in Romans 9—11 over the Jewish rejection of the gospel and the future of his people.

Considerable disagreement exists in scholarly circles about the status and extent of the Hebrew Scriptures (the term "Old Testament" was not introduced until the end of the second century A.D.). Basically, the issue is whether or not there was a threefold designation of "Law," "Prophets" and "Writings" during the time of Jesus and the apostolic age.[9]

Some scholars are convinced that the limits of the Hebrew canon were firmly established by the beginning of the first century, so that the Old Testament used by the early Christians was virtually identical with the one we have in our Bible today. Others, however, reason that the boundaries of the Old Testament canon may not have been decided until the Council of Jamnia (or Yavneh/Jabneh) around A.D. 90.[10] It does appear that first-century Judaism was not uniform in designating its "sacred Scripture." On one occasion Jesus asks: "Is it not written in your law [nomos] . . . ?" (Jn 10:34-35). But then he proceeds to quote from Psalm 82:6 and not the Law. There is no simple way of knowing whether the reference to "Psalms" in Luke 24:44 ("what is written in the law of Moses, the prophets, and the psalms") includes all the Scripture that became designated as the "Writings." We cannot be certain that the early church had a fixed body of these Scriptures at its disposal before the second century.[11]

3. The Septuagint (LXX)

Alongside the Hebrew Scriptures, the Jews studied and used a Greek translation known as the Septuagint[12] (from the Latin septuaginta, meaning seventy, abbreviated as LXX). Such a translation was necessary because of the large number of Jews who were living outside Palestine—the Diaspora. Some estimates suggest that as many as four and a half million Jews lived in different parts of the Roman Empire during the time of Caesar Augustus.

It appears that work on the LXX began in Alexandria early in the third century B.C. with the Pentateuch and continued into the second century B.C. with translations of the Prophets and Writings. External evidence for the existence of a Greek version of the Hebrew Scriptures in the second century B.C. is found in the book of Ecclesiasticus, also known as the Wisdom of Jesus the Son of Sirach (c. 200-180 B.C.). In its prologue, mention is made of the Law, the Prophets and the rest of the books.

The formation of the LXX was a gradual process spanning several centuries. Scholars have rightly judged that the Letter of Aristeas (c. 275-295 B.C.) is a legendary or romantic piece of Jewish propaganda about the origin of the LXX. In this document, the author narrates how King Ptolemy II Philadelphus (c. 284-247 B.C.) requested that priests in Jerusalem send seventy-two scholars, six from each of Israel's tribes, to begin translating the Law into Greek for the library in Alexandria. These translators were isolated on the Island of Pharos, near Alexandria, and after seventy-two days they completed identical translations. This was then read with great excitement before the Jewish community in Alexandria. And since this translation was done accurately and reverently, it was concluded that no revision or deletion of it should ever take place (*Letter* 310-11).

But the translation of certain parts of the Old Testament into Greek was not always done consistently and carefully. Some books differ considerably from our present Hebrew Bible. Jeremiah, for example, is about one-eighth shorter and Job about one-fourth shorter in the LXX than in our Old Testament. There also is a different order of materials in the Psalms and Proverbs. Joshua has a number of changes, including additions and omissions. These observations lead to the conclusion that the LXX is a collection of translations of the Hebrew Scriptures produced over several centuries by Jews of the Dispersion.

Another significant feature of the LXX is that it contains a number of additional books not found in the Hebrew Scriptures. Most of them are Greek translations of Hebrew and Aramaic, but others, such as the Wisdom of Solomon and 2 Maccabees, were originally composed in Greek.

These books, now known to us as the Old Testament Apocrypha, were written during the first and second century B.C. No one is certain, however, when they actually became part of the LXX. But given their early composition, their popularity with the Jewish people, the many allusions, parallels and ideas in the New Testament (see below), their use by the early church fathers, and their appearance in the best Greek codices of the Bible (such as Sinaiticus, Vaticanus and Alexandrinus), one can safely assume that they were part of the LXX in the first century A.D. and were, therefore, known to the Greek-speaking Christians and the writers of the New Testament. They were included in the Vulgate and thus continue to be part of the Roman Catholic Bible today.[13] The Protestant church, on the other hand, adopted the Hebrew canon of the Old Testament, which did not contain these Apocrypha books.

The most striking feature of the LXX for this study is that it was the predominant version of the Old Testament used by the early church and the writers of the New Testament. It would have been known in Jerusalem because there were many Hellenists (Greek-speaking Jews) in the city (Acts 6), as well as a synagogue of the Freedmen (Acts 6:9). Stephen, a Hellenist, is portrayed by Luke as using some form of the LXX when he disputed with the religious authorities in Jerusalem (Acts 7). Paul would have used the LXX when he visited the synagogues in the Diaspora in the hope that the Jews would come to believe that Jesus was the Messiah (e.g., Acts 13:17-18; 17:1-3). At least 80 percent of the Old Testament quotations found in the New Testament are taken from the LXX. In fact, there are many Old Testament passages in the New Testament which agree with the LXX but differ considerably from the Hebrew Old Testament (e.g., Amos 9:11-12 in Acts 15:16-17; Is 7:14 in Mt 1:23).

Once Christians began using the LXX for missionary and apologetic purposes, it began to lose favor with the Jews. Their earlier acceptance of this version waned when they found how consistently and effectively it was used against them in arguments. More and more the LXX became identified *as the Old Testament of the Christian church.* This led to a Jewish rejection of the LXX in its current form and the production of several other Greek versions that attempted to translate the Hebrew text more accurately. These revisions by Aquila, Theodotion and Symmachus in the early second century A.D. were produced roughly at the same time the Hebrew Old Testament canon was completed without the Apocryphal books.

Since the LXX was used so extensively by the early Christians, it is natural that certain portions of the New Testament contain echoes of its language and concepts. Theological terms such as *law, righteousness, mercy* and *truth* were taken over directly from the LXX by New Testament writers. By becoming the Bible of the early church fathers, the LXX influenced church dogma as well as the formation of the Old Testament. Even the Hebrew threefold division of Law, Prophets and Writings was replaced with the Greek fourfold division of Law, History, Poetry and Prophets.[14]

4. The Old Testament Apocrypha

This body of literature that is included in the LXX and the Roman Catholic Bibles became known as the Apocrypha (from the Greek "to hide," "to conceal"). Initially, this was a literary term applied to certain books that were to be kept from the public (thus hidden away, not read publicly) because of the secret doctrines and esoteric wisdom they were thought to contain. Currently, however, it is used more in the sense of spurious or noncanonical. Thus when we talk about the Apocrypha today, we mean a body of literature that is not regarded as canonical by Protestants. Roman Catholics accept these books as authoritative and prefer the term *deutero-canonical* to distinguish them from the "protocanonical books"—those found in the Hebrew Old Testament.

The books of the Apocrypha include

1. The First Book of Esdras
2. The Second Book of Esdras
3. Tobit
4. Judith
5. The Additions to the Book of Esther
6. The Wisdom of Solomon
7. Ecclesiasticus, or the Wisdom of Jesus the Son of Sirach
8. Baruch
9. The Letter of Jeremiah

10. The Prayer of Azariah and the Song of the Three Young Men
11. Susanna
12. Bel and the Dragon
13. The Prayer of Manasseh
14. The First Book of the Maccabees
15. The Second Book of the Maccabees

Most of these books originated during times of oppression and persecution, when the Jews in Palestine were ruled by such Greek despots as Antiochus IV Epiphanes (175-163 B.C.), John Hyrcanus (135-105 B.C.) and Alexander Jannaeus (104-78 B.C.), who sought to Hellenize Palestine at all costs. Many of the historical events of this era are recorded in the Apocryphal books. In others the authors attempt to provide a message of hope for God's people who were undergoing suffering and hardships or to write a "theodicy"—a vindication of the justice of God in the midst of evil in the world.

Besides giving valuable historical background material, the Apocryphal literature shows the development of some important concepts found in the New Testament such as demons, angels, resurrection, rewards, the kingdom of God and the Son of Man. Students of the Bible should become familiar with this literature and appreciate its significance as a bridge between the Old and New Testaments.

There are many passages in the New Testament that closely parallel, allude to and contain ideas from the Apocrypha and Pseudepigrapha. Scholars who have worked in this area have made extensive comparisons between books of the Apocrypha and sayings of Jesus in the Gospels, Romans, Hebrews, James and Revelation.[15] (See the examples in table 1.1.)

Several things need to be kept in mind when one evaluates the significance of the parallels, allusions and reminiscences between the Apocryphal literature and the New Testament.

First, the writers of the New Testament were influenced by the common literary expressions and religious ideas of their day and did not necessarily borrow everything from their predecessors. Analogy does not always mean genealogy!

Second, although the writers of the New Testament were familiar with the Apocryphal writings from the LXX, we do not know whether they gave any type of scriptural status to them. On the one hand, they nowhere quote any Apocryphal books as authoritative (see below for comments on Jude 9 and 14). But this does not prove anything decisive about their attitude toward the Apocrypha, because the New Testament also lacks quotations from several canonical books that were regarded as authoritative Scripture, such as Joshua, Judges, Chronicles and Ezra. "We cannot say with absolute certainty," asserts F. F. Bruce, "if Paul treated Esther

Table 1.1. Sample Parallels: New Testament and Old Testament Apocrypha

Matthew 11:28-30	**Sirach 51:23-26**
Come to me, all you that are weary and are carrying heavy burdens, and I will give you rest. Take my yoke upon you, and learn from me; for I am gentle and humble in heart, and you will find rest for your souls. For my yoke is easy, and my burden is light.	Draw near to me, you who are uneducated, and lodge in the house of instruction. Why do you say you are lacking in these things, and why do you endure such great thirst? . . . Put your neck under her yoke, and let your souls receive instruction.
2 Corinthians 5:1, 4	**Wisdom of Solomon 9:15**
For we know that if the earthly tent we live in is destroyed, we have a building from God, a house not made with hands, eternal in the heavens. . . . For while we are still in this tent, we groan under our burden, because we wish not to be unclothed but to be further clothed, so that what is mortal may be swallowed up by life.	. . . for a perishable body weighs down the soul, and this earthy tent burdens the thoughtful mind.
Romans 1:20	**Wisdom of Solomon 13:5**
Ever since the creation of the world his eternal power and divine nature, invisible though they are, have been understood and seen through the things he has made. So they are without excuse.	For from the greatness and beauty of created things comes a corresponding perception of their Creator.
James 1:19	**Sirach 5:11**
. . . let everyone be quick to listen, slow to speak, slow to anger.	Be quick to hear, but deliberate in answering.

or the Song of Songs as scripture any more than we can say if these books belonged to the Bible which Jesus knew and used" (*Canon*, 50).

Third, the *early* church fathers quoted from the Apocrypha in the same way they quoted from the books of the Old Testament. *Later* church fathers such as Origen (A.D. 185-243), Cyril of Jerusalem (A.D. 315-386) and Jerome (A.D. 340-420) sought to separate the Apocryphal books from the rest of the Old Testament as "outside books." Tradition, however, prevailed, and most of the Apocrypha was included in the Vulgate and eventually became an authoritative part of the Roman Catholic Scriptures.

5. The Old Testament Pseudepigrapha

Much of what has been said about the Apocrypha applies equally to the Pseudepigrapha. In reality, it would be better to designate this and other literature that was written during the postexilic period as "intertestamental literature" or simply "noncanonical literature."

The term *pseudepigrapha* literally means "false writing" and has come generally to designate books that were attributed "falsely" to ideal and/or heroic individuals from the Old Testament. Some books truly are pseudepigraphal (*1 Enoch, Revelation of Ezra, Apocalypse of Baruch, Testament of the Twelve Patriarchs*); others simply are anonymous (from an unknown author). James Charlesworth comments, "Contemporary scholars employ the term 'pseudepigrapha' not because it denotes something spurious about the documents collected under that title, but because the term has been inherited and is now used internationally."[16]

For the most part, these books were written in Palestine and areas of the Diaspora between 200 B.C and A.D. 200. Like the Apocrypha, they provide valuable information about Jewish history and the nature and variety of religious thought during that period. Themes that run throughout the books include perseverance in the midst of suffering, God's righteous character in spite of evil circumstances, resistance to Hellenism, and the exaltation of Judaism through commendations of faith, the Mosaic law and ancestral traditions. That these works were known and used by some elements of Christianity is reflected directly in the New Testament: Jude 14-15 quotes from *1 Enoch* 1:9, and Jude 9 alludes to the *Assumption of Moses*.

A special genre (classification) of literature within the Apocrypha and Pseudepigrapha is known as "apocalyptic" (Greek, "to unveil," "reveal," "uncover"), and it includes such books as *1 Enoch, 4 Ezra* and *2 Baruch*. Students of the Bible are familiar with this type of material from portions of the book of Daniel in the Old Testament and from Revelation (also known as "the Apocalypse of John") and apocalyptic sections such as Matthew 24, Mark 13 (sometimes called "the Little Apocalypse"), 2 Thessalonians 2:1-12 and 2 Peter 3:1-12 in the New Testament.

Apocalyptic literature characterizes the world as a battle between two opposing cosmic powers, God and Satan. The temporal evil age under Satan will eventually be overthrown by God, who will establish a perfect and eternal age where he will rule and the righteous be blessed forever. Much of the message of apocalyptic literature is couched in revelations, visions, prophecies, dreams, animal symbolism, numerology and astral influences (angels and demons). And although Christianity rejected or reinterpreted some of the teachings of Jewish apocalyptic, it also took over and incorporated many apocalyptic concepts into its theology. To this extent the New Testament writings provide a useful commentary on such apocalyptic doctrines as the resurrection of the dead, judgment, Messianism and the end of the present evil age.

The eschatological (i.e., end-time) expectations that the early Christians adopted from Judaism were reinterpreted in light of their belief that Jesus was the Messiah whose coming had inaugurated the new age. This new belief set

Table 1.2. The Books of the Old Testament Pseudepigrapha[17]

Apocalyptic Literature
1 Enoch
2 Enoch
3 Enoch
Sibylline Oracles
Treatise of Shem
Apocryphon of Ezekiel
Apocalypse of Zephaniah
4 Ezra
Questions of Ezra
Revelation of Ezra
Apocalypse of Sedrach
2 Baruch
3 Baruch
Apocalypse of Abraham
Apocalypse of Adam
Apocalypse of Elijah
Apocalypse of Daniel

Testaments
Testaments of the Twelve Patriarchs
☐ Testament of Reuben
☐ Testament of Simeon
☐ Testament of Levi
☐ Testament of Judah
☐ Testament of Issachar
☐ Testament of Zebulon
☐ Testament of Dan
☐ Testament of Naphtali
☐ Testament of Gad
☐ Testament of Asher
☐ Testament of Joseph
☐ Testament of Benjamin
Testament of Job
Testaments of the Three Patriarchs
☐ Testament of Abraham
☐ Testament of Isaac
☐ Testament of Jacob
Testament (Assumption) of Moses
Testament of Solomon
Testament of Adam

Expansions of the Old Testament and Legends
Letter of Aristeas
Jubilees
Martyrdom and Ascension of Isaiah
Joseph and Asenath
Life of Adam and Eve
Pseudo-Philo
Lives of the Prophets

Ladder of Jacob
4 Baruch
Jannes and Jambres
History of the Rechabites
Eldad and Modad
History of Joseph

Wisdom and Philosophical Literature
Ahiqar
Pseudo-Phocylides
3 Maccabees
4 Maccabees
The Sentences of the Syriac Menander

Prayers, Psalms, Odes
More Psalms of David
☐ Psalm 151
☐ Psalm 152
☐ Psalm 153
☐ Psalm 154
☐ Psalm 155
Prayer of Manasseh
Psalms of Solomon
Hellenistic Synagogal Prayers
Prayer of Joseph
Prayer of Jacob
Odes of Solomon

Poetry
Philo the Epic Poet
Theodotus

Oracles
Orphica

Drama
Ezekiel the Tragedian

Other
Fragments of Pseudo-Greek Poets
☐ Pseudo-Hesiod
☐ Pseudo-Pythagoras
☐ Pseudo-Aeschylus
☐ Pseudo-Sophocles
☐ Pseudo-Euripides
☐ Pseudo-Philemon
☐ Pseudo-Diphilus
☐ Pseudo-Menander

Philosophy	Pseudo-Eupolemus
Aristobulus	Cleodemus Malchus
Demetrius the Chronographer	
Aristeas the Exegete	**Romance**
	Artapanus
History	Pseudo-Hecataeus
Eupolemus	5 Maccabees

their theology at odds with the Jews, who were still awaiting the "Coming One." So while the church was using apocalyptic ideas more and more to clarify what had taken place with the coming of Christ, the Jews, on the other hand, found this literature less and less attractive and sought to distinguish themselves from the Christian faith. Many apocalyptic books were rejected and eventually destroyed.

6. The Dead Sea Scrolls

The discovery of the Dead Sea Scrolls began in 1946, when a young shepherd boy wandered into a cave in the wilderness of Judea to retrieve a wayward goat. Since that time, most archaeologists have concluded that the site at Khirbet Qumran, situated southeast of Jerusalem near the Dead Sea, was inhabited by a group of religious Jews that resembled the Essenes, a sect of Judaism that existed in Palestine from about the middle of the second century B.C. until the fall of Jerusalem in A.D. 70.[18]

This community probably had its origin in the second century B.C., when Judaism was going through some difficult religious and political struggles. The Hasmonean high priests of the time, John Hyrcanus and Alexander Jannaeus, were Hellenistic sympathizers, and Antiochus Epiphanes was a Seleucid ruler who ruthlessly imposed Hellenistic customs and ideas on the Jews. Among those who opposed Hellenism was a group of pious and conservative Jews known as the Hasidim. When they could no longer tolerate the persecution and compromises to their faith, they withdrew to the wilderness and set up their own type of eschatological community. By putting a special nuance on the prophecy of Isaiah 40:3 ("A voice cries out: 'In the wilderness prepare the way of the LORD, make straight in the desert a highway for our God' "), they believed that they were preparing for the coming day of the Lord. The community existed from the middle of the second century B.C. until A.D. 68, when it was finally destroyed by the Romans.

The discoveries at Qumran are significant for at least two reasons.

First, they provide information about the existence of a religious community during the time of Jesus and the early church. Archaeological reconstruction of the site shows that the facilities included a large meeting room for study and the common meal, a library, storerooms for food and deep cisterns to store water for drinking and for their baptismal rite. Extensive rules and regulations governing the community are described in the *Manual of Discipline* or the *Rule of the Community.*

Second, the caves yielded a marvelous treasure of religious documents. Some of the manuscripts included copies of the Apocryphal and Pseudepigraphal texts discussed earlier; other scrolls consist of hymns and psalms; another is a *War Scroll,* which outlines plans for the final eschatological battle between the forces of good and evil, represented by the Children of Light and the Children of Darkness. Two incomplete medieval fragments of the *Damascus Document* (also known as *Fragments of a Zadokite Work*) had been discovered in the Genizah (a storage chamber for unused manuscripts) of the Ezra Synagogue in Cairo in 1897. More extensive fragments of this document were recovered from the Qumran caves.

The most important manuscripts, however, are the numerous biblical texts. The scrolls contain excerpts from all the Old Testament books, with the exception of the book of Esther. The two scrolls of the book of Isaiah are a thousand years older than previously known manuscripts of the Hebrew Old Testament.

Since the Qumran community was contemporary with the early Christian movement, one has to wonder about any possible contact between the two. Scholars who have examined this question have noted both similarities and differences. Some suggest that John the Baptist belonged to this community because he lived in "the wilderness," practiced an ascetic way of life and gave teaching focused on baptism and repentance (cf. Mt 3:1-12 and parallels). Others note similarities with John's Gospel as well as between Jesus and the Teacher of Righteousness mentioned in the Scrolls. Both early Christianity and Qumran were apocalyptic movements which saw themselves as living in the last days and engaged in a battle against Satan and the powers of darkness. The dualism in the Qumran literature (light-darkness; good-evil) also has been compared with the language in the Gospel of John and the Epistle to the Hebrews.[19]

At this point it seems fair to say that there is no proof that Christianity and Qumran influenced each other directly. Many of the similarities are from their common heritage in Judaism and/or religious beliefs, expressions and practices during the time of Christ. Analogy, as mentioned earlier (p. 27), does not necessarily mean genealogy; nor should plausible, or even probable, theories be given more certainty than they warrant. It would be best to conclude that the influence of the Qumran community upon early Christianity as reflected in the New Testament is, at this stage of our knowledge, minimal. Nevertheless, the texts from Qumran are a valuable source of information for the milieu that gave birth to Christianity.

7. Greco-Roman Literature

Since Christianity emerged within a Jewish *and* Hellenistic environment, one would expect Greco-Roman literature to be an important component in reconstructing the composition of the New Testament. The discovery of the ancient papyri in Egypt at the turn of the century was just the tip of the literary iceberg. Since that time, other materials have been uncovered and published. Scholars continue to examine the Greco-Roman literary environment of the New Testament with renewed passion and have shown that the writers of the New Testament utilized the literary models, conventions, styles and practices of their day.[20]

This observation should not surprise or alarm us. The writers of the New Testament were familiar with this literary world and were seeking to communicate the good news about Jesus and to explain the nature of the Christian religion to a culture that used, understood and appreciated such forms.

At times the Greeks used the "diatribe," a form of Greek discourse and exhortation used by schools of philosophy such as the Sophists, Stoics and Cynics. "The distinguishing feature of the diatribe," writes David Aune, "is its dialogical or conversational character, a pedagogical method based on the model of Socrates."[21] It includes such distinguishing features as rhetorical questions, hypothetical objections and imaginary opponents.

We also know that the Greeks and Romans were great rhetoricians and that audiences were fascinated by the power of speech. Rhetorical "manuals" or "handbooks" were written by such important people as Aristotle (384-322 B.C.), Cicero (106-43 B.C.) and Quintilian (c. A.D. 35-95) and were an essential part of education in Greek and Roman society.

The aim in rhetoric is, of course, persuasion and response—a purpose similar to that of a speech or sermon today. And since much of early Christianity involved public preaching and teaching (see Jesus, Paul, the speeches in Acts, etc.), it would be natural to assume that rhetorical principles were utilized in oral and written communication.

Another major area of research has concentrated on letter writing among the Greek and Romans. Letter writing is one of Rome's most distinctive legacies to the literature of the world. Stanley Stowers has identified six distinct letter types from this period (friendship, family, praise and blame, exhortation and advice, mediation, apologetic) and has discussed their influence upon letter writing in the early church.[22] It would be fair to say that the research of Stowers and others has given us a deeper appreciation for the structure and meaning of letters in the New Testament. The same can be said for the relationship between the Gospels and ancient biography or history in the writing of Luke-Acts.

The importance of this research for our study is voiced by Stowers when he writes:

> Something about the nature of early Christianity made it a movement of letter writers. We possess more than nine thousand letters written by Christians in antiquity. Twenty-one of the twenty-seven writings in the New Testament take the form of letters. Two of the remaining works, the Acts of the Apostles and the Apocalypse, contain letters within them. If the interpreter is willing to understand early Christian letters as Greco-Roman letters, they can provide a fascinating window into the world of those Christians.[23]

In the following pages we shall gaze into this literary "window" and examine more specifically how the literature of the Greco-Roman world illuminates our understanding of the nature and composition of the New Testament.

PART II

THE GOSPELS

1. Jesus of Nazareth

Nearly all of what we know about the life and message of Jesus comes from the canonical Gospels.[1] In them we are told of his miraculous birth in Bethlehem to Mary and Joseph, a carpenter from the village of Nazareth in Galilee (Mt 1:18—2:23; Lk 2:1-40). After a stay in Egypt, the family settled again in their hometown, where Jesus ostensibly grew up as any other Jewish boy. This meant learning his father's trade, studying the Torah in the local synagogue, participating in social events and making occasional pilgrimages with his family to Jerusalem for special religious festivals. During these years, according to Luke, "the child grew and became strong, filled with wisdom; and the favor of God was upon him" (2:40, 52).

With the exception of a visit to Jerusalem to celebrate the Passover when Jesus was twelve years of age (Lk 2:41-51), the Gospels do not record anything about the adolescent and young adult years of Jesus. The mythical and imaginary stories that one finds in the apocryphal Gospels were attempts to fill these gaps. Scholars have rightly concluded that these are fictional accounts.

The Gospels present Jesus as an extraordinary person. Matthew understands his birth to be a special sign that God is with his people (" 'they shall name him Emmanuel,' which means, 'God is with us' "—1:23). Luke records the words of Simeon at the time of Jesus' purification in Jerusalem as a prophecy that this child Jesus was indeed God's agent of redemption for Jews and Gentiles alike (2:22-38).

The first indication that Jesus is about to make a public appearance comes through the prophetic activity of John the Baptist (Mt 3:1-12; Mk 1:1-8). John emerges from the wilderness, calling people to repentance and baptism, and announcing that the Messianic Age is about to be inaugurated by someone more significant and powerful than himself—someone who will baptize "with the Holy Spirit and fire" (Lk 3:16). Soon Jesus emerges from his home in Nazareth of Galilee and makes his way to Judea, where he is baptized by John in the Jordan River (Mt 3:13-17; Mk 1:9-11; Lk 3:21-22).

The baptism of Jesus when he is thirty years old (Lk 3:23) marks his first public appearance and is the occasion at which he confirms John's message, identifies himself with the nation of Israel and is anointed and empowered to fulfill his messianic task. The period of temptation in the wilderness that follows (Mt 4:1-11; Mk 1:12; Lk 4:1-13) reinforces the fact that Jesus' ministry will be characterized by complete obedience and dedication to the word of God and not by selfish security, cheap popularity or some compromising alliance with Satan.

The Gospels tell us that Jesus called a group of twelve disciples, with whom he often traveled and to whom he gave special instruction (Mt 4:18-22; Mk 1:16-20; Lk 5:1-11; Jn 1:35-51). We also know that he went about the regions of Judea, Galilee, Perea, the Decapolis and Caesarea Philippi teaching and performing miracles of healing and exorcism.

Several different terms are used to describe the public ministry of Jesus. In most cases (forty-five times) he is called a teacher because teaching was such a significant part of his life. On other occasions (fourteen times) he is addressed with the Aramaic title "rabbi," probably because his ministry of proclaiming divine law, teaching in the synagogues, debating with scribes and settling legal disputes was reminiscent of rabbinical activity. And from his prophetic pronouncements, working of miracles and signs and so on, he also was considered to be a "prophet" and "sage" (a wise man). A number of times during his ministry the people wondered whether he was Elijah, Jeremiah or one of the prophets (cf. Mt 16:13-14).[2]

The Gospels also permit us to observe different methods or techniques that Jesus used to communicate with people. While some were attention-getting devices to create an immediate reaction from his hearers (e.g., hyperbole), the majority were methods appropriate to the information he wished to communicate. All this confirms that Jesus was an exceptionally diverse teacher. Beyond that, he taught his listeners "as one having authority, and not as their scribes" (Mt 7:29).

When one reads the Gospels it does not take long to realize that there was a serious conflict between Jesus and the religious establishment of his day over the meaning and application of the Torah. This conflict, usually among the scribes, Pharisees and Sadducees, focused primarily on the "oral" law (Torah) that had developed in Judaism alongside the written. (Technically, "Torah" includes more than just the Pentateuchal law. It means the "teaching" or "direction" that God has revealed to his people.) Part of Torah is written and commonly is referred to as the "Law of Moses" or the Pentateuch, the first five books of the Old Testament; the other part of Torah is the oral tradition that became such an important part of Jewish religious life. This oral tradition, accepted by the Pharisees but not the Sadducees, is mentioned by Josephus:

> What I now explain is this, that the Pharisees have delivered to the people a great many observances by succession from their fathers, which are not written in the law of Moses; and for that reason it is that the Sadducees reject them, and say that we are to esteem those observances to be obligatory which are in the written work, but are not to observe what is derived from the tradition of our forefathers. (*Antiquities* 13.10.6)

Later rabbinical tradition even carried this revelation back to Sinai. Tractate *Pirqe 'Abot* ("Sayings of the Fathers") in the Talmud states:

> Moses received Torah from Sinai and delivered it to Joshua, and Joshua to the Elders, and the Elders to the Prophets, and the Prophets delivered it to the Men of the Great Synagogue. These said three things: Be deliberate in judging, and raise up many disciples, and make a hedge for the Torah.

In the New Testament, the oral tradition is referred to as "the tradition of the elders" (Mt 15:2; Mk 7:3, 5) or the "customs" of Moses and/or the "fathers" (Acts 6:14; 15:1; 21:21; 22:3; 26:3; 28:17; Gal 1:14).

The tradition of the elders goes back to the time of the exile in Babylon and the development of the scribal office within Judaism. Here the Jews gave increasing significance to the studying, gathering, editing, copying and guarding of the Torah.[3] A scribe was someone able to "cipher" (from the Hebrew *sōp̄er*, thus forming an authoritative body of teachers, the *sōp̄erîm*) or to interpret the meaning of Torah. Thus we have Ezra, "a scribe skilled in the law of Moses" (Ezra 7:6) who "had set his heart to study the law of the LORD, and to do it, and to teach the statutes and ordinances in Israel" (7:10). By the time of the New Testament, scribes (Lk 5:21) also were referred to as teachers (Lk 2:46) and lawyers (Lk 5:17; 7:30). The Gospels—and other historical records—do not always make a clear differentiation between scribes and Pharisees, so it is difficult to determine their role as teachers, interpreters and enforcers of the Law.

The rabbis discovered that the written Torah, with the "Ten Command-ments" and the additional 248 positive and 365 negative commandments they had identified, did not cover all the contingencies in life. For example, Moses said to "remember the sabbath day, and keep it holy" (Ex 20:8-11); but what constituted keeping it holy? In what type of work could one engage and not transgress this law?

Sabbath observance was one area of conflict between Jesus and the Phari-sees. Jesus was accused of breaking the Law by picking grain (Mt 12:1-8; Mk 2:23-28; Lk 6:1-5) and healing (Mt 12:9-14; Mk 3:1-6; Lk 6:6-11). Similar con-frontations arose over laws regulating purity, as in the case of washing one's hands (Mt 15:1-20; Mk 7:1-23), and social intercourse with tax collectors and sinners (Mt 9:11). Other conflicts took place on such issues as paying taxes (Mt 22:15-22), the resurrection (Mt 22:23-33) and divorce (Mk 10:2-12). Matthew (23:1-36) and Luke (11:37-54) contain a series of severe denunciations ("woes") of the scribes and Pharisees for their casuistry and hypocrisy concerning tithing and taking oaths and their lack of inner righteousness.

It is important to realize that Jesus is not condemning the Law of Moses as such—a law that he too would have regarded as divine revelation. He was opposing a religious system that overemphasized the legal and ceremonial dimensions of Torah at the expense of the moral. Matthew develops this concern when he clarifies that Jesus did not come "to abolish the law or the prophets . . . but to fulfill" them (Mt 5:17). In the antitheses ("You have heard that it was said . . . but I say to you . . .") that follow in the "Sermon on the Mount" it appears that Jesus' concern was with the inner and moral meaning of the law and not with the outward performance. The Pharisees had placed ritualistic and external observances above moral obligations and thus fell prey to legalism and formalism.

The oral Torah contained two types of material: that which defined proper conduct and gave guidance on rules for daily conduct is called *hᵃlākâh* (from the Hebrew *hālak*, "to go," "to walk"); the other is *haggāḏâh* ("the narrative," from the Hebrew verb *nāḡaḏ*, "to tell") and includes edifying material such as stories, parables and legends that describe the moral life lived according to the Law.

As this body of oral traditions grew, it became necessary for the rabbis to codify and put it into writing. This process began in earnest after the fall of Jerusalem in A.D. 70 and continued into the second century, when it finally was completed as the Mishnah (from Hebrew *šānâh*, "to repeat," "study," "teach"). The Mishnah contains sixty-three tractates that are grouped under six major divisions.

It did not take the rabbis long to discover that even the Mishnah did not have an answer for everything, so they added further commentary. Their comments and additions to the Mishnah are known as the *Gemara* (from *gᵉmar*, "to complete"—i.e., to complete knowledge that has been learned), which, together with the Mishnah, constitutes the Talmud (from *lāmad*, "to study"; *limmad*, "to teach," "to instruct").

Work on the *Gemara* took place in Palestine and Babylon and resulted in the

Table 2.1. The Talmud

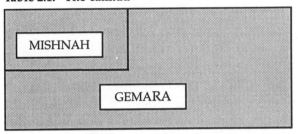

publication of the Jerusalem Talmud (fourth century A.D.) and the Babylonian Talmud (fifth century A.D.), the latter being the larger and more authoritative for rabbinical Judaism.

Besides the existence of written and oral Torah during the writing of the New Testament, there is evidence of rabbinical methods of interpretation and exegesis within the New Testament. This should not surprise us, since Christianity and Judaism shared so many common elements, and many writers of the New Testament were Jewish Christians. Paul, for example, was trained in rabbinical exegesis before he became a believer and employed some of the methodological principles of this discipline in his letters.

The most common method of interpreting Scripture among the Jews was *midrash* (from the Hebrew *dāraš*, "to search out," "to find something by exposition"). Jesus undoubtedly refers to this method when he states, "You search the scriptures because you think that in them you have eternal life" (Jn 5:39). The main focus of midrash was to apply the text to daily life. Examples of midrash in the New Testament include such passages as John 6:25-59 and Galatians 3:8-14.[4]

During Jesus' time the synagogue (from *synagōgē*, an assembly, a gathering) was the main center of Jewish activity for prayer, worship, instruction and civil and judicial matters (see Mt 10:17; Lk 4:16-20; 11:43; 12:11). Jesus would have received some of his religious education in a synagogue in Nazareth. Here, according to Luke 4:16, he actually inaugurates his public ministry: "When he came to Nazareth, where he had been brought up, he went to the synagogue on the sabbath day, as was his custom."

Although the Jewish scriptures were written and studied in Hebrew, the people of Palestine spoke a dialect of Aramaic as the *lingua franca* (common language) of the day.[5] This necessitated a translation from the Hebrew into Aramaic, known as a "Targum." Such interpretive translations were common in synagogue worship during the time of Jesus. In many ways, the Targumim may be compared to some current English translations of the Bible that paraphrase, annotate and to some extent even interpret Scripture (e.g., *The Living Bible*).[6]

Since Jesus was able to speak Hebrew, Aramaic and Greek,[7] scholars have debated whether some of the sayings of Jesus originally were written and circulated in Aramaic before they appeared in the Greek as we know them today. Some of the Aramaic words retained in our English New Testament include "Talitha cum" (Mk 5:41), "Ephphatha" (Mk 7:34), "Maran atha" (1 Cor 16:22), "Abba" (Mk 14:36; Rom 8:15; Gal 4:6) and "Eloi, Eloi, lema sabachthani" (Mk 15:34). However, any theories about an Aramaic Gospel or Aramaic originals behind our Greek Gospels remain highly conjectural.

2. The Formation of the Oral Tradition

In our age of literacy and literary activity it is difficult to imagine that the early Christians were part of a culture that passed on ideas orally more than by the written word. In first-century Judaism a significant amount of learning was accomplished through memorization. Scribes and rabbis would teach people in schools and synagogues to commit their instructions to memory and repeat them in their homes and public life.[8] Manuscripts were very costly to produce, so even individuals who could read were not able to afford their own private copies of the Scriptures. Only the scribes had access to the scrolls that were kept in the synagogue.

When Jesus gathered his twelve disciples, he communicated with them orally. The crowds who heard him came without notebooks and left without paperback copies of "The Good News According to Jesus." They simply had to retain his message by applying it to their daily life, retelling it and memorizing it. Learning by memorization may explain why Jesus used certain "forms" of teaching, such as parables and parallelism *(parallelismus membrorum)*. R. Riesner estimates that about 80 percent of Jesus' teaching utilizes parallelism, a characteristic of Hebrew poetry.[9] All this, however, should not lead us to conclude that the early Christians had "professional or semi-professional schools of memorizers who meticulously passed down oral tradition."[10]

After Pentecost, the early Christians in Jerusalem continued to pass on the stories and sayings of Jesus in their preaching and teaching. When they were asked questions about Jesus, such as who he was, what he said, why he was crucified, what he thought of the Torah, where he went and so on, they would rely upon their memory and the oral traditions that were developing within their communities. Christian centers in other parts of Judea, Galilee, and Damascus and Antioch in Syria would assemble oral collections of Jesus' sayings. Teachers and prophets in these communities (cf. Acts 13:1) would have appealed to these traditions for devotional, instructional and apologetic reasons.

Before we discuss the actual formation of the oral tradition, there are two important things to remember.

First, the Gospels as we have them today in our New Testament were not written until thirty to fifty years *after* the resurrection and ascension of Jesus and the founding of the church at Pentecost. New Testament scholars are fairly unanimous in dating Mark at around A.D. 65-70, Matthew and Luke around A.D. 85, and John around A.D. 95.[11] This means that Paul's letters—and most of the books of the New Testament—were written before the sayings of Jesus acquired their literary form. It is a mistake to assume that the Gospels were written first because of their order in the New Testament.

Second, during his earthly ministry Jesus obviously said and did much more than is recorded in the Gospels. One can read through any one of the Gospels in approximately one to two hours. Matthew's version of "the Sermon on the Mount" takes about five minutes to read. This, too, may surprise us, because we would expect such a significant sermon to be considerably longer. In a remarkable example of Near Eastern hyperbole John writes: "But there are also many other things that Jesus did; if every one of them were written down, I suppose that the world itself could not contain the books that would be written" (Jn 21:24). This raises the question of *why* certain deeds and sayings of Jesus were remembered while others were not recorded and are forgotten. What influences were at work in the early church which determined the selection of material that we have today?

After Jesus' death two important factors developed simultaneously in the early church that contribute to our understanding of the composition of the Gospels: one was the *content* of the proclamation or preaching about Jesus; the second was the *organization* of Jesus' sayings into certain forms by the worshiping believers.

■ **Early Christian Kerygma.** The Greek term *kērygma* ("that which is preached," hence the proclamation) is used to describe the content of the proclamation about Jesus. C. H. Dodd was one of the first New Testament scholars to define the nature of proclamation or preaching in the early church.[12] Following Dodd, most scholars discuss the contents of early Christian preaching under the heading "the mighty acts of God in Jesus Christ." These acts include

1. that the messianic age foretold by the prophets has arrived (Acts 2:16-21; 3:18, 24; 10:43; Rom 1:2)

2. that the fulfillment of the messianic age is demonstrated by the life, death and resurrection of Jesus (Acts 2:24, 31; 3:15; 5:30; 10:37-43; Rom 1:3-4; 4:24-25; 8:34; 1 Cor 15:3-4; 1 Thess 1:10)

3. that by virtue of his resurrection, Jesus is the exalted Lord (Acts 2:33-36; 4:11; Rom 8:34; 10:9; Phil 2:9)

4. that the presence of the Holy Spirit in the church is a sign of God's presence with his people (Acts 2:37-47; 4:31; 5:32; Rom 8:26-27; 1 Cor 12:1-11)

5. that Christ will return as Judge and Savior of the world (Acts 3:20-26; 10:42; 17:31; Rom 2:16; 1 Thess 1:10)

6. that the call to repentance includes an offer of forgiveness from sins and the reception of the Holy Spirit as a guarantee of salvation (Acts 2:38; 3:19; 10:43; 11:18; Rom 10:9)

Dodd's thesis is helpful for appreciating the unity of the kerygma in the early church. Subsequent research, however, has noted some diversity to this pattern.[13]

■ **Form Criticism.** Form criticism (from the German, *Formgeschichte*) is a method of determining the oral prehistory of written documents or sources and then classifying that material according to certain "categories" or "forms." It is an endeavor that has been applied to secular "folk literature" as well as to biblical literature.[14]

Form criticism seeks to identify the "form"—the literary structure or genre—of each Gospel section (or *pericope*) at a time when traditions concerning Jesus circulated by word of mouth. New Testament form critics work from a basic set of propositions or "axioms" that govern their research.

1. The stories of Jesus that constitute the Gospels are closer to "popular" or "folk" literature than to historical, biographical or classical literature. The authors (Evangelists) of the Gospels "were not historians employing modern methods of research, but receivers and transmitters of traditions cherished by Christian communities."[15]

2. The words and deeds of Jesus circulated orally throughout the Christian communities. Initially, these sayings would have circulated individually, in bits and pieces without local or temporal connections. "We cannot imagine," observes Travis, "the apostles giving a series of lectures in the temple precincts on the life of Jesus. Rather, they would use some particular story or word of Jesus to bring home some point in the course of their preaching."[16] Jesus was not a "systematic theologian" in the modern sense of the term, even though he taught consistently on certain themes and regularly utilized certain teaching methods, such as parables. What he taught was important and suited his audience; but the style was patterned after that of an itinerant teacher and prophet and not that of a classroom lecturer.

Form critics argue that these "random" sayings of Jesus gradually became more stereotyped and were organized into units. One early collection may have been the "Passion Narrative."[17] This part of our Lord's life was extremely important to the early church. In worship, believers would have recounted and rehearsed the events that led to his death and resurrection; in teaching, they would have found such a narrative essential for apologetic purposes. There were many questions about Jesus' death that needed explanation. Was he a heretic, a revolutionary, a criminal or a Zealot who deserved to die for political reasons? The Jews could not believe that their Messiah could be crucified. Believers had to explain why Jesus went to the cross and what his death accomplished for humankind. Mark's account of the passion (chapters 14—16), therefore, is an early connected narrative that he took over from tradition and incorporated into his Gospel.

The Passion Story was not the only material brought together before the actual composition of the Gospels. When Luke writes his Gospels he begins by saying:

Since many have undertaken to set down an orderly account of the events that have been fulfilled among us, just as they were handed on to us by those who from the beginning were eyewitnesses and servants of the word, I too decided, after investigating everything carefully from the very first, to write an orderly account for you, most excellent Theophilus, so that you may know the truth concerning the things about which you have been instructed. (Lk 1:1-4)

We do not know what Luke meant by "many have undertaken to set down an orderly account." Does he have Mark or Matthew in mind? Were there other Gospels similar to Mark and Matthew in existence around A.D. 85? Or is Luke referring to other collections like the passion narrative or the "Q" (from the German Quelle, "source") material as one of the "many"? One also wonders whether Mark had been aware of other sources when he wrote his Gospel fifteen to twenty years earlier.

There simply are no easy answers to some of these questions. The most we can say with guarded certainty is that Q and the passion narrative are exceptions to the composition of the Gospels at this early stage (c. A.D. 35-65) of transmission. On the other hand, C. F. D. Moule's suggestion is intriguing:

It is not difficult to imagine how self-contained units of Christian teaching came to be hammered out, first orally, then it may be, as written fly-sheets or tracts—often in several differing though related shapes, according to the contexts in which they were used. Unless, therefore, we follow Papias quite literally in his assertion that Mark omitted nothing that he had heard from Peter . . . we may guess that, when he sharpened his reed pen and dipped it in the ink to write, he had already behind him a considerable tradition of Christian speaking and possibly writing, by Peter and many others. He would know recognized patterns of argument and exhortation, of defense and attack, of instruction and challenge—from among which he might select his narrative material and his sayings. The earliest Christian writers were probably already heirs to a considerable body of tradition.[18]

3. The sayings that were retained and transmitted were those that met the missionary, preaching, apologetic and pastoral needs of the early church. Scholars refer to this sociological setting as the *Sitz im Leben* ("life setting" or "situation in life") and have concluded that Jesus' sayings passed through several chronological stages.

The first is the life setting of Jesus himself *(Sitz im Leben Jesu)* and the particular stories that he told to specific groups of people on certain occasions. Years later, the early church would have taken the same story and, unaware of its original life setting, applied it to a different setting in life—sometimes called the *Sitz im Leben Kirche* (life setting of the church).

Finally, the Evangelists who composed their Gospels used the material to fit into their own life setting and purpose in writing a Gospel. When one consults a "synopsis of the Gospels," for example, one quickly observes that many sayings of Jesus are edited and arranged by the Evangelist to support his purpose.[19] Note, for example, Jesus' saying "Foxes have holes, and birds of the air have nests; but the Son of Man has nowhere to lay his head." In Matthew 8:18-27, Jesus says this to a "scribe" and then proceeds to get into a boat and still the storm. In Luke, the statement is made to an unidentified man who is walking along the road with Jesus (9:57-58), but in Luke's chronology, this is *after* the stilling of the storm (8:22-25). Either Jesus used this saying on another occasion or Matthew and Luke were applying this pericope to different life situations.

The different accounts of the "sign of Jonah" (Mt 16:4; Mk 8:11-12; Lk 11:29-32) *may* illustrate how a statement of Jesus was interpreted and remembered differently so that the interpretation eventually became part of the saying itself. A possible scenario of this process is presented by Joseph Tyson:

> It is possible to say that Jesus once cited the sign of Jonah but did so without an interpretation, so that various hearers preserved the saying in the light of the significance it had for them. . . . Here an original statement of Jesus, subject to diverse understandings, has picked up different interpretations, which finally became part of the saying itself. Once the interpretation became attached to the saying, it would be difficult to distinguish between the two. Thus, the explanation came to be attributed to Jesus himself. This must have been the case when Matthew wrote. Aware of several forms of

the saying, the evangelist felt that Jesus said all of them. So he recorded both primary and secondary elements with no attempt at discrimination.[20]
It may help to reverse the sequence and ask the following questions:

a. What did a particular saying or story mean to the evangelist who inserted it into his Gospel?

b. What did a particular saying or story mean to the Christian community/communities who preserved it—the *Sitz im Leben Kirche* (life setting of the church)—before the Evangelist used it?

c. What did a particular saying or story originally mean in the life and teaching of Jesus—the *Sitz im Leben Jesu* (life setting of Jesus)?

The issues here have raised a number of significant questions about the historical reliability of Jesus' sayings. Some form critics, such as Rudolf Bultmann, believed that most of the sayings attributed to Jesus in the Gospels were creations of the church rather than the very words (*ipsissima verba*) of the historical Jesus. More moderate form critics, such as Vincent Taylor, challenged the skepticism of Bultmann by stressing the veracity of oral transmission and the role of eyewitnesses.

Taylor, for example, comments, "If the Form-Critics are right, the disciples must have been translated to heaven immediately after the Resurrection."[21] In other words, no one would have been around to check whether Jesus' sayings were distorted. James Dunn also has some insightful observations as to why the early church was concerned to preserve the memory of Jesus. "The Gospel traditions," he writes, "bear witness to a strong and widely prevalent concern among the first Christians to *remember* Jesus, to celebrate their memories, to retain them in appropriate forms, to structure their traditions for easy recall, but above all to remember."[22]

4. The final axiom is that the sayings can be classified into certain forms. While the technicalities of this axiom extend beyond the scope of our study, some examples will illustrate what the form critics mean. There is no universally accepted list of forms, but the classifications of three significant form critics may be observed in table 2.2.

Darrell Bock does a commendable job of integrating the classifications by

Table 2.2. Three Classifications of Gospel Forms

Dibelius	Bultmann	Taylor
1. paradigms	1. apophthegms	1. passion narrative
2. short stories	2. logia	2. pronouncements
3. legend	3. prophetic/apocalyptic	3. parables
4. paraenetic	4. legal sayings	4. miracle stories
5. myth	5. "I" sayings	5. stories about Jesus
	6. parables	

Dibelius, Bultmann and Taylor under several headings.[23]

a. Paradigms/apophthegms/pronouncement stories. These are sayings/stories where the climax comes at the end in the form of a punch line. For example, the key element in the "Pronouncement about the Sabbath" (Mk 2:23-28) is not the story about Jesus and his disciples plucking grain on the sabbath but rather the punch line, "The sabbath was made for humankind, and not humankind for the sabbath; so the Son of Man is lord even of the sabbath" (vv. 27-28). On another occasion, Jesus is accused of eating with "tax collectors and sinners" (Mk 2:13-17). In this passage, the climax is "Those who are well have no need of a physician, but those who are sick; I have come to call not the righteous but sinners." (Other examples are Mk 10:17-31; Lk 10:38-42; 11:27-28.)

b. Tales/Novellen/miracle stories. The terms *Novellen* and *tales* were first introduced by M. Dibelius to designate types of miracle stories. These categories now are expanded by other form critics to include exhortations (Mt 18:10; Lk 6:27-49), logia (i.e., "sayings" such as Mt 6:34b and 12:34b), metaphors (Mk 4:21), prophetic sayings (Mt 5:31-32; 6:14-15; Lk 12:10), similitudes (Mt 5:29-30; 7:13-14), parables (Lk 15:1-7) and miracles (Mk 1:40-45; 4:35-41).

c. Legends/stories about Jesus. Here, notes Bock, "either title is simply intended to describe an account that is interested in the life and adventures of Jesus for its own sake, without being concerned to recount his sayings or other such things."[24] This would include, for example, his temple visit when he was twelve years old, his baptism, transfiguration and triumphal entry, and Peter's confession. Bock also adds Dibelius's category of "myth," a term unfortunately often misunderstood, along with "legend," to imply something nonhistorical and therefore false. When used by scholars to designate a literary form, *myth* refers to events which transcend history and which fall beyond the scope of historical investigation, such as Jesus' resurrection and ascension or anything miraculous and supernatural.[25]

Although contemporary scholars continue to debate the classification and function of these "forms," they remain a helpful way of suggesting how certain sayings of Jesus may have circulated orally and eventually came to be written down.

3. From Oral to Written Gospel

■ **Why the Gospels Were Written.** There has been considerable speculation among scholars about *why* the Gospels were written. Some of the standard answers usually given include the following.

1. The expansion of the church. Through its missionary activity, Christianity

spread more and more into the Greco-Roman world. Since this was a literary culture, the custom of oral instruction so vital to the Jews would not have appealed to Gentile converts. William Barclay writes that when Christianity went into the Greco-Roman world, "it entered a world where books were familiar things and where publishing and book-selling were part of big business. . . . Christianity began to see the immense value of the written word; and it is not without significance that Mark, the first Gospel, was almost certainly written and issued in Rome."[26] Contact with other religions and philosophical movements also required some written traditions about Jesus.

Economic realities, however, did not always permit the rapid publication of materials. We must remember that the Gospels and letters initially were meant to be read aloud in the churches (for Paul's letters, cf. Col 4:16; 1 Thess 5:27; 1 Tim 4:13). Thus wordplays, repetitions, the sequencing of events, parallelism and so on would serve as aids to the hearer. In other words, writers would structure their material more conscious of the hearer than the reader. The texts, to use W. Kelber's term, were "hearer-friendly."[27]

2. The passing away of the eyewitnesses. After the middle of the first century, many of the original witnesses to the Jesus movement were passing away. The early church could live on its memory only as long as believers could appeal to these witnesses when there were important questions to be answered. But in a written record, the preacher of the gospel could be assured "that his preaching is in accord with the original revelation and that the answers he gives to the innumerable questions that he will be asked will be in accord with the mind of the Lord and of his followers."[28]

3. The response to new challenges. Several issues usually are considered in this category. For one, there was an external threat to the Christian church. As Christianity spread, it became increasingly necessary to defend its doctrines from other religious and philosophical systems. Here W. D. Davies wisely notes:

Men challenged it and could have perverted it by turning it into a metaphysical system or a Gnostic cult, without connection with the historic figure who gave it birth; i.e., they would have cut it from its root. To prevent this, the Gospels came into being; they kept the Church attached to its base—in the actualities of the ministry of Jesus; they preserved Christianity from degenerating into a theology of the Word or of an idea, and preserved the community rooted in the Word made flesh, that is, in the historically real Jesus.[29]

Second, there were threats within the emerging church in the form of false teaching. The New Testament documents are full of warnings against various kinds of heresies (cf. Colossians, the Pastoral Epistles, 2 Peter, Jude and 1 John, for example). The church needed a unified and authoritative standard of teaching regarding the person of Jesus to confront false christologies and other heresies.

Finally, there were apologetic and pastoral needs within the Christian community itself. Believers, especially during times of persecution and martyrdom, would find comfort and guidance from Jesus' own suffering and the predictions that he made about their impending trials (e.g., Mt 5:11-12, 44; 13:20-21 and parallels). A central theme in Mark's Gospel is that believers are called to suffer even as their Master suffered. An account of Jesus' life could also assure Roman authorities that Jesus was not some kind of revolutionary figure and that his followers were not a subversive movement preparing to commit treason.

4. The need for standard instruction. As the church grew it became necessary to instruct and strengthen the believers. The stories and sayings of Jesus were treasured by the believers as tools for evangelism and instruction in the faith and not for their nostalgic value. New converts needed instruction in Christian doctrine and practice to understand the changes that had taken place in their life so that they could accept the privileges and responsibilities of belonging to the body of Christ.

Although these reasons may have some validity, we need to remember that they are no more than hypotheses. The fact is that we simply do not know exactly *why* the Gospels were written *when* they were. Any one of them could have been composed at an earlier or later stage in the life of the church. It is doubtful that the delayed return *(parousia)* of the Lord contributed to the writing of the Gospels, because apocalyptic enthusiasm continued in the church even after they were written. Of the Synoptic writers, Luke is the only Evangelist who gives a specific purpose for his Gospel—so that Theophilus "may know the truth concerning the things about which [he had] been instructed" (1:4). John has a definite evangelistic motive for his Gospel: "These are written so that you may come to believe that Jesus is the Messiah, the Son of God, and that through believing you may have life in his name" (20:31).

The appearance of the written Gospels did not bring all oral traditions about Jesus to an abrupt halt, because oral tradition continued throughout the Mediterranean world even after Mark had written the first Gospel. "There is considerable evidence," writes W. J. Ong, "that oral and written cultures existed side by side in the ancient world, particularly since writing tended to be used as a help to memory rather than as an autonomous and independent mode of communication."[30] And C. F. D. Moule reminds us that the Gospels were written as supplementary and explanatory material for early Christian preaching: "It [each Gospel] ministers to Christian witness: it is the supplementation of a herald's announcement."[31]

■ **How the Gospels Were Written.** So far we have established that by the time Mark wrote his Gospel (I shall consider this the earliest one, written c. A.D. 65-70[32]), he had access to various independent units of tradition, a Passion Story in narrative form, and possibly some other more substantial collections of sayings. In addition to this, Eusebius writes that Papias regarded the apostle Peter as Mark's informant:

Mark being the interpreter of Peter, whatsoever he recorded he wrote with great accuracy, but not, however, in the order in which it was spoken or done by our Lord, for he neither heard nor followed our Lord, but as before said, he was in company with Peter, who gave him such instruction as was necessary, but not to give a history of our Lord's discourses: wherefore Mark has not erred in anything, by writing some things as he has recorded them; for he was carefully attentive to one thing, not to pass by anything that he heard, or to state anything falsely in these accounts. (*HE* 3.39.15)

■ **The Synoptic Problem.** If we had only the Gospel of Mark, there would be no such thing as "the Synoptic problem." The term *synoptic* (Greek, "to view at the same time") dates back to J. J. Griesbach (1745-1812) and was attributed to the first three Gospels because they provide a common or similar outline of the story of Jesus. Basically, the "problem" is the interrelation of Matthew, Mark and Luke. How is it that they have so many similarities? And if they have so much in common, why are there so many differences?[33] To illustrate, observe the differences among the Synoptics in the accounts of the Lord's Prayer, the Beatitudes and the Confession at Caesarea Philippi in table 2.3.

Just a cursory study of these passages reveals a number of differences. Mark does not have any material that approximates "the Lord's Prayer" as found in Matthew and Luke. Luke's version has fewer petitions, and they are stated more briefly than in Matthew.

Only Matthew and Luke have the sections we refer to as "the Beatitudes." Matthew's account is longer and more structured and has a setting on "the mountain" (Mt 5:1), whereas Luke's version is set as a sermon on the plain ("a level place," Lk 6:17).

The confession of Jesus as the Christ at Caesarea Philippi is common to all three evangelists with some minor variations in word selection and order. The main difference, however, is Matthew's inclusion of Jesus' response to Peter and the role he is to play in the Christian community.

Attempted solutions to the synoptic problem by New Testament scholars have led to the study of literary relationships, referred to as "source criti-

Table 2.3.   Three Synoptic Parallels (RSV)

The Lord's Prayer

Matt 6.7-15	Mark 11.25 [26]	Luke 11.1-4
7"And in praying do not heap up empty phrases as the Gentiles do; for they think that they will be heard for their many words. 8Do not be like them, for your Father knows what you need before you ask him.		
		1He was praying in a certain place, and when he ceased, one of his disciples said to him, "Lord teach us to pray, as John taught his disciples." 2And he said to them, "When you pray, say:
9Pray then like this: Our Father who art in heaven, Hallowed be thy name. 10Thy kingdom come, Thy will be done, On earth as it is in heaven.		"Father, hallowed be thy name. Thy kingdom come.

11Give us this day our
    daily bread;
12And forgive us our debts,
  As we also have forgiven our
    debtors;
		3Give us each day our
		    daily bread;
		4and forgive us our sins,
		    for we ourselves forgive every one who is
		    indebted to us;

13And lead us not into temptation, But deliver us from evil.		and lead us not into temptation."
14For if you forgive men their trespasses, your heavenly Father also will forgive you;	25"And whenever you stand praying, forgive, if you have anything against any one; so that your Father also who is in heaven may forgive you	
15but if you do not forgive men their trespasses, neither will your Father forgive your trespasses."	your trespasses." [26"But if you do not forgive, neither will your Father who is in heaven forgive your trespasses."]	

Beatitudes

Matt. 5.3-12	Mark	Luke 6.20b-23

3"Blessed are the poor in spirit,
  for theirs is the kingdom of heaven.
		20b"Blessed are you poor,
		  for yours is the kingdom of God.

4Blessed are those who mourn,
  for they shall be comforted.
5Blessed are the meek,
  for they shall inherit the earth.
6Blessed are those who hunger and thirst for righteousness,
  for they shall be satisfied.
		21Blessed are you that hunger now,
		  for you shall be satisfied.
		Blessed are you that weep now,
		  for you shall laugh.

7Blessed are the merciful,
  for they shall obtain mercy.
8Blessed are the pure in heart,
  for they shall see God.
9Blessed are the peacemakers,
  for they shall be called sons of God.
10Blessed are those who are persecuted for righteousness' sake,
  for theirs is the kingdom of heaven.		

11Blessed are you when men revile you and persecute you and utter all kinds of evil against you falsely on my account. 12Rejoice and be glad, for your reward is great in heaven, for so men persecuted the prophets who were before you.		22Blessed are you when men hate you, and when they exclude you and revile you, and cast out your name as evil, on account of the Son of man! 23Rejoice in that day, and leap for joy, for behold, your reward is great in heaven; for so their fathers did to the prophets.

The Confession at Caesarea-Philippi

Matt. 16.13-20	Mark 8.27-30	Luke 9.18-21
		[18]Now it happened that as he was praying alone
[13]Now when Jesus came into the district of Caesarea Philippi, he asked his disciples, "Who do men say that the Son of man is?" [14]And they said, "Some say John the Baptist, others say Elijah, and others Jeremiah or one of the prophets."	[27]And Jesus went on with his disciples, to the villages of Caesarea Philippi; and on the way he asked his disciples, "Who do men say that I am?" [28]And they told him, "John the Baptist; and others say, Elijah; and others one of the prophets."	the disciples were with him; and he asked them, "Who do the people say that I am?" [19]And they answered, "John the Baptist; but others say, Elijah; and others, that one of the old prophets has risen."
[15]He said to them, "But who do you say that I am?" [16]Simon Peter replied,	[29]And he asked them, "But who do you say that I am?" Peter answered him,	[20]And he said to them, "But who do you say that I am?" And Peter answered,
"You are the Christ, the Son of the living God." [17]And Jesus answered him, "Blessed are you, Simon Bar-Jona! For flesh and blood has not revealed this to you, but my Father who is in heaven. [18]And I tell you, you are Peter, and on this rock I will build my church, and the powers of death shall not prevail against it. [19]I will give you the keys of the kingdom of heaven, and whatever you bind on earth shall be bound in heaven, and whatever you loose on earth shall be loosed in heaven."	"You are the Christ."	"The Christ of God."
[20]Then he strictly charged the disciples to tell no one that he was the Christ.	[30]And he charged them to tell no one about him.	[21]But he charged and commanded them to tell this to no one.

cism," and the study of theological intentions, referred to as "redaction criticism."

■ **Source Criticism.** As the name suggests, source criticism is concerned with identifying the sources that the Evangelists used to produce their Gospels.[34] Table 2.4 illustrates material that is common and unique to each Synoptic Gospel.

One useful and popular solution to the Synoptic problem is the "Two-Document Hypothesis," a theory based on the priority of Mark.[35] As the diagram shows, approximately 90 percent of Mark is reproduced in Matthew and 57 percent in Luke. But what about the material *common to Matthew and Luke* which is not in Mark? What is the source for this information about Jesus, which consists of approximately 230 verses?

Certain German New Testament scholars contemplating this question rea-

Table 2.4. A Comparison of Synoptic Material

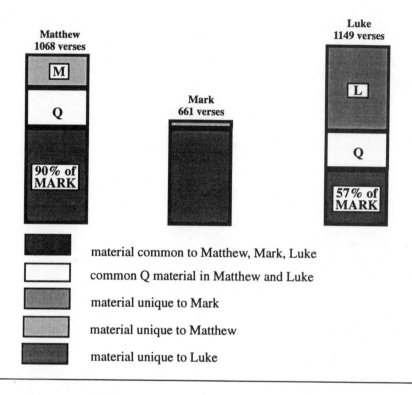

material common to Matthew, Mark, Luke

common Q material in Matthew and Luke

material unique to Mark

material unique to Matthew

material unique to Luke

Table 2.5. The Q Hypothesis

soned that there had to be another literary "source," hence the German word *Quelle* (source) and the abbreviation Q, as it commonly is known in New Testament studies.[36] On this hypothesis one can visualize the composition of the Gospels as illustrated in table 2.5.

Issues related to the nature, transmission, purpose and theology of Q go beyond the scope of our discussion.[37] After a rather detailed study of the topic, G. N. Stanton arrives at the following conclusions:

We may now be reasonably certain that Q existed as a written document; its 230 or so sayings of Jesus were used and partly reinterpreted by both Matthew and Luke. But we can be less certain about Q's earlier history, literary genre, overall theological perspective and purpose. Although clusters of traditions with related themes can be identified, Q contained such varied material that it is unwise to claim that it has *one* primary theological perspective or that it was used in the early church in any *one* specific way.[38]

Nevertheless, theories on the priority of Mark and the existence of Q do not account for all the material in the Synoptics. Our earlier diagram indicates that there is still some material peculiar—in the sense of unique—to both Matthew and Luke. What is the source of this material? At this point, B. H. Streeter has advanced our study of sources to another level with his famous "Four-Document Hypothesis" (see table 2.6).

Table 2.6. The Four-Document Hypothesis

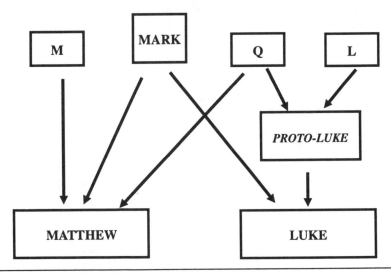

In Streeter's schema, *M* and *L* represent the material that is unique to Matthew and Luke respectively. Unfortunately, there is no way of knowing whether this material was from written or oral traditions.[39]

Table 2.7 may help for visualizing the process by which the oral traditions of Jesus were passed on and collected as different sources before they were composed by the Evangelists.[40]

As helpful as the study of sources may be, it still does not solve the Synoptic problem or answer other pressing questions about the composition of the

Table 2.7. From Jesus Tradition to Written Gospels

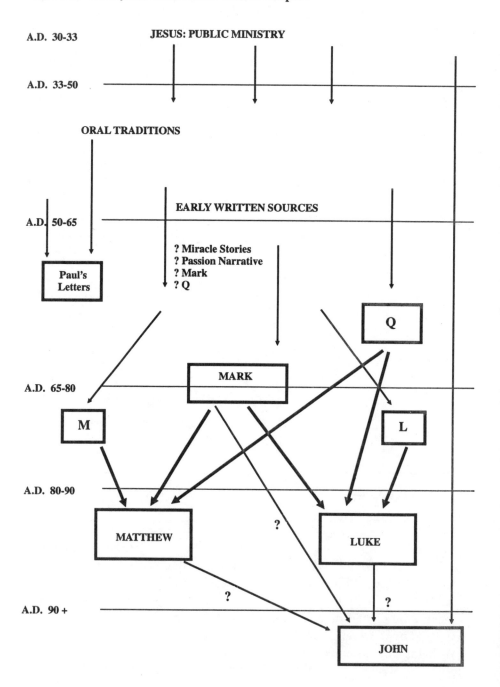

A.D. 30-33   JESUS: PUBLIC MINISTRY

A.D. 33-50

ORAL TRADITIONS

A.D. 50-65   EARLY WRITTEN SOURCES

? Miracle Stories
? Passion Narrative
? Mark
? Q

Paul's
Letters

Q

MARK

A.D. 65-80

M

L

A.D. 80-90

MATTHEW   ?   LUKE

A.D. 90 +   ?   ?

JOHN

Gospels. From a comparative study of the Gospels we notice that even though the Evangelists used much of the same material, they often used it differently. How does one account for the additions, omissions, rearrangements, connecting links, different applications and theological perspectives in the Gospels?

Some early form critics, such as W. Wrede, K. L. Schmidt, M. Kähler, R. Bultmann and M. Dibelius, saw the Gospels as little more than a series of formerly unconnected and loosely assembled stories (pericopes) artificially strung together with no apparent unifying theme. Later scholars who examined the Gospel material discovered that the Evangelists were more than just collectors of traditions about Jesus. They have led us to appreciate that each Evangelist had definite theological and historical interests that shaped his Gospel.

■ **Redaction Criticism.** Redaction criticism (from the German, *Redaktionsgeschichte*, also referred to as "editorial" or "composition" criticism) moves our observations on the making of the New Testament a step forward by viewing each Gospel as a whole, composed not by a mere collector of stories and events but by a theologian with a well-defined purpose. As R. Stein describes it, "The evangelists were not merely 'scissors and paste men.' On the contrary, the 'scissors' were manipulated by a theological hand, and the 'paste' was impregnated with a particular theology. . . . Each had a theological purpose in writing his gospel."[41]

Redaction criticism seeks to discover the theology and setting of a writing by studying the ways the redactor or editor changed the traditions he inherited and the connections that he used to link those traditions together. By studying the Gospels as unified wholes or individual entities, and not as random collections of stories, we are able to appreciate *why* the Evangelists introduced certain changes into their Gospels. The material in each is arranged and interpreted according to the theological understanding and intention of the author.

The insights of redaction criticism have had a number of positive effects upon our understanding of the composition of the Gospels.

First, they help us understand *why* and *how* the Evangelists used the traditions that were at their disposal. A pericope such as "The Stilling of the Storm" is found in all three Synoptics (Mt 8:23-27; Mk 4:35-41; Lk 8:22-25), but is arranged and applied differently in each. This is a good example of the third *Sitz im Leben* (life setting) discussed earlier in regard to what a particular pericope might mean to the Evangelist who put it into its final form.

Second, they enable us to appreciate the Gospels as products of individual authors who deliberately sought to interpret Jesus' words and deeds to serve their theological intentions. Hence, concerning the Synoptics, we have three distinct "theologies" in the form of the Synoptic Gospels or, as Robert Guelich so creatively put it, three "portraits" of the *one* gospel, which is the good news of salvation in Jesus Christ.[42] Grant Osborne's observation also is worth quoting:

> Now we can see how God inspired the evangelists to select, highlight, and emphasize certain aspects of the life of Jesus in order to speak to their readers. For the first time these writings have actually become "gospels," not just biographical accounts but "history with a message." These inspired authors did not just chronicle historical events but produced historical sermons, as God inspired the evangelists to take virtually the same set of stories and weave out of them individual tapestries of theological truth.[43]

This reality helps us to appreciate that each Gospel has a central theme that depends upon the inclusion, structure and application of certain materials. Mark's Gospel, for example, may be built around the theme stated in 10:45 that "the Son of Man came not to be served but to serve, and to give his life a ransom for many." If true, this would at least partially explain Mark's concern with the passion of Jesus and its significance for Christian discipleship.

Luke, on the other hand, emphasizes the universality of the gospel: "that repentance and forgiveness of sins is to be proclaimed in his name to all nations, beginning from Jerusalem" (24:47). This observation explains why Luke universalizes certain sections and presents Jesus as "the Son of Man [who] came to seek out and to save the lost" (19:10). Matthew's Gospel has the appearance of a teaching manual for a Jewish Christian community to demonstrate that Jesus is, in fact, the royal Davidic Messiah ("This is Jesus, the King of the Jews"—27:37). This may explain why he arranges the genealogy as he does, uses so many Old Testament proof-texts, and emphasizes how Jesus fulfills the law and the promises made by God to Israel. John's style, tone and theology are certainly different from that of the Synoptics while at the same time serving his evangelistic purpose (20:31). W. Barnes Tatum suggests that Mark portrays Jesus preeminently as the "Crucified Christ," Matthew as the "Teaching Christ," Luke as the "Universal Christ" and John as the "Eternal Christ."[44]

Third, redaction criticism helps us to focus on the community for which each Evangelist wrote. In this way we gain a new understanding of and appreciation for the early church in several geographical settings. These settings provide an opportunity for theology to be developed "through living relationships and enacted in dynamic events, thus producing a sort of case study workbook for theological understanding. In other words, the Gospels are not just theology taught but theology lived."[45]

Although many of the steps that led to the composition of the Synoptic Gospels apply to the Fourth Gospel, it should be noted that there are some unique and complex features surrounding the latter. G. N. Stanton describes the Fourth Gospel as "a stream in which children can wade and elephants swim . . . full of poignant and dramatic moments . . . appreciated by . . . untutored readers, but it also engages minds well-versed in the philosophical ideas of the ancient world. Behind a veneer of simplicity lies profundity."[46] In many ways the Gospel of John hardly resembles the Synoptics in literary style, language and content. Johannine scholars remain divided over the dependence and/or independence of the Fourth Gospel in relation to the Synoptic tradition.

Those who believe that John knew and used these traditions often have concluded that John's Gospel is a relatively distinct and somewhat independent representation of early Christianity. It is quite common to view John's Gospel (and the Johannine Epistles) as coming from a Christian community that possessed certain traditions about Jesus which it shaped for its own particular needs.

Raymond Brown has adopted a theory of composition for the Fourth Gospel which includes five stages: stage 1—the existence of a body of traditional material similar to but independent of the Synoptic tradition; stage 2—over a period of several decades, these traditional materials were "sifted, selected, thought over, and molded into the form and style of the individual stories and discourses that became part of the Fourth Gospel"; stage 3—the organization of the traditional material into a continuous gospel by "the Evangelist"; stage 4—a process of reediting the Gospel several times by the Evangelist to address certain issues of the day; stage 5—a final edition by a "redactor," a probable close friend or editor of the Evangelist.[47]

The theory of John's independence from the Synoptic Gospels has become widely, although not universally, accepted. On this basis, differences between John and the Synoptics may be due to traditions—both oral and written—exclusive to the Johannine community. Similarities could be attributed to traditions available to all four Evangelists. At any rate, Brown's reconstruction of transmissional and redactional activity behind the Fourth Gospel represents a plausible theory of its composition.

So far our inquiry into oral and written traditions has taken us through several major disciplines of New Testament study: source, form and redaction criticism. We discussed the uniqueness and limitations of each discipline while attempting to affirm that collectively they are useful for understanding the composition of the Gospels. We also saw that even though scholarly opinions vary on certain matters, we have a fairly good idea of how and when the oral traditions of Jesus were written down in a literary form that has come to be known as a "Gospel."

4. The Gospel Genre

The Gospels as we now know them were anonymous—that is, they were written and subsequently circulated for approximately fifty years before specific names were attached to them. The readers probably knew their identity, but evidently the *content* of the material as "the good news of Jesus Christ" (Mk 1:1) was more important than by whom it was written.

Note also that the writings of the Evangelists did not have the title "Gospel" as part of the original manuscripts. Initially, the term *gospel* was used exclusively for the oral proclamation of the message of salvation and not for a *written* document such as a book or a letter. It is only from the second century onward that reference is made to "Gospels" as something written. (See Justin's *First Apology* 66: "For the apostles in the memoirs composed by them, which are called Gospels, thus handed down what was commanded them." Eusebius, in *HE* 3.37.2, refers to "the books of the holy gospels.") We can appreciate that this was a natural development within the life of the church: "Since the preaching bears witness to Christ and His words and acts, and since these constitute the essence of the Gospel, the writings which contain the life and words of Jesus come to be given the name 'gospel.' "[48]

The term *gospel* is the English translation of the Greek *euangelion*, meaning "the good news." In secular literature the term was used as a technical term for the good news of political victory and private messages that brought joy to someone. For Paul, *gospel* meant the good news of what God had done in Jesus Christ on behalf of humanity (Rom 1:1, 3-5, 9; 15:16, 19; 1 Cor 9:12; 2 Cor 2:12; 9:13; 10:14; Phil 1:27; 1 Thess 3:2). For Mark, it is the good news preached by Jesus that the kingdom of God has come near (1:14-15) and will be proclaimed to all nations (13:10). Matthew uses the term by qualifying it as "the good news of the kingdom" (4:23; 9:35; 24:14) or in 26:13 simply as "this good news." In Luke-Acts the term is found only in Acts 15:7 and 20:24 and is used for the apostolic preaching.

Our familiarity with the term *gospel* tends to cloud what Mark intended by the term. What did he have in mind when he wrote in 1:1: "The beginning of the good news [*archē tou euangeliou*] of Jesus Christ, the Son of God"? Did he have any literary models to guide him in his composition? Would his contemporaries have found it strange to designate the *written*—rather than the oral—story of Jesus as "The Gospel According to Mark"?

Unfortunately, we do not know the precise answer to some of these questions. It seems evident that Mark utilized oral traditions about Jesus and that he was the first writer to put the good news (gospel) into written form. And it appears likely that his Gospel was the model Matthew and Luke used for their Gospels. But we are less certain about defining his material and deciding where it fits into the Greco-Roman literary world.

Scholars are unanimous in referring to the Gospels as a literary "genre" (from the French, "kind," "species" or "gender," hence a specific category or type of literature) with certain affinities to Hellenistic biographical and narrative literature. Some research near the turn of the century concluded that the Gospels were similar to popular Greco-Roman biographical literature. This opinion was almost immediately challenged by claims that the Gospels are absolutely *unique* among the literature of the world and that they have no literary parallels. According to this view the Evangelists created something "out of nothing" (*de novo*, or *sui generis*).

New research beginning in the 1970s modified this position considerably. Scholars began to study the literature of the Greco-Roman world with a passion like that of ancient knights in search of the Holy Grail, hoping in this case to find some clues that would illuminate the nature of the Gospels.[49] They concluded that there are significant analogies between the Gospels and ancient biographical and narrative writings. But they also noted certain differences. For example, the presentation of Jesus differs in purpose, emphasis and structure from popular biographies. The setting that led to the writing of the Gospels was not the Greco-Roman literary world but the early Christian community. They were written to address certain needs and answer specific questions of the early believers. Their focus, observes Larry Hurtado, was on Jesus "as the personal vehicle of revelation and redemption" and not his inner personality. We should, concludes Hurtado, "see them as church documents with a certain biographical character rather than as biographies with a religious tone."[50]

Very few doubt that the Evangelists were influenced by the literary conventions of their day or that certain features of ancient literature help us to understand the nature of the Gospels more clearly. But the significant differences have led most contemporary scholars to characterize the Gospels as a "subgenre," "subtype" or "subgroup" of ancient literary forms. As such, they constitute a distinctive—but not unique—genre among ancient writings.[51] They could be described as "theological handbooks"[52] or "theological biography."[53] Basically, this means that they focus on Jesus Christ as the one whom God sent to be Israel's Messiah and the church's Lord, or, to quote Mark himself, they constitute a literary genre whose form and content is "the good news [gospel] of Jesus Christ, the Son of God."

5. Summary

Up to this point we have made the following observations about the making of the Gospels:

1. Jesus, an itinerant teacher/prophet who went about the regions and cities

of Judea and Galilee teaching and preaching, left no written record of his sayings.

2. After Jesus' death and resurrection, the early church recalled his words and deeds and circulated them orally as independent units within the context of their worship—which included preaching, teaching and apologetic activity.

3. The units of tradition gradually assumed certain forms or classifications according to the function they served within the Christian community.

4. Before the first Gospel was written, there may have been several partial and different collections of Jesus' sayings.

5. The existence of these forms, however, still did not complete the story of the making of the Gospels. Someone, whom we now identify as an Evangelist, took this material and put it together into what has come to be called a "Gospel."

6. The main motivation for writing the Gospels lies with the author's intention to provide his readers with a certain historical and theological perspective on the person and teaching of Jesus.

7. In spite of certain limitations, the disciplines of source and form criticism assist us in understanding how the traditions of Jesus gradually were collected and how the Evangelists made use of these materials in the composition of their gospels.

8. Redaction criticism, when properly understood and applied, helps us to explain certain questions raised by a comparative study of the Gospels (the Synoptic problem).

9. The availability of four portraits of Jesus actually enriches our appreciation of the gospel message—namely, that Jesus is God's way of salvation for humankind.

10. In a number of ways, the written Gospels represent a distinct literary genre in the ancient world.

If readers of the Gospels are to give them a fair hearing, they must interpret them for what they are and not attempt to fit them into some false or preconceived framework. A serious and impartial study of the nature, composition and purpose of the Gospels will enlighten and enrich our understanding of them as reliable witnesses of the good news of Jesus Christ.[54]

6. The Fourfold Gospel Collection

As previously noted, the Gospels were not written until thirty to fifty years after the resurrection and ascension of our Lord. This meant that his sayings were passed on orally within the early Christian communities for several decades before they took written form. The early apostles and teachers, therefore, had to rely upon these oral traditions in their ministry to the church.

Paul, for example, appealed directly to the "word of the Lord" (Acts 20:35; 1 Cor 7:10-11; 9:14; 11:23-26; 14:37; 1 Thess 4:15-17). Peter uses language in his First Epistle which approximates sayings found in the Synoptics (2:12, 19-20; 3:9, 14, 16; 4:14). And there are at least eight places where James utilizes sayings that belong to the Synoptic tradition (1:5; 2:5; 4:2-3, 9, 10; 5:1, 2-3, 12).

Writers in the postapostolic age also testify to this authority by utilizing such phrases as "he said to them," "let us recall the words of the Lord," "remembering what the Lord said," and so on (cf. *1 Clement* 13.1-2, 46.7-8; Ignatius *Letter to the Smyrneans* 3.2; *Barnabas* 5.9; Polycarp *Letter to the Philippians* 2.37.29). The *Didache*, an early Christian teaching manual composed at the turn of the first century, admonishes believers to "pray . . . as the Lord bid us in his gospel" (8:2) and to remember what "the Lord said" (9:5).

7. The Need for a Collection

There were a number of factors during the first and second centuries which made it necessary for the church to establish a canon of authority for the written words of Jesus.

First, there was the gradual spread of the Gospels throughout the churches. Since the Gospels initially were written to meet the liturgical, didactic, apologetic and pastoral needs of a specific community, it follows that they remained in a certain church(es) or region. In time, however, each Gospel eventually reached other churches and areas throughout the empire. This expansion forced the church to decide whether it would acknowledge all four Gospels instead of just one.

Second, there was the proliferation of other gospels circulating throughout the churches. Documents such as the *Gospel of Thomas, Gospel of Philip, Gospel of Peter, Gospel of the Egyptians* and *Gospel of Truth* also claimed to record the words of Jesus and thus laid claims to authority for the church. Decisions had to be made on the legitimacy of such claims, because some of these materials were used by some churches or groups within churches to support heretical ideas, as for example, the Gnostics. The history of the Gospel of John shows that it took longer to be accepted by the church than the other Gospels because it was misused by the Gnostics and Montanists. Now the church had to decide which of all the current Gospels were to be regarded as authoritative. Eventually a conscious decision was made to retain only those that were apostolic in origin or could be associated with the apostolic age. In time, the others were relegated to "apocryphal" status and were not canonized (cf. discussion in part five).

Third, the church reacted to Marcion and his so-called canon, which included an edited (rather, mutilated) version of Luke's Gospel plus ten letters of Paul. This list was determined by Marcion's rejection of anything that smacked of Judaizing tendencies in the Gospels plus his admiration for Paul as the only apostle who championed a true and law-free gospel (see such references to "gospel" in Gal 1:6, 7, 11; 2:2, 5, 7, 14). Marcion probably included Luke's Gospel because Luke was an associate of Paul and the Gospel places a lot of emphasis on the Gentiles. In Marcion's version of the third Gospel, Luke was more consistent with Paul's theology.

How did the church respond to Marcion's list, coming as it did from someone who had been excommunicated for his unorthodox views? Frankly, scholars are divided on the impact that Marcion had on the formation of the Christian canon. Some, like Campenhausen, Harnack and Goodspeed, believe that Marcion virtually forced the church to decide on its Scriptures. Others, such as Gamble and Bruce, think that Marcion's role in the formation of the New Testament canon has been exaggerated. Nevertheless, it must be said that Marcion's list is a definite and unique attempt to define the Christian canon.

Fourth, there was the existence of the four Gospels themselves. Separately, they each had authority in the localities where they were written and circulated. When they were brought together and compared, a new problem was created. Why were there such differing accounts of the life and teachings of Jesus? How was the church to deal with the apparent contradictions and discrepancies (for example, the different genealogies in Matthew and Luke or the differences between the Synoptics and John with respect to the date of the Passover and the cleansing of the temple)?

The particularity of the Gospels raised the question of authority in the face of different accounts. This concern begged for a different solution, and several were offered: it may have compelled Marcion to select only one Gospel, Luke; it may lie behind the formation and popularity of Tatian's *Diatessaron*, where everything was harmonized into a continuous narrative; and it may have inspired Irenaeus to develop his elaborate allegorical justification for the four Gospels. In the final analysis, however, the collection "was due to the dominating importance of apostolic witness and apostolic testimony. No document which bore the name of Matthew or of John, no document which was held to go back to Peter or Paul could possibly be discarded. The Gospels were apostolic, and were, therefore, the essential documents of the Christian faith."[55]

8. The Stages of Collection

In addition to the references to the words of Jesus by the apostles and in some early Christian literature cited above, church history records some further steps that led to the fourfold collection and canonization of the Gospels.[56]

■ **Papias (c. 70-140/60).** The words of Papias, bishop of Hierapolis, are preserved in the *Ecclesiastical History* of Eusebius, bishop of Caesarea:

But if I met with any one who had been a follower of the elders any where, I made it a point to inquire what were the declarations of the elders. What was said by Andrew, Peter or Philip. What by Thomas, James, John, Matthew, or any of the other of the disciples of the Lord. What was said by Ariston, and the presbyter John, disciples of the Lord; *for I do not think that I derived so much benefit from books as from the living voice of those that are still surviving.* (*HE* 3.39.4, emphasis added)

Papias also indicates that these written documents are associated with the names of either apostolic authors or individuals associated with the apostles. On Mark he writes:

And John the Presbyter also said this—Mark being the interpreter *[hermeneutēs]* of Peter, whatsoever he recorded he wrote with great accuracy, but not, however, in the order in which it was spoken or done by our Lord, but as before said, he was in company with Peter, who gave him such instruction as was necessary, but not to give a history of our Lord's discourses: wherefore Mark has not erred in anything, by writing some things as he has recorded them; for he was carefully attentive to one thing, not to pass by anything that he heard, or to state anything falsely in these accounts. (*HE* 3.39.15)

And about Matthew Papias said, "Matthew composed his history in the Hebrew dialect, and every one translated it as he was able" (*HE* 3.39.16). Some other translations read: "Matthew composed the Logia *[ta logia]* in the Hebrew tongue and everyone interpreted them as he was able." These names (i.e., Matthew and Mark), "which already guaranteed the trustworthiness of the oral tradition, are now used to assure the faithfulness of the written documents."[57]

Papias's mention of "the living voice of those that are still surviving" confirms that in some circles there remained a preference for eyewitness accounts over the written material. The publication of the Gospels did not initially bring oral tradition to an end. Rather, the Gospels were considered as supplementary material and no more authoritative than the oral traditions that were circulating. It is people—the oral transmitters of Christian tradition—and not books that dominate the scene during this stage.

■ **Justin Martyr (c. 100-163).** Justin (one of the earliest Christian apologists), writing only a decade after Papias, states: "And on the day called Sunday there is a meeting in one place of those who live in cities or the country, and the *memoirs of the apostles* [emphasis added] or the writings of the prophets are read as long as time permits" (*First Apology* 67).

These "memoirs of the apostles" are gospel writings (they were not called "Gospels" at this stage) that eventually became authoritative for the church (for additional references to "memoirs" cf. Justin *Dialogus cum Tryphone Judaeo* 100.4; 101.3; 102.5; 103.6, 8; 104.1; 105.1, 5, 6; 106.1, 3, 4; 107.11). Although most scholars believe that Justin was acquainted with Matthew, Luke and Mark, it is doubtful that he was familiar with John. Justin's knowledge of several Gospels does not necessarily mean that there was a full collection at this time. We do not know when, where or by whom each Gospel was brought into a collection. "The circumstances of the first edition of the fourfold gospel," concludes Bruce, "must be a matter of speculation, since historical evidence is lacking."[58] What we do know is that the Gospels became part of the canon as a collection and not individually.

■ **Tatian (c. 110-180).** Tatian was a Syrian Christian who studied with Justin in Rome before he returned to his native country, where he translated his Greek text into Syriac. His *Diatessaron* (literally, "through the four") was the first known "harmony" of the four Gospels (c. A.D. 150-160). By using the framework of John's Gospel (although not slavishly), Tatian arranged all the Gospel material into a continuous narrative on the life of Jesus.[59]

His work had tremendous popularity in the Syrian churches until the fifth century, when it finally was ordered to be replaced by the fourfold Gospel. Unfortunately, this led to a systematic destruction of many copies of this important work. A small parchment fragment about four inches square and containing fourteen lines is all that remains of the Greek text. Our knowledge of its content and arrangement is derived primarily from Ephraem's commentary in the Armenian language (fourth century), although parts of this commentary are also available in the original Syriac.[60]

Tatian's *Diatessaron* lends further proof to the circulation of all four Gospels by the middle of the second century. Scholars are divided on whether Tatian's use of the four Gospels implies that they already were regarded as authoritative by the church or whether each one had just attained a status on its own. Gamble, for one, believes that Tatian's free handling of the texts by omissions, additions and transpositions, as well as possible citations from other sources, demonstrates that he did not regard the Gospels as "sacrosanct."[61] Bruce Metzger, on the other hand, takes the position that "the *Diatessaron* supplies proof that all four Gospels were regarded as authoritative; otherwise it is unlikely that Tatian would have dared to combine them into one gospel account. At a time when many gospels were competing for attention, it is certainly significant that Tatian selected just these four."[62]

■ **Irenaeus (c. 130-202).** Further evidence for the existence of the fourfold Gospel comes from Irenaeus, bishop of Lyons in Gaul. Around A.D. 180 Irenaeus wrote the following thoughts in his principal work, *Against Heresies:*

> The Gospels could not possibly be either more or less in number than they are. Since there are four zones of the world in which we live, and four principal winds, while the Church is spread over all the earth, and the

pillar and foundation of the Church is the gospel, and the Spirit of life, it fittinglyhasfourpillars,everywherebreathingoutincorruptionandrevivi- fying men. From this it is clear that the Word, the artificer of all things, he who sits upon the cherubim and sustains all things, being manifested to men gave us the gospel, fourfold in form but held together by one Spirit. . . . For the cherubim have four faces, and their faces are images of the activity of the Son of God. For the first living creature, it says, was like a lion, signifying his active and princely and royal character; the second was like an ox, showing his sacrificial and priestly order; the third had the face of a man, indicating very clearly his coming in human guise; and the fourth was like a flying eagle, making plain the giving of the Spirit who broods over the Church. Now the Gospels, in which Christ is enthroned, are like these. . . . For the living creatures were quadriform, and the gospel and the activity of the Lord is fourfold. Therefore four general covenants were given to mankind: one was that of Noah's deluge, by the bow; the second was Abraham's by the sign of circumci- sion; the third was the giving of the Law by Moses; and the fourth is that of the Gospel, through our Lord Jesus Christ. (3.11.8)

It is difficult to know precisely how to interpret Irenaeus's comments. Is he simply confirming a concept that is well established in the churches? Or is he seeking to provide authority and legitimacy for one?[63]

We need to be reminded that the term *gospel*, which originally meant the "good news" that Jesus himself *taught* about the kingdom of God or the "good news" preached by the early believers about Jesus, came to mean the *written* words of Jesus. And what first was applied to each Gospel came to designate the fourfold Gospel collection as well. Once the four separate Gospels were brought together into a collection, it became necessary to distinguish one from another. By designating them as the "Gospel Accord- ing to Matthew," "Mark" and so on, the church developed "a system of nomenclature that respected both the oneness of the Gospel and the multi- plicity of the gospels."[64]

■ **The Muratorian Canon.** One final witness for the fourfold Gospel is the "Muratorian Canon," a Latin fragment possibly dating from the late second century A.D. and named after its Italian discoverer, L. A. Muratori. Although several lines are missing from the beginning of this manuscript, one can safely conclude that the author made reference to Matthew and Mark. It mentions that Luke is the third and that John is the fourth of the Gospels.[65]

The circumstances behind this document are difficult to reconstruct. Harry Gamble believes that the Muratorian Canon should be interpreted as an attempt to legitimize the collection because of a possible preference for only one Gospel in some circles and to endorse John's Gospel, which had been neglected by the church because of its misuse by Gnostics and Montanists to support their particular theological views.[66] Others, like F. Beare, share the view that in the Muratorian Canon "the divine inspiration and the essential unity of the four gospels could not be more explicitly affirmed."[67]

▪ **Final Stages.** From early Christian sources it seems reasonable to conclude that the fourfold Gospel collection was a well-known and accepted fact *by the end of the second century*. After Irenaeus, the evidence is even more compelling. Tertullian (c. 160-220), a native of Carthage in Africa, acknowledges all four canonical Gospels and indicates that they were written either by the apostles or by associates of the apostles (cf. *Adversus Marcionem* 4.2.2.).

Clement of Alexandria (c. 150-215), a contemporary of Tertullian and the esteemed director of the great catechetical school in Alexandria founded by Pantaenus, cites the four canonical Gospels as Scripture, although he acknowledges the existence of other gospels such as the *Gospel of the Hebrews* and the *Gospel of the Egyptians* as well. According to Bruce, "The fourfold gospel was part of the tradition that Clement has received and its contents were specially authoritative for him, but he has no objection to citing other gospel writings if it suited his purpose."[68]

Origen (c. 184-235), recognized as the greatest theologian and scholar of his day, knows of only four Gospels. Eusebius's comments on Origen are helpful here:

But in the first book of his Commentaries on the gospel of Matthew, following the Ecclesiastical Canon, he attests that he knows of only four gospels, as follows: "As I have understood from tradition, respecting the four gospels, which are the only undisputed ones in the whole church of God throughout the world. The first is written according to Matthew, the same that was once a publican, but afterwards an apostle of Jesus Christ, who having published it for the Jewish converts, wrote it in the Hebrew. The second is according to Mark, who composed it, as Peter explained to him. . . . And the third, according to Luke, the gospel commended by Paul, which was written for the converts from the Gentiles, and last of all the gospel according to John." (*HE* 6.25.4-7)

Finally, there is Eusebius himself, the bishop of Caesarea (writing c. 325-330), who firmly placed the fourfold Gospel in his list of "undisputed" writings: "And here, among the first, must be placed the holy quaternion of the gospels" (*HE* 3.25.1-2).

The opinions of these church leaders played an important role when the Gospels and the rest of the New Testament books were finally canonized by the Council of Carthage in A.D. 397.

9. The Authority of the Written Gospels

We saw earlier that the primitive church regarded the words of the exalted Lord as possessing ultimate authority for their faith and practice. This pattern also is evident in writings of the early church fathers, such as Clement, Ignatius and Polycarp, where Jesus' words are juxtaposed to citations from the Old Testament. The author of 2 *Clement*, for example, after quoting a passage from Isaiah, introduces a saying of Jesus with "And another Scripture says" (2.4). These, as well as other passages, show that "the authority of the Lord and his apostles was reckoned to be not inferior to that of the law and the prophets. Authority precedes canonicity; had the words of the Lord and his apostles not been accorded supreme authority, the written record of their words would never have been canonized."[69] In the same way, the "memoirs" mentioned by Justin would have possessed the same inspiration and authority as the "writings of the Prophets."[70]

On the other hand, it did take some time for the church to grant the same authority to the *written* Gospel. It may be that since the church already had authoritative Scripture with "the Law and the Prophets," there was no need for another "written" authority. Papias's preference for the oral tradition suggests that he did not regard what was written about Jesus as uniquely Scripture. The same held true for Justin's "memoirs," which appeared to be closer to historical records than inspired writings like the Old Testament. Tatian took the liberty to use and alter all four Gospels to compose his *Diatessaron*—a harmony on the life of Christ.

It is difficult to determine the exact status of the Gospels during the latter half of the second century. Although some scholars suggest that they were in a "highly fluid situation" and did not possess *exclusive* authority for the church before A.D. 200 even though they were considered apostolic, others are convinced that both the Gospels and the writings of Paul achieved the status of Scripture by the turn of the century.[71] This latter view is confirmed by Origen's statements that the Old and New Testaments are regarded as "divine Scripture."

The writings of Origen show that leaders in the early church were beginning to identify the Scriptures as the "Old" and "New" Testaments. Earlier, as in the writings of Irenaeus for example, the term *covenant* (Hebrew *b^erît*, Greek *diathēkē*) was used to distinguish the books of "the old covenant" that God made with Israel and those of "the new covenant" that was inaugurated in the life and ministry of Jesus. By the time of Tertullian (c. A.D. 160-220) the Greek *diathēkē* (covenant) was translated into Latin as *testamentum*, and the Christian writings familiar to Tertullian and the church at the end of the second century A.D. became known as the New Testament (*Novum Testamentum*) alongside the Old. From this time on, the church would recognize these two parts in its canon of Scripture.

PART III

THE
PAULINE
LITERATURE

1. Paul

Readers of the New Testament are introduced to Saul during the stoning of Stephen, the first Christian martyr (Acts 7:58). Here Saul is represented not only as one who approved the stoning (8:1) but as a Jewish zealot intent on destroying the early church as well ("Saul was ravaging the church by entering house after house; dragging off both men and women, he committed them to prison"—8:3; cf. also 9:1-3; 26:9-11; 1 Cor 15:9; Gal 1:13). According to Galatians 1:14, Saul's zeal for defending the traditions of his ancestors gained him advanced standing in Judaism. But after his conversion to Christianity his zeal was redirected toward his calling as an apostle to the Gentiles.

The conversion of Saul occurred approximately two years after the crucifixion of Jesus.[1] By all accounts this dramatic change in his life involved both a confession of Jesus as Messiah and Lord *and* a call or commissioning to be a missionary to the Gentiles (note how these two dimensions are included in the accounts of his conversion in Acts 9:10-17; 22:6-21; 26:12-18; Gal 1:15-16).

By piecing together Acts and biographical portions of Paul's letters, we know that his preparatory years for missionary activity included time in Damascus (Acts 9:10-25), Arabia (Gal 1:17), Jerusalem (Acts 9:26; Gal 1:18) and Tarsus (Acts 9:30).[2] To understand Paul fully, one has to appreciate his dual heritage. He was brought up as a pious Jew (Phil 3:4-6) and therefore had a thorough knowledge of Judaism and the Old Testament. But he was a Hellenistic Jew. This heritage helps us to understand his preference for the LXX, fluency in the Greek language, familiarity with Greek authors and the use of current literary forms in his letters. When it comes to his interpretation of the Old Testament, however, he often employs Jewish exegetical techniques that he learned from the rabbis.

Although Paul was involved with a number of early Christian communities and performed some missionary work during his early years (Acts 9:30; Gal 1:21), the commitment to his apostolic call really began when Barnabas brought him from Tarsus to the city of Antioch (Acts 11:25-26). The church at Antioch commissioned Paul (Saul) and Barnabas (Acts 13:1-2), and they launched what commonly is known as Paul's first missionary journey (Acts 13:1—14:28). This major Hellenistic city became Paul's "home base" and the center from which he carried out further missionary activity to the Gentile world (Acts 15:35-40), including such important cities around the Aegean Sea as Philippi, Thessalonica, Athens, Corinth and Ephesus. Approximately twenty-eight years elapsed from Paul's conversion to his imprisonment in Rome, around A.D. 60-61.

It was during these years of intense missionary and pastoral activity that Paul began his literary activity and became one of the most prolific writers of the New Testament. His letters make up one-fifth of the New Testament. One-half of the book of Acts is devoted to him. This means that approximately one-quarter of the New Testament is attributed to the apostle Paul.

2. Paul and Greco-Roman Literature

It is very interesting to look at the way in which the literary world of Paul's day helped shape the form and content of his letters.

An early and serious study of ancient Greco-Roman letters began with Adolf Deissmann and the publication of his magisterial work, *Light from the Ancient East*.[3] Deissmann, who studied a mass of papyri and inscriptions from the garbage dumps of ancient Egypt, was one of the first scholars of this century to distinguish "letters" (or "real letters") from "epistles" ("nonreal letters"). According to Deissmann, letters are nonliterary compositions used for private and common matters. Epistles, on the other hand, are public, written in good literary form and intended for posterity.

This means that Paul's "letters" should be considered as personal and informal notes rather than as literary and theological essays. Many scholars, however, have modified Deissmann's rigid classification and have come to appreciate the *public* nature of Paul's letters, noting that they were addressed to communities of believers who read them publicly and even circulated them among other communities. At the same time, they must not be regarded solely as dogmatic theological essays. Current scholarship "has reached something of a balance between treating Paul's letters as purely occasional, contextual writings, directed only to specific situations, and as attempts to express a Christian understanding of life which had ramifications for theological expression beyond the particular historical situation."[4]

Many significant advances have been made in understanding types of ancient letters since Deissmann's time.[5] Stanley Stowers has identified letters of friendship, family, praise and blame, exhortation and advice, mediation, and apologetic (cf. part one). Another scholar, David Aune, classified letters under the headings of (1) private or documentary, (2) official and (3) literary. William Doty utilizes the categories of (1) business, (2) official, (3) public, (4) nonreal (i.e., pseudonymous) and (5) discourse. All of these authors provide examples of each type of letter and are helpful in showing where the New Testament letters—or portions of them—fit.

Recognition of different "types" of letters is helpful in understanding and interpreting the writings of the New Testament. In Aune's development of these types, for example, he suggests that "the character of the communication is determined by the relationship between sender and receiver."[6] On this basis he attributes the following categories to certain letters: 1 Thessalonians—a paraenetic letter; Galatians—a deliberative letter; 2 Corinthians—a composite letter; Philippians—a letter of gratitude and paraenesis; Philemon—a letter of recommendation; Hebrews—a hortatory sermon; Romans—a combination of diatribe, epideictic and protreptic; 1 Peter—a paraenetic encyclical.

Time and space do not permit any extensive analysis of these types and comparisons with all the literature of the New Testament. Interested readers are advised to consult some of the excellent resources listed in the footnotes. However, two examples illustrate the methodology at work: diatribe and rhetoric.

Although no one book of the New Testament can be called a diatribe, Paul's letter to the Romans appears to utilize diatribal features more than any other book in the New Testament. Some specific examples include his use of an imaginary opponent (2:1, 3; 9:20) and phrases such as "then what" (3:1) or "what then" (3:9; 6:1, 15; 7:7; 9:14). Other passages in the New Testament that mirror diatribal style include 1 Corinthians 6:12-20; 15:29-41; Galatians 3:1-9, 19-22; James 2:1—3:12; 4:13—5:6.[7]

A significant number of scholars have focused on ancient rhetoric and examined Paul's letters for rhetorical and artistic features.[8] The most vivid example involving the use of rhetoric in the New Testament takes place between Paul and the Corinthians (1 Cor 1:17—2:5). Apparently the Corinthians were enamored of wisdom and public oratory, because when Paul proclaimed the gospel to them they criticized him for his lack of rhetorical skills. The reality is that Paul probably studied some rhetoric as part of his education and that he was capable of using it when appropriate. Although the Corinthians judged his speech "contemptible" (2 Cor 10:10), one cannot miss the irony of his response in 2 Corinthians 11:6: "I may be untrained in speech [literally, an idiot *(idiōtēs)* in words] but not in knowledge."

The point of Paul's reply to the Corinthians about "eloquent wisdom" (1 Cor 1:17), "the wisdom of the wise" (1:19-20) and "debater of the age" (1:20) is that *content is more important than form.* If "the medium is the message" (Marshall McLuhan), we can appreciate the apostle's concern to proclaim the gospel in a way that would focus on the message of the cross of Christ and *its* power and not the eloquence of the speaker (1 Cor 2:4-5).

The focus on rhetoric has led to a method of biblical interpretation known as "rhetorical criticism" by which the Gospels and letters are examined according to the canons of ancient rhetoric. Basically, the procedure is to discern where certain authors of the New Testament used the phenomena of language, speech, communication, order, persuasion and so on in their writings. Virtually every book—and many sections of books—in the New Testament has been examined by this relatively new "science" of interpretation.[9]

When we discussed "Gospel genre" in part two, we observed that even though the Evangelists utilized biographical models from their literary environment, the Gospels are distinctive literary creations because of the way they present Jesus and the good news. Much the same can be said about the apostle Paul and his letters. Paul was a Hellenistic Jew and quite naturally employed the oral forms of communication and literary conventions of letter writing that were common in the first century. Current research is helping us to understand what Paul's readers already knew and took for granted because they recognized such models, forms and styles in his writings.

This is not to say, however, that Paul's letters are exactly what scholars claim; it is interesting to notice how these scholars have major disagreements as to *what* Paul's models were. Perhaps Paul was guided but not bound by any models. He appears free to modify his style according to the life setting of his churches.

What is new and different about Paul's letters and distinguishes them from contemporary ones is that *they are Christian letters.* In some respects, therefore, Paul creates a new literary genre—the apostolic letter—in order to pass on apostolic tradition and communicate the Christian faith. First Thessalonians (assuming it is the earliest epistle) would then be the first of many such apostolic letters (Greek *epistolai*) which would, in the process of canonization, become epistles for the universal church.[10]

3. The Form of Paul's Letters

The *basic* form of ancient letters contained a threefold division of (1) an introductory section, (2) a main body and (3) a concluding section. This structure can be observed in an early letter written "to Isidorus":

> To Isidorus, my brother, greetings. Upon reaching Antinoöpolis, I received your letter, through which I experienced the feeling of seeing you. I therefore urge you to keep writing continually, for in this way our friendship will be increased. When I am slow to write to you, this happens easily because I am not able to find anyone traveling your way. Write to me about any need you might have since you know that I will comply without delay. If you write me a letter, send it to my friend Hermes at the house of Artemis so that he may deliver it to me. Hermes himself and his sister Tausiris send you many greetings. Farewell.... Deliver to my friend Isidorus in Philadelphia from . . . [11]

A careful comparison of Paul's letters with ancient forms reveals that the apostle did not feel bound to follow these patterns slavishly. Many modifications are discernible in his letters due to the circumstances and conditions under which he wrote. In a general way, however, his letters follow a similar format:

1. the opening salutation (sender, addressee, greeting)
2. the thanksgiving or blessing (often with intercession)[12]
3. the body of the letter
4. the paraenesis (i.e., ethical instruction/exhortation)
5. the conclusion (greetings, doxology, benediction)

Table 3.1 helps us to visualize this pattern more clearly.

4. The Content and Context of Paul's Letters

When Paul actually sat down to write his letters, he had two main sources of information (this is not to discount the creative genius that he displays in the interpretation, application and development of early Christian doctrine). One was through a personal revelation from the Lord, as Galatians 1:11-12 indicates: "For I want you to know, brothers and sisters, that the gospel that was proclaimed by me is not of human origin; for I did not receive it from a human source, nor was I taught it, but I received it through a revelation of Jesus Christ."

Here, as well as in 1:16-17 ("I did not confer with any human being, nor did I go up to Jerusalem to those who were already apostles before me"), Paul wants to emphasize that his revelation of the gospel and the particular

Table 3.1. The Structure of Paul's Letters

OUTLINE OF LETTER STRUCTURE

	1 Thessalonians	1 Corinthians	2 Corinthians	Galatians	Philippians	Romans
I. Salutation						
A. Sender	1:1a	1:1	1:1a	1:1-2a	1:1	1:1-6
B. Recipient	1:1b	1:2	1:1b	1:2b	1:1	1:7a
C. Greeting	1:1c	1:3	1:2	1:3-5	1:2	1:7b
II. Thanksgiving	1:2-10 2:13 3:9-10	1:4-9	1:3-7	—	1:3-11	1:8-17
III. Body	2:1—3:8 (possibly 3:11-13)	1:10—4:21	1:8—9:14 (letter incomplete) 10:1—13:10 (letter fragment)	1:6—4:31	1:12—2:11 3:1—4:1 4:10-20	1:18—11:36
IV. Ethical exhortation and instructions	4:1—5:22	5:1—16:12 16:13-18 (closing paraenesis)	13:11a (summary)	5:1—6:10 6:11-15 (letter summary)	2:12-29 4:2-6	12:1—15:13 15:14-32 (travel plans and closing paraenesis)
V. Closing						
A. Peace wish	5:23-24	—	13:11b	6:16	4:7-9	15:33
B. Greetings	—	16:19-20a	13:13	—	4:21-22	16:1-15(?)
C. Kiss	5:26	16:20b	13:12	—	—	16:16(?)
Apostolic command	5:27	16:22	—	6:17	—	—
D. Benediction	5:28	16:23-24	13:14	6:18	4:23	16:20(?)

interpretation he is setting forth in this letter was a special disclosure from the Lord. Such statements are intended to establish his legitimacy as an apostle and prevent his readers from turning "to a different gospel" (1:6-7).

Paul's second source of information was the traditions of the early church. Earlier, in the discussion of the Gospels, I showed how Paul utilized the early Christian kerygma in his ministry (part two). These were theological truths that Paul inherited through his association with early Christian communities. We need to remember that during Paul's formative years as a Christian—and even after—he was part of a worshiping and teaching church. His contacts with the believers in Damascus, Tarsus, Antioch and Jerusalem exposed him to the ideas and practices of early Christianity. Thus it was natural that as an apostle of Christ he would accept such traditions and pass them on through his teaching and preaching.

One important key to this reality is the use of the terms *receive (paralambanō)* and *deliver (paradidōmi)*. There are two striking examples of this usage in Paul:

For I *received* from the Lord what I also *handed on* to you, that the Lord Jesus on the night when he was betrayed . . . (1 Cor 11:23-25)

For I *handed on* to you as of first importance what I in turn had *received*: that Christ died for our sins. (1 Cor 15:3-4)

In addition to these classic examples, studies of Paul's letters reveal other places besides the kerygma where the apostle is indebted to early Christian traditions. In broad categories these include the following:

1. *Early Christian creeds and confessions* (Rom 10:9; 1 Cor 16:22; 1 Cor 15:3-4; 1 Tim 3:16—also a hymn)

2. *Early Christian liturgical expressions* (hymns, baptismal formulas, prayers: Rom 6:1-11; Eph 5:14; Phil 2:6-11; Col 1:15-20; 1 Tim 3:16; 2 Tim 2:11-13; Tit 3:4-7)

3. *Early Christian paraenesis* (this includes many references where Paul urges his readers to keep believing and doing what they were taught, e.g., 1 Cor 11:2; Phil 4:9; Col 2:6; 1 Thess 4:1; 2 Thess 2:15; 3:6)[13]

Thus a significant amount of the material that Paul used in his letters he inherited from the early church and then passed on to his congregations. This is not to imply that Paul lacked creativity. He simply adapted traditional material to current problems and issues. Tradition, for Paul, was "a dynamic reality coming out of a living past, impinging directly on the present, and anticipating the future."[14] No one doubts that Paul was the most significant Christian theologian of the first century. Without his missionary zeal, pastoral concerns and the theology developed in his letters, Christianity might have remained a sect of Judaism.

By reading Paul's letters in the New Testament one can arrive at the following conclusions: (1) thirteen (excluding Hebrews) letters are attributed to Paul; (2) most of his letters were occasional or particular, that is, they were written to specific local congregations for a definite purpose (e.g., believers in Rome, Corinth, Philippi, Thessalonica, Colossae, Ephesus, Galatia, etc.); (3) other letters were written to individuals (Philemon, Timothy and Titus); (4) Paul's letters were read in the church, probably in the context of worship (Col 4:16; 1 Thess 5:27; cf. Justin *First Apology* 67); (5) some letters were intended to be circulated to other churches (Gal 1:2; Col 4:16); and (6) not all the letters that Paul wrote have been preserved (1 Cor 5:9; 2 Cor 2:4; Col 4:16). At the time of writing, Paul had no idea that his letters would be collected or become authoritative and canonical for the universal church as they are today.

5. The Writing of Paul's Letters
Any discussion about the composition, collection and canonicity of Paul's letters takes place between two certainties: one is that the apostle Paul wrote letters to a number of individuals and churches; the other is that by A.D. 397, the church had canonized fourteen epistles attributed to Paul along with the other books that make up our canon of the New Testament.

What happened between the first and the fourth centuries, however, is open to considerable speculation and debate. Sources for reconstructing the status of Paul's letters during this period are either nonexistent or subject to a variety of interpretations. There is very little scholarly consensus on what could and did happen. Hypotheses abound, and in many cases we are left with a bewildering number of probabilities. W. Schmithals expressed this uncertainty well when he wrote: "The question as to the form of the *earliest collection of Paul's epistles* has occupied the exegetes and historians so often and with so much ingenuity that one takes up this question with only slight hope of new convincing results."[15] Nevertheless, we may proceed with the conviction that there are some valuable insights that help us to appreciate the process by which Paul's single letters became part of a larger corpus and, eventually, the canon of the New Testament.

■ **Paul as Sole Author of His Letters.** Most readers of Paul's letters conclude that Paul is the sole author of the letters that have been attributed to him. After all, these letters have internal comments about authorship, such as, "I Paul . . . to . . ." or "Paul and Timothy . . ." etc. Hence many versions of the New Testament introduce each letter with the heading "The Letter of Paul to the . . ."

This often leads to the impression that Paul had all the necessary writing materials at his disposal and sat down to write these letters as the occasion demanded. Some were written while he was en route from one place to another, others when he was settled in a place for a longer time, and still others while he was in prison (cf. various "introductions" to the New Testament for suggestions regarding place, date and occasion of writing).

■ **Paul's Use of a Secretary (Amanuensis).** A careful reading of some of Paul's letters indicates that he followed the literary conventions of his day by employing a secretary—or, to use the more technical term, amanuensis (from the Latin *manu*, a slave with secretarial duties).[16] Some of this secretarial help may have come from the coworkers that Paul includes in the salutations of his letters. Timothy is mentioned in 2 Corinthians, Philippians, Colossians and Philemon; Silvanus and Timothy in 1 and 2 Thessalonians; and Sosthenes in 1 Corinthians. One gets the impressions that these "cosenders" may have had some role as "coauthors." More specific examples, however, are embedded within the text of certain letters:

I Tertius, the writer of this letter, greet you in the Lord. (Rom 16:22)

I, Paul, write this greeting with my own hand [the implication being that the rest of the letter was written by someone else]. (1 Cor 16:21)

I, Paul, write this greeting with my own hand. This is the mark in every letter of mine; it is the way I write [a comment necessitated by his concern in 2:2 that a fictitious letter in his name had been circulating in the Thessalonian church]. (2 Thess 3:17)

See what large letters I make when I am writing in my own hand! [Here he is apparently drawing attention to his own script in the final admonition and benedictions in 6:11-18. Paul would not have written the entire letter in "large letters."] (Gal 6:11)

I, Paul, write this greeting with my own hand. (Col 4:18)

Secretaries in the ancient world were used in a number of different situations and ways. There were royal secretaries responsible for official correspondence and private secretaries for the upper class. Famous writers such as Cicero, Pliny and Seneca employed secretaries to write, copy and edit their materials. Some secretaries recorded verbatim the dictation of the author; others functioned much like an editor or coauthor who would make a final draft from the author's oral presentation or written notes; in other cases the secretary was simply instructed to compose a letter for a specific purpose.[17]

Obviously, the task of determining *how* the amanuenses contributed to Paul's letters—i.e., as recorder, editor, coauthor, composer—is a complex issue that exceeds the limits of this study, but one that should be pursued by other disciplines of New Testament study. I concur with E. R. Richards's observation that "even if Paul exercised much control over his secretary, there was more influence possible from a secretary than many modern exegetes have allowed."[18]

■ **Pseudonymity and the Deutero-Pauline Hypothesis.** Although Paul's use of a secretary in writing some of his letters is apparent, the extent to which he employed such individuals and the influence they may have had on the final "draft" of his letters remains unclear. But *Paul is still regarded as the author* and is responsible for the style and content, whether or not all of it came from his mind or pen.

The situation is similar to many modern authors who use people on their staff to collect, draft, write and edit material for a book. Such individuals may—or may not—be acknowledged in the "preface" or "foreword," but usually one person is regarded as the author (e.g., a book by Billy Graham). Much the same is true for the president of the United States, whose speeches are written by a well-trained staff, but the president receives the credit.

There are two widely held theories about Pauline authorship. The traditional view regards Paul as the author of the thirteen letters that bear his name. This means that all of them fit into his ministry and were written before he was executed in Rome around A.D. 62-64. The other theory, which arose with the ascendancy of critical scholarship in the nineteenth century, questions the authenticity of certain letters and proposes that they are *pseudonymous*, that is, attributed to Paul but written sometime after his death by another author—a "second," or "deutero," Paul. The letters in question include 2 Thessalonians, Colossians, Ephesians and the Pastorals (1 and 2 Timothy and Titus).

This approach, identified as the deutero-Pauline hypothesis, is built upon several assumptions: (1) that pseudonymity was an accepted literary practice in the ancient world; (2) that subtle differences of language, style and doctrine (particularly christology, ecclesiology and eschatology) in these letters attributed to Paul can best be explained by positing authors other than Paul; and (3) that certain letters—notably Ephesians and the Pastorals—reflect a historical setting subsequent to Paul's death. If this hypothesis is true, it changes the way one reconstructs the chronology of the composition and collection of Paul's letters.

Proponents of the deutero-Pauline hypothesis argue that during Paul's lifetime, he and some of his closest coworkers may have formed some type of theological school where his theology would have been discussed at great length—perhaps in Ephesus, where he spent three years. Then, after Paul's death, certain individuals felt led to write letters in his name. Their motives would have been to commend Paul's theology and apostolic authority to later generations of believers.

According to this theory, readers would not have considered these letters as forgeries nor regarded their authors as impostors or charlatans. In the case of the deutero-Pauline literature we need to conceive of an individual (or individuals)—possibly a pupil (or pupils) of Paul—who assumed his master's name and who firmly believed that such a practice would in no way dishonor the apostle or God or deceive his readers. Pseudonymity would not have prevented a letter from being considered inspired, authoritative and worthy of canonical status.[19]

Quite the opposite is argued by scholars who support the traditional authorship of Paul's letters. One objection raised against the deutero-Pauline hypothesis is historical. Even though pseudonymity was practiced by Jewish and Christian writers and was common for Gospel and apocalyptic writings, there is no conclusive evidence that any pseudepigraphic *letters* were accepted by the church.

A second objection is moral or ethical. Scholars in this camp view pseudonymity as a deceptive and fraudulent enterprise, a dishonest attempt to pass off a forged document as the genuine article. How could a Christian writer, they argue, aware of the many moral exhortations in Scripture to be truthful and honest, to practice goodness and avoid hypocrisy, be involved in a scheme to dupe his readers? And would not the readers themselves be aware of Paul's death and reject outright any later letter purporting to be from the apostle? Paul actually warned the Thessalonians about a false letter claiming to be from him (2 Thess 2:2) and asked them to examine his letters for their authentic greeting (2 Thess 3:17).

A third factor involves the relationship between apostolicity and canonicity. Here some scholars argue that the church categorically rejected any book that was pseudonymous, even if its contents were judged to be orthodox. In other words, only apostolic writings, or those associated with apostles such a Mark with Peter and Luke with Paul, were accepted into the canon.[20]

Time and space do not permit a lengthy defense or refutation of these hypotheses. The secondary literature shows that both positions have their strengths and limitations. Credible arguments have been presented for both the Pauline and the deutero-Pauline authorship of certain letters. But in most cases there simply is not enough hard evidence to make a definitive decision either way.

Disagreements on matters of authorship should not separate Christians into theological camps, as if one position were right and the other wrong, or as if one represented a higher view of Scripture than the other. Certain epistles, such as Ephesians or the Pastorals, for example, do not lose their canonical status, value and authority for the church today if they are judged to be written by someone other than Paul.

■ **Editors, Interpolators and Redactors of Paul's Letters.** Another issue raised by New Testament scholars is whether any editorial and/or redactional changes were made to Paul's letters between the time they originally were written and the earliest extant copies, which are found in an incomplete papyrus manuscript (P[46])[21] dated around A.D. 200. (These editorial changes need to be distinguished from mistakes made in the process of copying manuscripts and the occasional insertion of marginal notes or glosses into the text—cf. part six.) Theories of such possibilities abound, and discussions of various hypotheses can be found in most major introductions to the New Testament and commentaries on certain books.

It has, for example, been suggested that 1 and 2 Corinthians are a combination of several letters that Paul wrote to Corinth at different times and were edited by someone after Paul's death. Some think that Paul's very first letter to the church, referred to in 1 Corinthians 5:9, either is lost or may be part of 2 Corinthians 6:14—7:1. First Corinthians, then, would actually be Paul's second letter. References to a harsh letter (2 Cor 2:3-4, 9; 7:8-12) may partially be preserved in 2 Corinthians 10—13. Second Corinthians 1—9, or 1:1—6:13, according to some, is Paul's fourth letter.[22]

Others have been puzzled by some internal and textual features of Paul's letter to the Romans (for example, the omission of "in Rome" in some manuscripts at 1:7 and 1:15) and its ending. It has been proposed that Romans originally consisted of chapters 1—15, with chapter 16 added later from a piece of Paul's correspondence to the believers in Ephesus.[23]

Theories have been proposed about the unity of Philippians because of the impression that it consists of *three* separate Pauline letters (1:1—3:1; 3:2—4:9; 4:10-20) joined together by an unknown editor.[24] And there also are questions about Ephesians. Was it written as a "circular letter" for the churches in Asia Minor before it found a permanent home in Ephesus? Both the "general" nature of the letter and the textual problems related to its destination "in Ephesus" (1:1) suggest such a possibility.[25]

The study of interpolations and glosses in Paul's letters is highly subjective, and great care needs to be exercised in determining the validity of certain proposals. Victor Paul Furnish rightly observes that "so far no firm and convincing techniques or criteria have been developed to aid in the identification of glosses and interpolations. . . . Highly subjective judgments about content and tone are intermixed with often-questionable generalizations about the apostle's style and vocabulary. What emerges is a Paul created in the interpreter's own image."[26]

6. The Collection of Paul's Letters

■ **From Paul to Clement (c. A.D. 64-96).** Clement, an early bishop of the church in Rome, appears to have been acquainted with several epistles of Paul.[27] His "Letter of the Church of Rome to the Church of Corinth" *(1 Clement)* reflects an acquaintance not only with Paul's "Epistle to the Romans" (as we would expect) but with our 1 Corinthians as well. This means that Clement had access to 1 Corinthians either from a personal visit to Corinth, where he read the letter, or from a copy which had found its way to Rome. One wonders if this presupposes the existence of a limited collection of Paul's epistles by the time of Clement's writing.

What happened between the time of Paul and Clement is shrouded in mystery. The evidence we possess does not indicate any significant knowledge of Paul's letters at the end of the first century. Luke does not mention them in Acts, even though he focuses on the life of the apostle Paul. This silence is puzzling no matter whether one dates Acts in the sixties or in the eighties. One has to suspect that Luke knew of Paul's letters but that his interest in Paul at this point in time was biographical. Or perhaps he intended to collect Paul's letters at a later date and publish them as a third volume, along with his Gospel and Acts.

■ **Theories of Collection.** If Paul's letters were known during this time (as appears from 2 Pet 3:15-16), it is indeed puzzling why there is no further evidence of their use, circulation and collection.[28] However, given that they ultimately were circulated, collected and canonized, it is obvious that some kind of process was at work during this early stage. Two theories have emerged to explain the phenomenon.

The Gradual Collection Theory. Although some of Paul's correspondence may have been lost, such as the "sorrowful letter" to Corinth (2 Cor 2:4) and a possible letter to the Laodiceans (Col 4:16), it is legitimate to infer that his letters were preserved by the churches to which they were written because they were written by the *apostle* Paul and had practical, pastoral value. As such letters were read and reread in the church, new copies would be made for other congregations that also accepted the letters' apostolic authority and theological significance.

The letter that Paul addressed "to the church of God that is in Corinth" (1:2), for example, probably circulated among a number of house churches along the Corinthian isthmus and not just within one church in a certain part of the city. Letters could have been carried and circulated by significant church leaders in the same way that Paul had his letters delivered by messengers such as Timothy.[29]

The circulation of letters and their limited collection may have begun in such regional areas as Asia Minor (Colossae, Ephesus, Hierapolis, Laodicea), Macedonia (Thessalonica, Philippi), Achaia (Corinth) and Italy (Rome). Then at some point these regional collections came to constitute the Pauline corpus.[30] Unfortunately there is no hard evidence that such early regional collections existed.

It is difficult to imagine this early circulation and collection of Paul's letters without the guidance of some significant individual(s). The apparent editorial and redactional activity in the Corinthian correspondence, and possibly in Philippians and Romans, confirms that *someone* was working on the letters. True, Paul may have recognized the timeless value of his own letters and initiated the process of collection himself.[31] But the credit, according to this theory, most likely belongs to such individuals as Luke, Timothy and Onesimus. Or perhaps Marcion was the first person to set this process in motion. On the other hand, Marcion may simply have taken over an existing list and edited it to fit his theological agenda.

It is also suggested that the process of collecting and editing Paul's letters may have come from a "school" of Paul.[32] This envisions a process, sometime after Paul's death, when a group of his disciples or coworkers met together for the purpose of passing on the theological traditions they had inherited from their master. They would have remembered what Paul said (*ipsissima vox Pauli*—Paul's very voice) as well as had access to fragments of his correspondence or entire letters (*ipsissima verba Pauli*—the very words of Paul).

Those epistles designated as "deutero-Pauline" would be attempts of the school, or certain individuals within the circle, and under the convention of pseudonymity, to interpret, reinterpret and apply Paul's theology to later generations by appealing to Paul's apostolic authority.[33] Luke often appears on the top of the list as the most likely candidate for collecting, editing and augmenting the Pauline corpus.

The utilization of Paul's name and authority would have been especially significant as the church confronted various forms of false teaching and needed to establish "sound doctrine and practice." Certain individuals within the school, like Luke, Tychicus and Onesimus, may actually have been responsible for the writing of some epistles. Ephesians often is attributed to Luke or Onesimus. Suggestions for the authorship and/or final editing of the "Pastorals" range from a Paulinist like Luke to Polycarp, bishop of Smyrna, around the middle of the second century. Most scholars are content simply to designate the author as "the Pastor," someone who stands firmly within the Pauline heritage.

Scholars attempting to reconstruct the formation of the Pauline corpus identify Ephesus (Goodspeed, Knox, Mitton), Corinth (Harnack, Zahn, Schmithals) or Alexandria (Zuntz, Grant, Bruce) as the place for this editorial activity. Bruce, following the reasoning of Zuntz, affirms that the corpus shows definite signs of dependence on "the traditions of Alexandrian scholarship."[34]

This collection theory is, of course, hypothetical. We are not always sure how much Paul was appreciated and how widely his theology was used in the early church. And although the reference to "all his letters" in 2 Peter 3:16 and the reminiscences of Paul in the early fathers testify to a steady and growing appreciation of Paul—as would the phenomenon of the deutero-Paulines—*the fact remains that there is no evidence for a collection of Paul's letters during the first century* (even if 2 Peter is dated around the turn of the century, the "all" could mean all those that were generally known at the time).

E. J. Goodspeed's Theory. Part of E. J. Goodspeed's reconstruction of the Pauline corpus[35] involves what commonly is referred to as "the theory of lapsed interest."[36] Rather than envisioning a sustained and growing apprecia-tion of Paul and the gradual collection of his letters, Goodspeed believed that because Paul's letters were occasional, they had little value for anyone else, were stored in church chests and gradually fell into obscurity. Goodspeed suggested that there was little apparent interest in Paul between the time of his death and the latter part of the first century. Only after the publication of the Acts of the Apostles (for Goodspeed, c. A.D. 90) was interest in Paul revived. Anyone reading this history of the early church would have been fascinated with Paul and undoubtedly would have asked questions about the apostle's literary activity. Goodspeed, followed by J. Knox and C. L. Mitton, identifies Onesimus (Paul's friend in the letter to Philemon and later the bishop of Ephesus) as the one who eventually collected and published Paul's letters as a corpus. They also posit that Ephesians was written as a cover letter for that corpus.

Goodspeed's theory is challenged by those who believe that Paul's letters continued to exert considerable influence upon the life and theology of the early church immediately after the apostle's death. Perhaps someone like Timothy was responsible for collecting and publishing Paul's letters. (Cf. 2 Tim 4:13: "When you come, bring the cloak that I left with Carpus at Troas, also the books, and above all the parchments.") And the reference to "all his [Paul's] letters" (2 Pet 3:16) could be taken as proof that at least *some* of Paul's letters were known to Peter before A.D. 68. Whether one regards Goodspeed's theory as "a romantic embellishment" (Bruce) or an "imaginative reconstruction" (Martin), one can readily concur with Zuntz, who commends Goodspeed for "the liveliness of his imagination and the persuasiveness of his presentation."[37]

Paul as Editor and Collector. Up to this point I have presented theories which reconstruct the formation of the Pauline corpus as a process that began near the end of the first century with the circulation and gradual collection of some of Paul's letters but that left no discernible evidence of any kind of list. Some current studies, however, are challenging these views by arguing that Paul himself began to edit and collect some of his letters before his death.

E. Randolph Richards's hypothesis for the editing and collecting of Paul's letters arises from his study on the use and role of the secretary in Greek and Roman letters. Drawing analogies mainly from the practices of Cicero and his secretary Tiro, Richards argues not only that Paul utilized secretarial assistance for his letters but that he also kept notes and had personal copies of most of his letters made before they were delivered to their respective churches. The reference to "scrolls" and "parchments" in 2 Timothy 4:13 ("When you come, bring the cloak that I left with Carpus at Troas, and my scrolls, especially the parchments" [NIV]) confirms this procedure for Richards.

From this interpretation of 2 Timothy 4:13, Richards suggests that the *first* collection of Paul's letters consisted of these personal copies rather than one which emerged by someone's rounding up copies of manuscripts from various churches at a later time. There is, writes Richards, "a higher probability that a secretary would have access to the letters of Paul during Paul's lifetime than would a disciple after the death of Paul. . . . For a collection to be available to a later disciple implies an early collection (and veneration?) of Paul's letters in the last half of the first century, which is less likely."[38] E. Earle Ellis supports this reconstruction and believes that Paul's own editorial activity accounts for some of the textual variations in his correspondence. His argument also gives credibility to the Pauline authorship of the Pastorals.[39]

A similar conclusion is reached by David Trobisch, who uses analogies of letter collections from Roman sources (particularly Cicero and Pliny) to argue that the editing and collecting of Paul's letters began with the apostle himself or at his request.[40] After his death the original collection would have been subject to further editorial activity and expansion.

In another study, Trobisch proposes that the collection of Paul's letters moved through three significant editorial stages: first, the "authorized recensions" of the author himself which included Romans, 1 Corinthians, 2 Corinthians and Galatians; second, some "expanded editions" with more letters added by editors after the apostle's death; third, the "comprehensive editions" containing a thirteen-letter corpus of Paul's letters.[41] However, it appears that Trobisch's conclusions depend more upon analogies from the editing and collection of Cicero's writings than on the internal evidence in Paul's letters.

In the preceding discussion I have attempted to present a number of hypotheses that deal with the collection of Paul's letters. Hypotheses can be frustrating because they leave us with possibilities rather than certainties; they challenge rather than comfort; but they also enlarge rather than restrict our vision. The nature of the material we have examined makes it impossible to determine with certainty whether Paul or a later disciple/editor initiated a collection of his letters and what form it took. As students of the New Testament, we are left to determine which theory best fits the evidence. The following discussion, however, is less hypothetical, because it deals with more tangible evidence.

■ **From Clement to Justin (A.D. 96-165).** An examination of the events and literature of the first half of the second century sheds some further light upon our subject. References and allusions to most of Paul's epistles can be found in Ignatius, bishop of Antioch (c. 50-107), and Polycarp, bishop of Smyrna (c. 69-155). Ignatius does not refer to 2 Thessalonians, Philemon or the Pastorals, while Polycarp has no allusions to 1 Thessalonians, Colossians, Titus or Philemon.

The writings of Papias and Justin (second century) and the *Epistle of Barnabas* (written between A.D. 90-130) bear no trace of Paul's epistles. Such omissions are puzzling, and caution is necessary when arguing from silence. Papias *may* have omitted quotations from Paul because, as he admits, he treasured oral tradition ("a living and continuing voice") much more highly than written sources, and Justin, an apologist, was not necessarily writing to Christians.

The possession of most of Paul's epistles by church fathers, however, signifies a further development in the collection of a Pauline corpus. Polycarp is aware of some kind of collection in the Philippian church: "When absent he [Paul] wrote you letters that will enable you, if you study them carefully, to grow in the faith delivered to you" (*Letter to the Philippians* 3.2). This statement, however, does not prove the existence of a collection of Paul's letters in the Philippian church, because "letters" may refer only to Paul's correspondence with that community. But Polycarp's additional comments in 13.2 ("We are sending you the letters of Ignatius, those he addressed to us *and any others we had by us,* just as you requested"—italics added) may indicate that the Philippian church was involved in some kind of activity that included the collection of letters.

From the above observations it is obvious that Paul's letters were becoming more widely known and used among the churches during this time. However, there is less certainty regarding the status of a single authoritative collection (corpus). A number of scholars feel confident that the collection—and the circulation *as a collection*—began early in the second century.[42] G. Zuntz, although he doubts that Clement would have had access to a Pauline corpus in Rome, believes that "it may conceivably have been circulating in, say, Asia Minor or Egypt for some time; but hardly for long. Thus, c. A.D. 100 is a probable date for the collection and publication of the *Corpus Paulinum;* that is forty or fifty years after the Epistles were written."[43]

■ **Marcion (c. A.D. 100-165).** This early church leader in Rome was expelled from the church around A.D. 144 because of his rejection of the Old Testament, his unorthodox views of God and the contradictions that he saw between the Old and New Testaments. Nevertheless, he remains a crucial figure in our understanding of the collection and canonicity of Paul's letters because of the corpus of ten letters which appears in his *Apostolikon* (Gal, 1 and 2 Cor, Rom, 1 Thess, 2 Thess, Eph [which he called the "epistle to the Laodiceans"], Col, Philem and Phil).

Reaction to the significance of Marcion's list varies considerably among scholars because there is no way of knowing with certainty what his intentions were. It is doubtful that he planned to produce a "closed canon" of Scripture as this term was understood by the church at a later date. Adolf von Harnack and H. von Campenhausen see him as the compiler of the first list; others believe that he is indebted to an earlier collection or collections.

The argument for there having been a pre-Marcionite collection rests on the likelihood of an earlier hypothetical "seven-churches edition" which Harry Gamble thinks had a genetic relationship to Marcion's list.[44] This supposed collection may have arisen from the need for the church to "generalize" or "universalize" Paul's letters. Earlier, I mentioned that Paul's letters were "occasional" or "particular"—that is, each one was written to a local church and addressed specific issues related to that congregation. But when Paul's letters began to circulate more widely, the concern arose as to how these specific letters could be relevant and helpful to other communities.

This question of particularity may have led to the creation of an early "seven-churches" collection. The possibility of this having occurred depends upon several important factors: (1) that the number seven—a biblical symbol of completeness or universality—was utilized for this purpose (note the letters to the *seven* churches in Revelation); (2) that the collection combined letters written to the same locality, and thus the two Corinthian and Thessalonian letters would each form one unit; and (3) that the letters were arranged according to the principle of decreasing length. This would produce a sequence of Corinthians, Romans, Ephesians, Thessalonians, Galatians, Philippians and Colossians (possibly including Philemon because it was addressed to the same locality).

Gamble uses this order of decreasing length to suppose a "genetic relationship" between this seven-churches list and Marcion's edition, even though there are several discrepancies between the two.[45] The significance of the similarities, however, allows for the possibility that the earliest collection of Paul's letters consisted of ten letters that were presented as a seven-churches edition.

Much of this is, of course, speculative. Perhaps the most we can say is that Marcion's list represents a deliberate selection of Paul's letters that supported his rejection of the Old Testament. This, in turn, may have driven the church to expand the collection at a later time by including other recognized epistles of Paul.[46]

▪ **P[46].** This manuscript, known as the Chester Beatty Codex (c. A.D. 200), is recognized as the earliest extant copy of the Pauline letters. Although only 86 of its original 104 leaves have survived, it remains a significant witness for the status of the Pauline corpus at the beginning of the third century. It contains Romans (beginning at 5:17), Hebrews, 1 and 2 Corinthians, Ephesians, Galatians, Philippians, Colossians and 1 Thessalonians. Metzger suggests that "the seven leaves lost from the end probably contained 2 Thessalonians but would have been insufficient for the Pastoral Epistles."[47]

Some scholars have thought that Hebrews and its alleged agreement with Codex Alexandrinus suggests that it is a product of the Eastern church, possibly Alexandria. But this is far from certain. Nevertheless, P[46] is the most significant tangible piece in the puzzle of reconstructing the Pauline corpus. It *may* well represent (though it should not necessarily be identified as) the earliest collection of Paul's epistles from which all subsequent collections were made. Nevertheless, there is no way of knowing whether this document was representative of the entire Eastern church.[48]

▪ **The Muratorian Fragment.** The significance of the Muratorian Fragment[49] for the reconstruction of the collection and canonicity of Paul's letters mainly depends upon its dating. Historically, the Fragment was considered to be the product of the Western church (Rome?) near the end of the second century. Paul's epistles to the Corinthians, Ephesians, Philippians, Colossians, Galatians, Thessalonians, Romans, Philemon, Titus and "two to Timothy" are included among the New Testament epistles (twenty-two of the present twenty-seven canonical books). As such, the Fragment could be a significant testimony to an early collection of Paul's letters.

The euphoria surrounding the value of the Fragment has been diminished in recent scholarship. A. C. Sundberg's detailed analysis led him to propose a fourth-century date and an Eastern setting. Chief among the problems that an early date created for Sundberg is the lack of similar lists until the time of Eusebius in the fourth century.[50]

Not everyone, however, has been persuaded by Sundberg's critique. Both Bruce[51] and Metzger[52] are confident that E. Ferguson has adequately answered, refuted and even "demolished" (to use Metzger's term) Sundberg's opposition to an early date.[53] Thus, in some circles at least, the Fragment is regarded as an authoritative list of New Testament books in the Roman church by the end of the second century. Metzger expresses considerable caution when he writes: "Perhaps the most that can be said is that a member of the Roman

Church, or of some congregation not far from Rome, drew up in Greek toward the close of the second century a synopsis of the writings recognized as belonging to the New Testament in his part of the Church."[54]

■ **Some Later Church Fathers (c. A.D. 150-254).** Significant individuals during this period include Tatian (c. 110-180), Irenaeus (c. 130/150-202), Clement of Alexandria (c. 150-215), Tertullian (c. 160-220) and Origen (c. 185-254). The consensus among scholars is that these church fathers recognized and accepted either thirteen or fourteen (if Hebrews is included) epistles of Paul. Tatian appears to reject 1 and 2 Timothy, and neither Irenaeus or Clement mentions Philemon. Origen often uses the phrase "Paul said" or "Paul says." Thus one can safely conclude that by the middle of the third century there was a fairly uniform consensus concerning the contents of the Pauline corpus. However, final confirmation of this has to wait for evidence derived from the next century.

7. Summary
1. In the composition of his letters, Paul utilized a significant number of traditional materials that were in circulation in the church.

2. Paul relied upon a secretary in writing certain letters. This may account for some of the differences in style and vocabulary.

3. A careful critical, textual, literary and theological study of Paul's epistles reveals the possibility of some editorial and redactional activity by Paul and/or editors after Paul's death.

4. There is sufficient evidence to conclude that by the end of the first century *some* of Paul's letters were being circulated and collected in various churches.

5. The deutero-Pauline hypothesis envisions that the writing and publication of some letters attributed to Paul constituted a conscious attempt by an individual or individuals within the Pauline circle to appeal to Paul's apostolic authority and commend his theology to later generations.

6. The circulation/collection of Paul's letters indicates that they were valued for their universal and not just their local significance.

7. We do not know how and when the editor(s) obtained copies of Paul's epistles. The collector/editor may have received them from Paul, picked them up during his travels or had them sent to his place of residence through the normal process of exchange and circulation.

8. After the first century, Paul's letters circulated as a collection and not (with possible minor exceptions) as individual letters. Although P[46] represents the earliest *extant* evidence of such a collection, it may be only one of several independent collections. These other collections may have included as many as seven, ten, thirteen or fourteen epistles of Paul. For a brief period of time

some later collections also included *Third Corinthians* and the *Epistle to the Laodiceans.*

9. References/allusions to Paul's epistles by church fathers from the second century onward indicate an increasing appeal to Paul's authority and theology in the church, so that by the middle of the third century the content of the Pauline corpus was pretty well decided. We must *not* assume that the fathers felt obliged to mention all the letters they knew or that they intended to construct a "canon" of authoritative Scripture.

10. The significance of the Muratorian Fragment needs to be tempered in the light of criticisms made by Sundberg and others. If it is authentically from the second century, the apparent absence of similar lists until the fourth century is puzzling.[55]

8. The Canonicity of Paul's Letters

Enough has been said to indicate that the collection of Paul's letters was a significant factor in their ultimate canonicity. Although originally addressed to specific congregations, they increasingly were valued for their universal applicability and apostolic authority. One can safely conclude that a Pauline corpus of thirteen letters existed by the beginning of the third century. These, along with the Gospels and the other letters that make up the New Testament, were declared "canonical" by the Council of Carthage in A.D. 397.

There are a number of confluent factors that led to the canonization of the entire New Testament generally and of Paul's letters specifically (see part five). Externally, there was the problem of false teaching. The heterodoxy that Paul faced during his own lifetime, which is reflected throughout the Pauline corpus, became more acute in the postapostolic age with the development of Gnosticism and other heresies. This syncretistic milieu continually forced the church to appeal to an authoritative and widely accepted body of literature to define its theology.

The theory that certain letters (e.g., the Pastorals) are deutero-Pauline fits into this development. Certain features of these letters, such as the emphasis on keeping "the faith" and "sound teaching" and guarding "the truth" and the "good deposit" suggest that they are facing off against post-Pauline challenges. Perhaps the earliest collection and editing of Paul's letters was motivated by an attempt to provide a universal body of Paul's letters to serve as an authoritative weapon against Gnosticism and/or other heresies.

Marcion played a significant role in the development of the Pauline canon when he published his list of ten Pauline letters in the mid-second century. The question whether he created this "hyper-Paulinist" list or utilized an earlier collection is secondary to the insight that it provides on the status of Paul and his letters in the church of Marcion's day. It may have stimulated the church to clarify and enlarge its position on the content of the Pauline corpus, because succeeding lists contain additional letters. However, too little is known about the effects of Marcion's canon to suggest that it *forced* the church to formulate a canon of its own in opposition to his. Montanism (c. A.D. 140-180), on the other hand, with its claim of new revelations, prophecies and inspiration, undoubtedly made it necessary for the church to establish tighter norms of acceptability and authority.

The *internal* criteria that determined the canon include such factors as apostolicity, orthodoxy and catholicity (see part five). Since Paul was regarded by the church as a legitimate and inspired apostle, his letters would have been considered part of the "apostolic deposit of faith" and thus authoritative for the church. This reverence for Paul helps us to understand why a deutero-Paulinist might appeal to his apostolic authority in addressing the theological needs of later generations (Ephesians, Pastorals).

Nevertheless, there were factors other than inspiration and apostolicity at work in the second and third century. Certain apocryphal gospels, letters and apostolic histories claimed to be apostolic (Peter, Thomas, Philip, etc.) but were rejected because much of their teaching differed from that of the accepted Gospels. Even Paul's *Epistle to the Laodiceans* was judged to be spurious and hence was not included among the canonical letters of Paul. Other factors noted earlier, including the antiquity of a document (i.e., whether it was written during the apostolic age), its orthodoxy and its usage in the church, also helped to shape the canon. The Muratorian Fragment, for example, rejects the *Shepherd of Hermas* because it was written too recently—that is, too long after the time of the apostles.[56]

In spite of a "general" consensus regarding the canonical status of Paul's letters by the end of the second century, there were a few interesting debates that continued into and beyond the fourth century. We noted above that the Pastorals were not included in such early collections as those by Marcion or P[46]. Philemon also is missing from P[46], although it, along with 2 Thessalonians, may have been part of the missing seven leaves at the end.

The book of Hebrews (as noted earlier) had a curious and checkered history. In Alexandria (the Eastern church) it was held in high regard and considered to be Pauline. Hence it was included in P[46] as one of Paul's letters. Rome (the Western church), on the other hand, doubted its apostolic (Pauline) authorship and did not include it among the Pauline letters. This may account for its absence from the Muratorian Fragment, a creation of the Western church. It was not until the fourth century, and only due to the persuasive influence of Athanasius, that Rome consented to include Hebrews in the Pauline corpus.[57]

PART IV

OTHER
NEW TESTAMENT
LITERATURE

1. The Acts of the Apostles

The composition of Acts is best understood by comparing it with the Gospel of Luke. Both books are anonymous—that is, the name of the author is not stated within the text itself. The identification of the author as Luke is a product of second-century scholarship based upon internal and external evidence. This tradition also identifies the author as the companion whom Paul mentions in some of the letters attributed to him (cf. Col 4:14; 2 Tim 4:11; Philem 24). The "we" sections in Acts (16:10-17; 20:5-15; 21:1-17; 27:1—28:16) would then suggest that Luke himself was present on the occasions which are described in these passages.[1]

Both books also are addressed to the same person, Theophilus; the "first book" mentioned in Acts 1:1 is a reference to Luke's Gospel, where he decided "to write an orderly account" (Lk 1:3) of the life of Jesus. The similarities between the Gospel and Acts in literary style, vocabulary and theological ideas are striking and confirm that they are by the same author. These observations make it necessary to speak of Luke-Acts (rather than of each book separately) when considering Luke's contribution to early Christianity and to the canon of the New Testament. Acts begins to appear as a separate work under the title "The Acts of the Apostles" only around A.D. 150, after the Gospel of Luke became part of the fourfold Gospel collection. Initially, each book would have filled an entire scroll (about thirty-five feet according to Aune's calculation; the Gospel has 19,404 words or 2,900 stichoi [lines]; Acts has 18,374 words and 2,600 stichoi).

As a history of the early church, Acts provides an invaluable bridge between the Gospels and the letters of Paul. It contributes to our understanding of the relationship between the teaching of Jesus and the development of early Christian doctrine and world evangelism. In many ways Acts is not strictly an "Acts of the Apostles" insofar as it deals with so few of the apostles. Peter is the central figure in the first twelve chapters; the rest of the book is devoted to the apostle Paul.

It has been suggested—not inappropriately—that Acts should be called "The Acts of the Holy Spirit" because of its emphasis on the Holy Spirit. The word *spirit* (*pneuma*) occurs seventy times in Acts, which is approximately one-fifth of the total usage of *spirit* in the New Testament. The selection of *acts* ("deeds," "achievements") to designate the material in Acts conforms to ancient patterns of Hellenistic historiography. In writing, Luke used his rhetorical skills "as an appropriate literary vehicle for depicting the origins and development of Christianity."[2]

Studies in Luke-Acts can be characterized as the movement of a pendulum. At the turn of the century, largely through the research of Sir William Ramsay, the focus was on Luke's reliability as a historian.[3] Then, with the rise of critical German scholarship after World War II, the pendulum swung to the other extreme, and Luke-Acts was examined from a theological perspective. More recent scholars have come to the realization that this is not an "either-or" situation, that is, either history or theology; rather, Luke's writings need to be understood as theological history. Basically this means that the author approached his task as a historian but that he was not just a compiler of data and tradition: he gave a theological interpretation to his material.[4]

How did Luke go about writing his work as a historian-theologian? From the prologue to his Gospel (1:1-4) one concludes that he used *written records* ("since many have undertaken to set down an orderly account of the events that have been fulfilled among us . . . I too decided, after investigating everything carefully from the very first, to write an orderly account") and *oral reports* ("[events] handed on to us by those who from the beginning were eyewitnesses and servants of the word"). Since this prologue is intended to cover both of his writings, it is reasonable to assume that some information in Acts was derived from eyewitnesses as well. This means that by the time he composed Luke-Acts, Luke would have studied some written sources and contacted a number of individuals throughout the Mediterranean world about the history of the early church. He was not, quips Aune, "an armchair historian only."[5]

Much of the material in Acts comes from a number of different sources. I already mentioned that one interpretation of the "we" sections indicates that Luke obtained firsthand information while traveling with Paul. The rest of Acts is made up of speeches (according to Aune's calculations, thirty-two speeches, which add up to 25 percent of the book), travel narratives (38 percent of Acts) and many dramatic episodes.

In addition to chronological considerations, Luke's theological agenda is a significant factor in the selection, arrangement and extent of his material in Acts, in much the same way that it governs the composition of his Gospel. As noted earlier, Luke omits many of the apostles from Acts and devotes one-half of the book to Paul. The speeches in Acts were not intended to be complete—not even the major ones by Peter (2:14-40), Stephen (7:2-53) and Paul in Athens (17:22-31) or during his defense before Felix (24:10-21), Festus (25:8-11) and Agrippa (26:2-23).

Luke also omits a significant amount of material about the history of the church. This may perplex us because other events, such as Paul's conversion (repeated three times), his deliberate turning from the Jews to the Gentiles and the continual rejection of the gospel by the Jews, are emphasized repeatedly. All this leads us to conclude that in writing his history, Luke made a deliberate and conscious selection of persons, places, speeches and events.

From our perspective the ending of Acts is both puzzling and frustrating, for after spending so much time writing about Paul's life and theology, Luke leaves the reader wondering about the apostle's fate at the hands of the Roman authorities. Although several explanations have been proposed for this omission, the most one can say is that Luke's historical and theological purpose appears to be complete with Paul's arrival in Rome.[6] We must learn to accept and appreciate Luke-Acts as the composition of a historian-theologian who wrote a life of Jesus and a history of the early church to meet the needs of believers of the first century rather than those of the twentieth century.

2. The Catholic Letters

The term "Catholic Letters" (*catholic* in the sense of "universal" or "general") goes back to an early designation given by Eusebius (*HE* 2.23.24), who named them "catholic" because they lack a specific address (although 2 and 3 John are exceptions to this rule). They are also known as the "General Epistles." These letters include James ("to the twelve tribes in the Dispersion"—1:1), 1 Peter ("to the exiles of the Dispersion in Pontus, Galatia, Cappadocia, Asia, and Bithynia"—1:1), 2 Peter ("to those who have received a faith as precious as ours through the righteousness of our God and Savior Jesus Christ"—1:1), 1 John ("we declare to you"—1:1), 2 John ("the elder to the elect lady and her children, whom I love in the truth"—v. 1), 3 John ("the elder to the beloved Gaius, whom I love in truth"—v. 1) and Jude ("to those who are called, who are beloved in God the Father and kept safe for Jesus Christ"—v. 1). The letter to the Hebrews also lacks a specific designation. The most one can conclude from an internal examination of this letter is that it was written to Jewish Christians. After Hebrews lost its status as one of the "fourteen letters of Paul," it was not commonly considered along with the other Catholic Epistles.[7]

A study of these seven "catholic" letters reveals that each one had its own history and that they were not grouped together under this title until the fourth century A.D. Harry Gamble suggests that they "came finally to be grouped and arranged alongside the letters of Paul, perhaps in order to document the common witness of the primitive apostles, and especially of Paul and the 'pillar apostles' on the basis of Gal 2:9."[8] However, not all of them were accepted universally. The Syrian church excluded the four minor epistles (2 Peter, 2 and 3 John and Jude) from its authoritative version of the New Testament, the Peshitta.[9]

■ **1 Peter.** Although this letter is addressed to believers in certain geographical areas (Roman provinces), its message was relevant for all believers who were scattered throughout the world in the first century. Internal evidence (1:1; 5:1) and tradition strongly suggest that the author is the apostle Peter, with Silvanus, Peter's amanuensis (5:12), responsible for the actual writing. This possibly accounts for the good quality of the Greek and literary style.[10]

Most approaches to the composition of 1 Peter place it within a catechetical and/or liturgical framework. Classifications such as a "paraenetic encyclical" (D. Aune), a "baptismal document" (Hans Windisch), a "baptismal liturgy" (H. Preisker) and a "Paschal liturgy" (F. M. Cross) are discussed in most commentaries. These conclusions were reached by scholars who discovered that much of the material in this letter is hymnic, creedal, confessional and sermonic. What the author has done, therefore, is to incorporate fragments of this traditional material into his letter while at the same time expressing these ideas in his own language and style. The inclusion of so much traditional baptismal instruction, however, does not necessarily mean that the author engaged in wholesale borrowing from ancient liturgies.[11]

Disagreement over the many theories of composition should not blind us to the fact that 1 Peter is written to a group of believing "exiles" (1:1) who were experiencing some type of persecution (1:3-9; 3:13-17; 4:1-4, 12-19; 5:9) and needed a letter of hope and encouragement. This accounts for its emphasis on "a living hope," "an inheritance that is imperishable, undefiled, and unfading," and "a salvation ready to be revealed in the last time" (1:3-5). There is no record that the authenticity of 1 Peter was challenged in the early church, even though there is no explicit ascription of the letter to Peter until the time of Irenaeus. Polycarp quotes from it several times in his *Letter to the Philippians*, and Eusebius places it among the acknowledged parts of the New Testament canon of his day (*HE* 3.25.1-3).

■ **2 Peter.** Even an elementary study of 2 Peter—and Jude, a companion letter of sorts—introduces us to a bewildering number of theories regarding authorship, date and composition. Although this letter professes to be written by Simon Peter (1:1), someone who was an eyewitness of the transfiguration (1:16-18) and refers to Paul as his beloved brother (3:15), a majority of commentators seriously doubt that it was written by the apostle and consider it a pseudonymous letter.

Now while I readily acknowledge that a "majority opinion" may not necessarily be a "correct opinion," even such a conservative and thorough scholar as Donald Guthrie admits that 2 Peter "is the most problematical of all the New Testament epistles because of early doubts regarding its authenticity and because internal evidence is considered by many to substantiate those doubts."[12] The issues usually debated include (1) differences in literary style and vocabulary from 1 Peter, (2) allusions to an earlier generation ("words spoken in the past . . . through your apostles" [3:2]; "ever since our ancestors died"[3:4]), (3) the reference to Paul's letters, implying a collection of some sort (3:15-16), and (4) the apparent incorporation of material from Jude.

After a lengthy discussion of arguments on both sides, Guthrie opts for the Petrine alternative partially because of his negative presuppositions regarding pseudonymity and his understanding of apostolicity as a criterion for canonicity. "That it ultimately became accepted universally," he reasons, "must have been due to the recognition not merely of its claim to apostolic authorship, but also of its apostolic content."[13]

Equally plausible is the view that the composition of this letter is by a pseudonymous writer, but one who may have had some personal connection with Peter. A recent commentator, R. J. Bauckham, argues that the author was a Hellenistic Jew who may have been a "colleague" of the apostle Peter in Rome. After Peter's death this unknown author became one of the members of a "Petrine circle" in Rome and wrote this letter ("testament") under the pseudonym of Peter in order "to be a faithful mediator of the apostolic message."[14]

Second Peter is often described as a "last will and testament," a "memorandum," because of its emphasis on "recalling" and "reminding" (from the Greek *mneia*, a remembrance, thus to remember, recall; 1:10, 12, 13, 15, 19; 3:1-2, 14, 17-18). Ralph Martin's suggestion that a disciple from the Petrine circle "has been at work in assembling and publishing, in his master's name, a testament of that teaching in response to the pressing needs in the church" seems a reasonable solution to the questions of composition. Associating this letter with the apostle Peter undoubtedly aided in its rather turbulent history of canonicity— "the slow and cautious reception of 2 Peter into the canon."[15] It was one of Eusebius's disputed or spurious books (*HE* 3.3.4). It was never "received with authority among the Syrian churches [i.e., the Eastern church]. In the West, Hippolytus knew it, but Irenaeus, Tertullian and Cyprian did not, and it does not appear in the Muratorian Canon. It found acceptance in the West around 370-380."[16]

■ **Jude.** The extensive literary, verbal and conceptual similarities between 2 Peter and Jude are noted by most commentators. Those analyzing these similarities generally conclude that Peter borrowed from Jude, although it is possible that both writers incorporated several independent tracts that were circulating in the Christian communities. Both letters have stern warnings about false teachers—probably Gnostics—who are bent on disturbing and destroying the Christian church. In no other letters of the New Testament are false teachers described and denounced so vehemently as they are in 2 Peter and Jude (cf. Jude 5-23; 2 Pet 2).

Opinions on authorship ("Jude, a servant of Jesus Christ and brother of James") vary. Many see no reason to doubt that Jude and James were brothers of Jesus (see Mt 13:55; Mk 6:3) and wonder why a later author would use Jude as a pseudonym.[17] Others consider the letter pseudonymous, reasoning that the author is not a contemporary of the apostles (note v. 3: "the faith that was once for all entrusted to the saints"; v. 17: "remember the predictions of the apostles of our Lord Jesus Christ") and that those who are causing divisions (v. 19) correspond to a schism that emerged in the church after the apostolic age.[18]

As mentioned, the purpose of the letter is to expose the false teachers and in doing so to encourage a besieged and bewildered group of believers to stand firm in the faith: "Beloved, while eagerly preparing to write to you about the salvation we share, I find it necessary to write and appeal to you to contend for the faith that was once for all entrusted to the saints" (v. 3). On these grounds, the letter basically is an exhortation. Beyond that, the form of Jude gives little appearance of a letter. It is addressed "to those who are called, who are beloved in God the Father and kept safe for Jesus Christ" (v. 1), and it ends with a liturgical benediction (vv. 24-25).

Unlike 2 Peter, Jude was at first well received by the early church and regarded as canonical by Tertullian and Clement of Alexandria. Later, however, its canonical status was questioned, with Eusebius and Jerome including it among the "contested" writings. It appears that doubts arose about the letter because of Jude's use of Apocryphal books (cf. vv. 9, 14). But the identity of the author as a member of the holy family (Mt 13:55; Mk 6:3) would have given apostolic credibility to the letter as a defense against forms of Gnosticism threatening the early church.

■ **James.** It has been observed that the letter of James is the least Christian and most Jewish book in the New Testament. It opens by naming James, "a servant of God and of the Lord Jesus Christ," as the author (1:1). "Aside from 2:1," observes R. P. Martin, "this text is the only verse in the entire letter with a distinctively Christian flavor—which has led to speculation that this is a Christian edition of a work originally Jewish." Martin also concurs with scholarly consensus that James is not a letter in the regular sense of the term but a selection of exhortations "loosely strung together."[19]

A number of commentators identify James as the brother of Jesus who became a prominent leader in the Jerusalem church and a representative of a conservative Jewish Christianity (cf. Acts 12:17; 15:1-21; 21:18; Gal 2:9, 12). This would then date the epistle before A.D. 62, when tradition states that James was executed. A current—and attractive—reconstruction of the composition of James proposes that even though much of the material comes from the early period of the Christian church (mid-forties), it circulated for a number of years before being put into its current form. At some point an editor collected the sayings and discourses of James and circulated them as a general letter. The literary style, according to one commentator, is clearly "oral discourse, like the Greek diatribe, the synagogue homily, or a sermon."[20]

Studies on the history of James in the early church reveal that the letter received recognition rather slowly.[21] Although James and Jude were on Origen's and Eusebius's "disputed" list, they may have been granted canonical status because they were considered to be writings of the Lord's brothers. James first was included in Athanasius's Festal Letter (A.D. 367) and then endorsed by the Councils of Rome (A.D. 382) and Carthage (A.D. 397, 419).

Many of us are familiar with Luther's concerns about James, a letter that he disparagingly called "a straw epistle" because it fell short of the canonical standards that he had set. The questions that Luther raised about the teaching of James so many years ago reappear in some circles of critical scholarship today as individuals seek to discern its teaching and justify its inclusion in the canon of the New Testament. However, "acceptance of both the brother of the Lord and the Epistle of James by the church," observes Martin, "bore witness to his continuing value for it. In a different time and setting, he became regarded—for the Great Church—as a bearer of authoritative tradition and a faithful martyr for Christ."[22]

3. Hebrews

The title "The Letter to the Hebrews" is somewhat misleading, because this document lacks some of the literary structure that was typical of Paul's letters. The exposition begins without any kind of epistolary introduction and is followed by a hortatory section which does not come at the end of the letter as in most of the letters of Paul. Also, the exposition is interrupted repeatedly by paraenetic passages. Such observations have led some scholars to conclude that Hebrews is "atypical as a letter for it has an epistolary postscript but no prescript" and that on literary grounds it "stands in a class of its own in the New Testament library."[23]

There are a number of current theories on the nature and composition of this document.[24] David Aune, a specialist in analyzing literary genre, calls it "a hortatory sermon"[25] on the strength of 13:22, where the author asks his readers to "bear with my word of exhortation." This observation is supported by a number of commentators. Donald Hagner, for example, also concludes that the literary genre of Hebrews is an "exhortatory sermon" or, even more specifically, "a sermon-treatise because of its distinctive combination of exhortation and argumentative discourse, but a letter because it is written for and sent to a specific community of Jewish Christians, probably in Rome."[26] It is significant that the exhortations which conclude each section of the letter all express in varied ways a single appeal: "Do not forsake your faith in Christ, but endure to the end."

There is no way of knowing how this anonymous author composed the letter (suggestions for the author have included Paul, Luke, Clement of Rome, Apollos, Barnabas, Silvanus, Timothy, Epaphras and Priscilla). Does this letter have congregational worship as its setting? Was it intended to be read in one sitting, or would readers have recognized certain distinctive sections (dogmatic and paraenetic) and meditated on them individually? Those who have examined the structure and content in detail concede that the author draws freely from liturgical, cultic and confessional elements of the church. It is not unreasonable to suppose that the final composition is the result of a number of "exhortatory sermons" that were brought together into one letter.

With respect to its canonicity, the letter to the Hebrews was known and already accepted by the Eastern church in the second century and by the third century was regarded as canonical and Pauline. The Western churches did not acknowledge it as Pauline until the fourth century, and then only at the persuasion of Athanasius. According to W. G. Kümmel, "It is only from the second half of the fourth century on, through the influence of interchange between Western and Eastern theologians, that the Western canon became equivalent to the Eastern, and Hebrews was recognized as the fourteenth Pauline letter."[27]

4. The Johannine Literature

■ **The Epistles of John.** The Johannine literature is the name given to a rather distinctive group of five books in the New Testament whose authorship is attributed to the apostle John (the Fourth Gospel, 1, 2, 3 John and the Apocalypse). Of these five books, Revelation is the only one that specifically identifies the author (1:4). Later church tradition attributed the rest of the literature to John and indicated that after his leadership in Jerusalem, he moved to Ephesus where he lived to an old age and died a natural death (e.g., Irenaeus, *Adversus haereses* 3.3.4).[28]

When one studies the Johannine literature critically, one is faced with a bewildering array of questions:

1. What is the relationship between the Fourth Gospel and the Synoptics?

2. Is the author of all the literature attributed to "John" the same person, and is he to be identified as the apostle John? Or does the term *elder* in 2 and 3 John introduce a different individual?

3. What is the relationship of the "letters" of John to the Fourth Gospel and Revelation?

4. What is the relationship of the letters to each other, and in what sequence were they written?

5. Were the letters written after or before the Fourth Gospel?

6. Why were the letters written? Should they be considered as interpretations and/or supplements to the Gospel?

7. Was there a "community" or "school" of disciples associated with the apostle John in Ephesus near the end of the first century?

8. What literary genre best describes the letters and the Apocalypse?

These questions of authorship and the relationship between the Four Gospels and the letters are complex. Some scholars confidently affirm that the apostle John is the author of *all* the literature attributed to him and that it follows chronologically the sequence found in the New Testament. Others believe that an editor(s) from within the Johannine community utilized and reinterpreted traditions that originally came from the beloved disciple. In this case, the literature probably attained its final form in Ephesus some time after John's death near the end of the first century.[29]

Questions continue to be raised about the nature of the so-called letter of 1 John. Since it lacks some of the necessary features of a letter, such as personal names, a prescript and greetings, it gives the impression of not being a letter at all. For this reason it could be considered a tract or homily for all believers.

Although doubts about the authorship of these letters existed in the early church (see Eusebius *HE* 3.25.3), a study of their history reveals that they were known and used by a number of early church fathers. Irenaeus, near the end of the second century, accepted 1 John as a work of John, the disciple of the Lord (*Adversus haereses* 3.16.5, 8). The Muratorian Canon included letters of John, but doubt exists whether *all* of them were intended. Origen and Eusebius included them as "disputed" books.

■ **The Revelation to John (the Apocalypse).** The first word of this New Testament book tells us that it is a "revelation" (from the Greek *apokalypsis*—"a revelation"). The main focus of apocalyptic literature is eschatology (Greek *eschaton*, meaning "the last," or "the end"). Writings of this genre, therefore, stress the cosmic drama that will occur to replace the current evil world order with a new and perfect one. A good example is found in Revelation 21:5: "And the one who was seated on the throne said, 'See, I am making all things new.' " The message of how this will be accomplished is communicated through visions, symbolism, numerology and accounts of cosmic catastrophes and a final judgment of the wicked.

Some of the circumstances which called for the book of Revelation include the claims of certain Roman emperors to be gods (e.g., Domitian's title "our Lord and God") and the strong promotion of emperor worship in cities of Roman Asia. John, like Paul, sees these phenomena as "the secret mystery of lawlessness . . . already at work" (2 Thess 2:7)—a forerunner of the spectacle of a world divided by allegiance to the Christ of God and the Christ of the devil.

Recent analysis of the Apocalypse has emphasized that it contains more than just "revelations" mediated by an otherworldly being (God, angels) to a human receptor. The prophetic and epistolary genres also are a significant component of the book. John, in this case, is the human messenger through whom God is revealing his future plan. A number of passages describe the letter as prophecy (1:3; 22:7, 10, 18-19), contain visions that enable the messenger to accomplish his task (1:9-20; 4—5; 10:8-11), announce prophetic judgment (upon the seven churches, 2—3) and constitute oracles of woes (8:13; 12:12).

Chapters 2 and 3 contain the letters to the seven churches in Asia Minor. These recipients are introduced in the opening salutation (1:4). Characteristics of the letter form are obvious in the opening salutation, which identifies the recipients and the sender (1:4) and offers a blessing (1:4-5) with a doxology (1:5-6). The book ends with a final greeting (22:21).[30]

Research into the composition of Revelation confirms that more is involved than the author just sitting somewhere on the island of Patmos and passively writing down words from some heavenly voice (1:9-20). The use of the past tense—"was on the island called Patmos" (1:9)—probably indicates that this is where he initially received his vision when he was exiled but is not necessarily where the letter was written. Thus George Beasley-Murray notes that "John's banishment gave opportunity to receive the word of God and testimony of Jesus Christ that came to him in Patmos and subsequently to publish it."[31] The actual composition of the letter may have taken place in Ephesus, where, according to tradition, John made his home after Emperor Nerva (A.D. 96-98) freed him from his banishment (cf. Eusebius *HE* 3.20.9).

Basically, there are two ways to look at the composition of Revelation: one is to see the letter as a direct revelation from God without the use of any literary sources; the second is to acknowledge that in addition to "direct revelation" (1:1; 19:10; 22:8, 19) the author was consulting existing sources that he edited and incorporated into his composition at appropriate places. Historically, this second view has led to a variety of compilation, revision and incorporation theories. A number of current studies on Revelation have concentrated on the liturgical-hymnic material and motifs as sources.

As a book, Revelation was popular in the West as early as the second century. The Eastern church, however, questioned both its authorship and content, so that its canonicity was still a matter of dispute in the fourth century, when Athanasius endorsed it. It was listed as canonical by the Third Council of Carthage in A.D. 397 and officially ratified at the Third Council of Constantinople in A.D. 680. In spite of this, Robert Wall notes, "today, there are still some non-Chalcedon (i.e., Nestorian) Christian communions who reject the canonicity of Revelation and follow the Peshitta, an ancient Syriac version of the Bible that excludes Revelation along with 2 Peter, 2-3 John and Jude. The Eastern Orthodox do not include readings from Revelation in their liturgy—tantamount to a rejection of its canonicity."[32]

It seems appropriate to end this section on the making of the New Testament with the last book of the canon. Part of our journey has taken us from the time of Jesus and the first disciples in the mid-thirties to John's Revelation near the end of the first century. These seventy years were exciting and important ones for the early church, for it appears that this was the period during which all the twenty-seven books of the New Testament were written.

5. Summary

Throughout my discussion I have noted that a number of different authors contributed to writing the New Testament. Their writings, in turn, were grouped according to a specific genre and/or other factors. Table 4.1 gives a visual summary of how each part of the New Testament contributes to the whole.[33]

Table 4.1. Types of Literature

Gospels: 47%
Acts: 13%
Paul's Letters: 23%
Hebrews: 4%
Catholic Letters: 6%
Revelation: 7%

Another way to appreciate the New Testament is to realize that approximately 72 percent of its content is *attributed to* three individuals (see table 4.2): Luke (Luke-Acts), Paul (thirteen letters) and John (Fourth Gospel, three letters, the Apocalypse). Although the authorship in some cases is disputed, this does indicate the significance church tradition attached to certain figures.

Table 4.2. Literature Attributed to Authors

Luke (28%)	Paul (23%)	John (21%)	Other (28%)

The seventy years following the death of Christ saw the writing of all the New Testament books and also marked the beginning stages of the collecting, editing and publishing of some writings. However, we have to wait until the second and third centuries A.D. for more substantial evidence on these matters. It is evident that the Gospels were brought together into a collection near the end of the second century. With Paul, the evidence is a little more ambiguous. It is possible that the apostle was involved in collecting, editing and publishing some of his early letters. But we are left to admit that the collection of his letters *into a corpus* cannot be dated with any certainty prior to A.D. 200. Most of the Catholic Letters do not appear in any canonical lists until the third and fourth centuries.

In the course of this story of the making of the New Testament I have made passing reference to such concepts as apostolic authority, tradition and canonicity. In the following chapter I want to define these terms more clearly and discuss the process by which the twenty-seven books of the New Testament were canonized.

PART V

THE CRITERIA OF CANONICITY

Up to this point our inquiry into the making of the New Testament has led to a number of significant observations:

1. The early church inherited a body of authoritative literature known as the Hebrew Scriptures.

2. All the documents which make up the New Testament were probably written before the end of the first century.

3. Each of the four Gospels was included in the fourfold Gospel collection by the end of the second century.

4. Paul's letters became part of a thirteen-letter corpus by the beginning of the third century.

5. The Catholic Letters initially circulated independently but were brought together under this title by the fourth century.

6. The copying, circulation, collection and use of these books during the first four centuries shows that nearly all of them had universal appeal and authority for the church before the final canonical list was made in A.D. 397.

The historical and creative process by which the twenty-seven books came to make up the New Testament is known as *canonization* and took four centuries to complete. The word *canon* (from the Greek *kanōn,* a loan word from the Semitic languages, meaning "reed" or "straight rod") initially was used by the early church fathers for a *norm* or *rule* of faith (Latin *regula fidei,* "rule of faith"). But by the fourth century it referred to lists or tables and in this sense was applied to the books which were given *canonical* status by the church.[1]

In examining the criteria that were used in the formation of the New Testament canon, several observations should be kept in mind: First, the most important criterion appears to be whether or not a document was a trustworthy witness to the apostolic faith. Second, for the most part, the other criteria should be understood as operating *inter*dependently or concurrently rather than independently or sequentially. This means that one should not attempt to rank them in importance. Third, certain criteria were given different weight by some churches and leaders—a phenomenon which explains why a few books took longer to gain universal acceptance.

Following is a brief discussion of the criteria that were used.

1. The Authority of Jesus

The New Testament teaches that the ultimate authority for the early church was the authority of the resurrected and exalted Lord (cf. references in part two). Followers of Jesus remembered him as one who spoke from God ("Never has anyone spoken like this"—Jn 7:46) and whose words carried the message of eternal life (Jn 6:68). Although no evidence exists that Jesus committed any of his thoughts to writing, his spoken words were extremely important to his followers. He was considered a "standard" or "canon" of authority long before his words were written down, collected and officially canonized by the church. F. W. Beare is quite correct in stating that in oral transmission, the church had in germ the essential canon of the New Testament prior to having any literature to canonize. And when the Gospels were written down and gradually came into general use in the churches, the authority they acquired was accorded to them not in the first instance as holy books, but as books containing the holy words of Jesus. The authority of the words was primary; that of the books was secondary and derivative.[2]

2. Apostolicity

On the surface, this criterion suggests that the documents of the New Testament were written by apostles and would, therefore, fall within the apostolic age (c. A.D. 30-65). This would be the case, for example, with the Gospels attributed to Matthew and John or letters written by Paul, Peter and James.

Further study, however, reveals that the concept of apostolicity implied for the early church more than just apostolic authorship. Certain writings which claimed to be written by apostles (for example, the *Gospel of Thomas, Gospel of Philip, Gospel of Peter, Preaching of Peter, Apocalypse of Peter*) or which claimed apostolic authority (*The Teaching of the Twelve Apostles, Letter of Barnabas*) were not canonized. On the other hand, some documents were included in the canon because they were *indirectly* connected with an apostle. This appears to be the case with Mark and Luke, who were not apostles but whose writings were given apostolic authority on the basis of their association with Peter and Paul, respectively.

This rather elastic concept of apostolicity may explain why other letters of the New Testament were canonized. According to current historical-critical study, Hebrews appears to have gained general acceptance once it was attributed to Paul; James and Jude may have been included because they were regarded as written by brothers of the Lord; and the letters of 2 and 3 John were associated with the apostle who wrote the Fourth Gospel and the book of Revelation. Second Peter was considered to be the work of the apostle Peter, author of the first epistle bearing his name.

Contemporary scholars, however, were not the first to question authorship. Martin Luther questioned the apostolicity of James. "As for 2 Peter," reasoned Calvin, "if it is canonical and therefore trustworthy, it must be accepted as having come from Peter—'not that he wrote it himself, but that one of his disciples composed by his command what the necessity of times demanded.' "[3] The same can be said about other books in the New Testament whose authorship is uncertain today. Those noncanonical books which claimed apostolic authority probably were not canonized because their doctrine was considered unorthodox—that is, it was not sound apostolic teaching.

3. Usage in the Church

It appears that the books that finally were canonized are those that enjoyed a special status and were utilized both frequently and universally by the church. In other words, believers accepted certain Christian writings as authoritative for their faith because they transcended the immediate or particular situation for which they initially were written. Those that possessed only a temporary importance were not given canonical status. This criterion appears to be more significant in canonizing a writing than either apostolicity or catholicity.

Again, we need to remember that there were regional differences in the early church. The churches in the West used Revelation, but not those in the East; the East accepted Hebrews and regarded it as Pauline, while the West took many more years to come to a similar position. Up to the fifth century, the Syrian church preferred Tatian's harmony of the Gospels (known as the *Diatessaron*) over the fourfold Gospels. And there is no doubt that some of the churches used noncanonical books. First Clement, for example, was read in the Roman church long after it initially was sent there (cf. *HE* 4.23.11). In A.D. 367, when Athanasius, bishop of Alexandria, wrote his "Festal Letter" to the churches under his jurisdiction, he acknowledged that *The Teaching of the Twelve Apostles* and *The Shepherd of Hermas* were read in the church along with the books he was commending as canonical.

4. Orthodoxy

The church existed under the threat of false teachings and found it necessary to protect the truth of the gospel (see Gal 1:6-9) from such heresies as Gnosticism, Docetism and other heterodox movements of the late first and early second centuries. In the first century this was done by appealing to apostolic teaching and traditions (Col 2:6, 8; 2 Thess 2:15; 1 Jn 1:5), the word of truth (2 Tim 1:14; 2:15; 3:8), good doctrine (1 Tim 4:6), sound teaching and doctrine (1 Tim 6:3; 2 Tim 1:13; 4:3; Tit 1:9, 2:1), the faith (2 Tim 4:7; Jude 3, 20) and testing the spirits (1 Jn 4:1-4). These early appeals to orthodoxy led to a conformity to the "rule of faith" (Latin *regula fidei*) in the second and third centuries. Orthodoxy, however, does not mean that there was a sterile or even uniform theology in the early church. Recent studies have helped us to appreciate the diversity as well as the unity of early Christian theology.[4]

5. Inspiration

Initially, the concept of inspiration was not crucial to the canonicity of the New Testament. The early Christians believed that the Holy Spirit was the possession of every believer and thus inspired the entire community and not only the writers of their sacred literature (Acts 2:17; Rom 8:9; 1 Cor 2:14-16; Rev 2:7). The author of the book of Revelation is the only writer of the New Testament who expressly claims that his words are prophetically inspired (see 1:1; 3:22; 22:18-19). It was only during the second and succeeding centuries that the utterances of church leaders and teachers gave way to the apostolic testimony contained within certain Christian writings.

The Gospels and letters that were canonized were considered to be authoritative and reliable witnesses of the saving events of our Lord. Gradually the church came "to recognize, accept, affirm, and confirm the self-authenticating quality of certain documents that imposed themselves as such upon the church."[5] With the exception of prophetic and apocalyptic documents, inspiration was attributed by the church to a book only *after* it was recognized as canonical; it was considered a corollary of canonicity rather than a criterion of canonicity. According to K. Stendahl, "It was not until the red ribbon of the self-evident had been tied around the twenty-seven books of the New Testament that 'inspiration' could serve theologians as an answer to the question: Why are these books different from all other books?"[6]

The concept of inspiration was not restricted to the New Testament. The statement in 2 Timothy 3:16 that "all scripture is inspired by God [literally, 'God-breathed']," refers to the Old Testament, but we have no way of knowing whether "Scripture" meant the canon of the Old Testament as we have it today. It was only later, when the New Testament writings were included with the Old Testament, that the term *inspired* was attributed to them as well. Clement of Rome claims "inspiration" for his works (1 Clement 63.2), as does Ignatius (*To the Romans* 8.3). Bruce Metzger refers to a commentary on "the first six days of creation" by Basil (c. 330-379) that was considered "divinely inspired."[7] In sum, at no time was inspiration considered the unique or primary criterion to determine which writings of the New Testament should be canonized. With the exception of the author of Revelation, the writers of the New Testament do not base their authority on inspiration.

The role and nature of inspiration with respect to the canonicity of the New Testament continues to be debated in many circles today. There is no unanimous agreement on the definition of the term *inspiration*. Such statements as "a book was included in the canon because it was believed to be inspired" and "a book was believed to be inspired because it was in the canon" reflect the circular reasoning often evident in the debate. Students of the New Testament and early church history must define their terms carefully and not impose any preconceived ideas of inspiration and authority upon the text.[8]

There were, to be sure, other factors that contributed to the formation of the New Testament canon. Persecution and martyrdom, for example, may also have motivated the church to finalize its sacred and authoritative writings. And, as much as we believe in the divine element at work during this period of history, we cannot disregard the human factor. Who knows what went on behind the scenes with bellicose bishops, stubborn scholars and coercive councils! Our own experience testifies that being possessed by the Spirit does not always mean living by the Spirit (Rom 8:4-8; Gal 5:16-26). Perhaps the architects of the New Testament canon felt like the participants at the Jerusalem Council (Acts 15:1-35), who, after lengthy debates and passionate arguments, were able to say, "It has seemed good to the Holy Spirit and to us" (v. 28).

It is important to note that the Council of Carthage did not settle all the issues of the canon for Christendom, because different opinions on the status of certain books continued to exist in both the Eastern and Western churches. Some manuscripts appear which either lack one or more of the twenty-seven books (e.g., Hebrews) or add some books that originally were not included (e.g., *The Epistle to the Laodiceans*). Codex Sinaiticus (fourth century) includes *The Epistle of Barnabas* and *The Shepherd of Hermas* on its list; Alexandrinus (fifth century) has 1 *Clement* and 2 *Clement* 1:1—12:5; and the sixth-century Codex Claromontanus mentions *The Epistle of Barnabas, The Shepherd of Hermas, The*

Acts of Paul and *The Apocalypse of Peter* in its list. We do well to listen to Bruce
Metzger, for whom "it would be a mistake to represent the question of the
canon as finally settled in all Christian communities by the beginning of the
fifth century."[9]

Significant debates on the New Testament canon also took place during the
Renaissance and the Reformation. Martin Luther questioned the apostolic and
canonical status of Hebrews, James, Jude and Revelation and relegated them
to the end of his 1522 edition of the New Testament (he called James "an epistle
of straw"). Calvin, on the other hand, accepted the traditional form of the New
Testament canon. The Roman Catholic Church made its final decision on the
canon of Scripture, including the Apocrypha, at the Council of Trent in 1546.
The important fact, however, is that all of these confessions acknowledge the
same twenty-seven books of the New Testament.

Questions about the canon of the New Testament continue to be raised
today.[10] Which form of the text is canonical? Is the canon open or closed? Is
there a canon within the canon? Responses to these questions, however, go
beyond the purpose of this study. For our historical survey on the making of
the New Testament it seems wise to end this section with the judicious words
of F. F. Bruce, a scholar who devoted much of his life to a study of the canon:

> That the New Testament consists of the twenty-seven books which have
> been recognized as belonging to it since the fourth century is not a value
> judgment; it is a statement of fact. Individuals or communities may consider
> that it is too restricted or too comprehensive; but their opinion does not
> affect the identity of the canon. The canon is not going to be diminished or
> increased because of what they think or say: it is a literary, historical and
> theological datum.[11]

Excursus: The Arrangement of the New Testament Books

Once students of the New Testament appreciate the criteria used to determine
which twenty-seven books were canonized, they often wonder *why* the books
are placed in the order in which they are found. Who determined this arrangement? When? Why? Was it always this way, or did different sequences exist at
different times in history? Is there something "sacred" about this order? Did
God lower it this way from heaven on a golden string? In this section we will
explore some of the principles of arrangement that were at work with early
editors and attempt to answer the questions posed above.

The arrangement of the books that we have in our current English translations and Greek editions of the New Testament is often referred to as the
"canonical order." Some believe that it can be traced to Erasmus of Rotterdam
and the twelfth- and thirteenth-century manuscripts that he used to produce

his 1516 edition of the Greek New Testament. Others have suggested that the current arrangement goes back to the lists produced by Eusebius (c. 264-340) and the Council of Carthage. However, these two lists differ from the order in our New Testament.

The Gospels are placed first, probably because they deal with the words and deeds of Jesus. However, they are arranged differently in a number of manuscripts.[12] Augustine (A.D. 354-430), and other early church fathers, taught that the current canonical order of the Gospels was based on the *chronological order* in which they were believed to have been written—i.e., Matthew, Mark, Luke and lastly John (his theory has come to be known as the "Augustinian Hypothesis").[13] Eusebius records a statement by Clement of Alexandria that those Gospels "which contain the genealogies were written first" (*HE* 6.14). This would place Matthew and Luke up front.

But there are other interesting proposals. Goodspeed suggested that the Gospels were arranged from *the most Jewish to the most Greek*.[14] Bruce conjectures that the primacy of Matthew is due to its *catholic nature*—in other words, not chronological considerations but as "a proper catholic introduction to a catholic gospel collection and, in due course, to the catholic New Testament."[15] Metzger notes that in Codex Bezae (D) "the Gospels stand in the so-called Western order, with the two apostles first and the two companions of the apostles following (Matthew, John, Luke, Mark)."[16]

H. Conzelmann and A. Lindemann, although skeptical about attributing any theological value to the sequence of letters, nevertheless state that "it is not by accident that the Gospel of Matthew—highly esteemed by the early church—was placed at the beginning of the canon, while the disputed Apocalypse was placed at the end."[17] Unfortunately, they are unable to suggest any specific concerns that led to the current order.

The book of Acts did not always assume its current position in the list of canonical books. In Codex Claromontanus (sixth century) it appears after Revelation. The Cheltenham Canon (c. 350) and Codex Sinaiticus (fourth century) place it after the epistles of Paul and before the Catholic Epistles. One wonders if the editors of this arrangement felt that Acts, with its history of such church leaders as Peter, James and John, was an appropriate introduction to letters which bore the name of these apostles.

Another possibility is that Acts and the Catholic Letters were just bound together because they formed a codex. According to Bruce, "The placing of Acts after the Pauline epistles and before the catholic epistles reflects the earlier practice of binding Acts and the catholic epistles together in one smaller codex."[18] But why, then, did others relocate it before Paul's letters? Another author suggests that Acts, with its positive presentation of Paul, was placed between the Gospels and Paul's letters as a "bridge" to guarantee the true apostolicity of his letters.[19] Although this comment regarding apostolicity is questionable, there is no doubt that Acts eventually found its place into the canon between the Gospels and Paul *as a link* between the two collections. The unfortunate consequence was that Acts was severed from its companion volume, the Gospel of Luke. Hence most readers fail to appreciate the unity of Luke-Acts.

Although the order or sequence of Paul's letters varies in many lists, there is enough similarity and tangible evidence to offer the following suggestions.

1. The earliest collection of Paul's correspondence may be the "seven-churches" edition of ten letters, arranged according to the principle of decreasing length, with letters to the Corinthians and Thessalonians considered as a single unit.[20] Table 5.1 charts these letters according to the number of stichoi, or lines.[21]

Table 5.1. The Earliest Collection of Paul's Letters

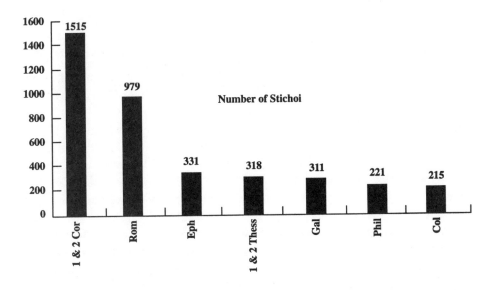

2. The expansion of Paul's letters to thirteen (or fourteen when Hebrews is included) was arranged by length, first according the congregations to whom they were written (Rome, Corinth, Galatia, Ephesus, Philippi, Colossae, Thessalonica), and second to individuals (Timothy, Titus, Philemon). Table 5.2 illustrates this arrangement.

Table 5.2. The Expanded Collection of Paul's Letters

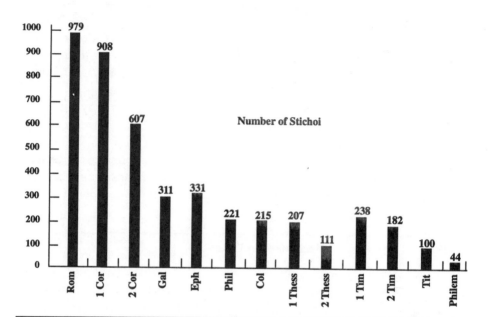

Two items require a brief comment.

1. The principle of decreasing length is not violated with the Pastorals (1 and 2 Timothy, Titus) if one considers that letters addressed to individuals were treated separately from those addressed to congregations.

2. The one exception to the rule is that Galatians precedes Ephesians even though it is shorter (by twenty stichoi). Did the editor fail to detect this slight variation? This seems doubtful, because the principle is followed with Philippians and Colossians, where the difference in length is even smaller (six stichoi). Who knows what led the first compiler of this arrangement to place Ephesians this way?[22]

The Catholic Epistles also appear in some interesting sequences. Some early Greek manuscripts place them immediately after Acts but before the Pauline epistles (Vaticanus, Alexandrinus; but Sinaiticus has Paul, Acts, Catholic Letters). Perhaps this was because they "were attributed to apostles who had been associated with Jesus . . . and partially because they were addressed, not to individual churches, but to any and all Christians."[23] One observes further that whereas James commonly stood first, Peter, because of his primacy in the church at Rome, assumes this position in lists from the West (cf. Council of Carthage). The principle of decreasing length is not used with these individual letters; otherwise, one would expect Peter (403 stichoi), John (332 stichoi),

James (247 stichoi) and Jude (71 stichoi) in that order. Athanasius also arranges Paul's epistles after Acts and the Catholic Epistles. But Eusebius, the Council of Carthage and most subsequent lists place Paul's epistles between Acts and the Catholic Epistles.

Hebrews, due to doubts concerning authorship and lack of appreciation by the Western churches, appears in a number of different places.[24] The four oldest Greek manuscripts (Sinaiticus, Alexandrinus, Vaticanus, Ephraemi) regard Hebrews as Pauline and place it after 2 Thessalonians because it is addressed to a congregation (at least a "group" called "Hebrews") and not to an individual.

The book of Revelation (the Apocalypse), due in part to its teaching on "the last things," appropriately comes at the end of the canon. Yet Metzger's point that Revelation occasionally follows the Gospels because it contains "the words of the heavenly Christ directed to the seven Churches" is well taken.[25]

It is not clear whether any systematic theological presuppositions—or prejudices—were used to determine the place of any books in the New Testament. Because the order varies in so many lists, one is forced to assume that there were a number of different factors at work. In addition to those already mentioned, church usage in worship and liturgy may have been a factor. And F. W. Beare make a cautious but intriguing suggestion that the change from a roll to the codex form of manuscripts required a serious and deliberate decision as to which particular books should be placed together. Collections like the Four Gospels and Paul's letters could each form a single codex. Bound into codex form, these and/or other materials would be viewed as a unity.[26]

These brief—and incomplete—observations show that there was no consistent or authoritative pattern employed by those who arranged the books of the New Testament canon. The decision to include these twenty-seven books did not specify how they were to be arranged. The one discernible exception is the principle of decreasing length applied to Paul's letters written first to congregations and then to individuals. Other arrangements were determined by questions of authorship, apostolic primacy, ecclesiastical preferences, codex production, scribal errors and editorial decisions that may have been based on some theological grounds which are not discernible to the modern reader.

If anything, the above discussion should prevent us from making any dogmatic statements and conclusive pronouncements about the order of the New Testament before the sixteenth century. From that time on, most editions of the English Bible have followed the traditional order that first appeared in the authorized Great Bible of 1539.[27]

PART VI

WRITING, COPYING & TRANSMITTING THE NEW TESTAMENT MANUSCRIPTS

1. Paleography

Paleography (literally, "old writing") is the study of ancient inscriptions and writings. People in early civilizations wrote on such materials as stone, wood, metal and clay tablets, and ostraca, which are broken pieces of pottery. Stone appears to have been used in all ages and in most areas. While the surfaces of rocks, cliffs, tombs and caves provided a natural place for early pictographs and writing, many inscriptions were carved on special monuments. For example, the Code of Hammurabi (Hammurabi was an ancient king of Babylon 1792-1750 B.C.) is carved on a large pillar of stone (known as a *stela*) in cuneiform (Latin *cuneus*)—that is, wedge-shaped letters. The hieroglyphics (literally, holy or sacred carvings) of Egypt were often carved on stone or tablets. Clay was readily available and widely used in Mesopotamia and other areas of the ancient Near East. Archaeologists have discovered thousands of such clay tablets at certain ruins. At Nuzi, an ancient city in what is now northeastern Iraq, twenty thousand clay tablets have been unearthed since 1925. The ruins that were discovered at Ebla in northern Syria in 1947 have also yielded approximately twenty thousand tablets. D. J. Wiseman notes, "By the time of Moses eight different languages were recorded in five different writing systems."[1]

The ancient Hebrews would have utilized the writing materials of their time. Thus we have references to writing on wood (Num 17:2-3; Ezek 37:16-17) and on either metal or wooden tablets that probably were covered with wax (Is 30:8; Hab 2:2). Later materials would have included papyrus (Jer 32:10-14; 36:21-23) and leather. Most of the Dead Sea Scrolls that were discovered at Qumran were written on leather. By the time of the New Testament, papyrus and parchment had become the most widely used materials. These eventually were replaced by paper, which came into prominence around the twelfth to thirteenth centuries A.D.2

2. Materials for Writing

■ **Papyrus.** The papyrus plant is a reed that flourished in the marshy areas of the Nile river delta in Egypt. The writer of the book of Job was aware of this when he asked the question: "Can papyrus grow tall where there is no marsh? Can reeds thrive without water?" (8:11). The stalk of the plant is triangular in shape and can grow to a height of ten to twelve feet.

The process of making writing material from the papyrus plant is vividly described by the Roman historian Pliny (A.D. 23-79) in his *Natural History* (13. 21-27). First, the hard outer shell was stripped away to expose the softer pithy center *(biblos).* The biblos was then split into very thin strips and laid vertically on a flat surface. Another layer of strips was placed horizontally over the vertical strips, and both layers were rubbed together until they formed one large sheet. After the sheet dried, it was cut into smaller sheets, each ranging in size from 6 to 9 inches high and 12 to 18 inches wide.

Table 6.1. Papyrus Sheets

It is estimated that the use of papyrus as a writing material spans a period of about 3,500 years. Since 1778, there have been many valuable archaeological discoveries of papyri in the sands and rubbish heaps of Egypt. Some papyri consist of a vast amount of nonliterary works such as personal letters, love notes, deeds and receipts; others are fragments of such important literary works as Homer's *Iliad* and the Old and New Testaments.

The dry and warm weather of Egypt was conducive to the preservation of papyrus manuscripts (manuscript, from *manu*, "by hand"; *scriptum*, "written") and accounts for the fact that outside Egypt there virtually are no New Testament papyri. In addition to the early finds at the town of Oxyrhynchus (see part one), an important discovery occurred in 1945 at Nag Hammadi in Upper Egypt by peasants digging for nitrates to fertilize their fields. Subsequent archaeological exploration verified that this was the site of a significant library. Thirteen papyrus codices in the Coptic language, a form of late Egyptian written in Greek characters and used by the early Christians in Egypt, have been recovered, translated and edited.[3] The majority of these papyri contain texts that reflect Gnostic theology and heterodox ideas after the second century.

Currently, there are ninety-seven papyri of portions of the New Testament cataloged and available to textual scholars. All of these are listed in the introduction to the United Bible Societies' *Greek New Testament* (hereafter *GNT[4]*), giving manuscript number (siglum), content, present location and date.[4] (See table 6.2 for examples.)

Table 6.2. Sample New Testament Papyri

Manuscript	Content[5]	Location	Date
P^1	Gospels	Philadelphia	III (century)
P^9	Catholic Epistles	Cambridge, Mass.	III
P^{16}	Paul's epistles	Cairo	III/IV
P^{29}	Acts	Oxford	III
P^{47}	Revelation	Dublin	late III
P^{74}	Acts and Catholic Epistles	Cologny	VII
P^{76}	Gospels	Vienna	VI

Some of these papyri are part of collections and are named after their owners: P^{45}, P^{46} and P^{47} were owned by Sir Chester Beatty of London; P^{66}, P^{72}, P^{74} and P^{75} were acquired by M. Martin Bodmer and are kept in the Bodmer Library of World Literature in Cologny, a suburb of Geneva. P^{52} is the oldest (c. A.D. 125) and smallest (about two and one-half by three and one-half inches of text from John's Gospel, 18:31-33; 37-38) extant fragment of the New Testament known today. Its discovery in Egypt shows that the Gospel of John had circulated in this area by the first half of the second century A.D. This is quite amazing when one considers that the Gospel was written in

Ephesus near the end of the first century A.D.

It is important to remember two things about these New Testament papyri. First, none of them contains the New Testament in its entirety. This means that we are dependent upon all of them to help us reconstruct the text of the New Testament. Second, although they are the oldest—that is, the earliest manuscripts that we have of the New Testament—they are not necessarily the most reliable witnesses to the New Testament text. Many were copied carelessly and are not too dependable in matters of detail.

■ **Parchment.** Parchment was the other chief writing material at the turn of the first century A.D. Since it was made from the skin (Greek *derma*, root for the English *dermatology*) of animals such as goats, sheep, calves and antelopes, it was more universally available than papyrus, which flourished only in the area of the Nile in Egypt. The literary world soon discovered that parchment had other commendable features: it was more durable, especially in cool and damp climates; both sides could be written on more readily than with papyrus; and corrections and erasures were more easily made. In some cases the parchment of a manuscript was used more than once. The original writing would be scraped off and the surface prepared for new material. Such a manuscript is called a palimpsest (literally, scraped again). While we may applaud this early form of recycling, there is no doubt that much early and valuable information was lost because of it.[6]

Although papyrus continued to be used in some literary circles, scholars estimate that parchment replaced papyrus by the fourth century A.D. and continued to be used into the twelfth century, when paper became common in the West. This means, therefore, that the autographs of the New Testament were written on papyrus, but the best and most complete manuscripts we now possess are on parchment from the fourth and fifth centuries.

Parchment should not be confused with ordinary leather. The use of leather for writing goes back to many centuries before Christ. J. Harold Greenlee notes that "the oldest leather scroll presently known is one written in 1468 B.C. describing the victory by King Tuthmosis III at Megiddo in that year."[7] Most of the Dead Sea Scrolls were written on leather. The *Letter of Aristeas* (second century B.C.) implies that the books brought to Alexandria from Jerusalem to be translated into Greek were written on leather.

Parchment is a form of animal skin that is far superior to leather. Steps in preparing it included "soaking the skin in lime water, scraping off the hair on the one side and the flesh on the other, stretching and drying the skin in a frame, smoothing it with pumice, and dressing it with chalk."[8] An even finer and more expensive form of parchment, called vellum, was made from calfskin and normally was used for special projects and deluxe volumes. Eventually, the terms *vellum* and *parchment* were used interchangeably.

The city of Pergamum is credited with the development and production of parchment. According to Pliny (*Natural History* 13.21f.) this came about because the king of Pergamum (Eumenes II, 197-159 B.C.) intended to build a library to rival the famous one in Alexandria. To avoid this, King Ptolemy of Egypt placed an embargo on the export of papyrus. Although this story is somewhat romanticized, it may well reflect the preeminence of the city of Pergamum in the manufacture and distribution of good quality parchment. Our English word *parchment* is derived from the Greek word for Pergamum.

It has been estimated that it took the hides of 4,500 animals (calves, sheep, goats, antelopes) to make the vellum for just fifty Bibles.[9] For a manuscript known as Codex Gigas, Metzger says, "the hide of 160 asses was required for its production."[10] When one adds the cost for the preparation of the parchment and the scribal fee for production, one can easily appreciate that this involved a "small fortune" and that only the very wealthy could afford such a project. Barclay, on the other hand, notes that copying by the process of dictation made materials much more plentiful and affordable than one would expect.[11] Yet elsewhere he calculates that a copy of Luke-Acts would have cost approximately today's equivalent of $150 to produce, making it quite clear that "for ordinary people books at that price were out of the question."[12]

■ **Pens.** Ancient scribes would have used a stylus made of metal, ivory or bone for writing on waxed tablets. With papyrus and parchment, however, a reed pen was developed. This basically was a thin reed, sharpened to a point with a slit in the middle—an instrument not unlike the old straight pen and nib used by children and adults before the invention of the ballpoint pen. The reed pen was supplanted by the more versatile quill pen, which became the preferred instrument for writing on vellum from about the fourth century A.D.

■ **Ink.** The word *ink* comes from the Greek word meaning "black" because the earliest ink was carbon-based and made from soot, gum and water. Improvements in quality and color were made over the centuries.[13] The New Testament refers to writing with "pen and ink" (3 Jn 13), with "paper and ink" (2 Jn 12) and with "ink" (2 Cor 3:3).

Besides parchment, pens and ink, a scribe would require some additional implements such as a knife, a whetstone, some pumice stone for smoothing rough spots on his parchment sheets, and a sponge for erasing and wiping his pen.

3. The Form of Books

■ **The Roll.** Ordinarily, about twenty individual sheets of papyrus were fastened together with glue and wound around a stick to make a roll. If a longer

Table 6.3. Writing and Writing Materials

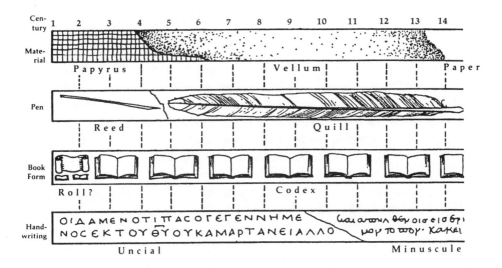

scroll was desired, additional sheets could be added. Since a roll normally did not exceed thirty-five feet in length, longer literary works would be separated and each section placed on a single roll.

Long books in the New Testament, like the Gospel of Matthew, Luke and the book of Acts, would have filled a roll of approximately thirty-one to thirty-two feet in length. Upon completion, papyrus rolls often were wrapped in cloth or leather and stored in some kind of container, usually a jar. Since *volumen* in Latin means "something rolled up," a scroll often was referred to as a "volume." A single scroll of a multivolume literary work was regarded as "a cutting" (from the Greek *tomos*, "a cutting"). This explains our reference to a single volume of an author's larger work as a "tome."

Writing was normally done only on the front (*recto*) side of a sheet of papyrus in columns about $2\frac{1}{2}$ to $3\frac{1}{2}$ inches because it was easier to follow the horizontal lines than write across the vertical lines on the back (*verso*) side. Revelation 5:1 refers to a scroll written "on the inside and on the back" and Ezekiel to one that had writing "on the front and on the back" (Ezek 2:10). Such a scroll was known as an *opisthograph* (from the Greek, a "writing behind") but was more of an exception than a rule, probably made necessary by economic factors.

The written product on a papyrus roll was called a *biblos* or a *biblion* because the material was made from the *biblos* of the plant. Thus Luke, in 3:4, refers to a scroll of Isaiah as the "book" of the "words of the prophet Isaiah" or, as in Acts 1:20, to the "book" of Psalms. The words "in the scroll of the book" in Hebrews 10:7 are a quotation from the Septuagint of Psalm 40:7 (LXX 39:8) and further confirms the use of *biblos* as a book in the form of a roll.

Historically, *biblos* was applied to the papyrus plant, the scroll and then the codex. The plural, *biblia*, eventually came to designate the entire collection of Old and New Testament books, hence our "Bible." According to F. F. Bruce, Chrysostom, bishop of Constantinople from A.D. 397 to 407, "appears to be the first writer to use the phrase 'the books' (Greek, *ta biblia*) of the two testaments together; in Christian usage the phrase had previously been restricted to the Old Testament writings. Chrysostom's usage is the origin of our word 'Bible'; while *biblia* ('books') is a plural word in Greek, it was taken over into Latin as a singular, *Biblia*, 'the Bible.' "[14]

Matthew begins his Gospel by calling it "the book of the genealogy of Jesus Christ" (1:1; RSV translates as "book" but NRSV as "account" and NIV as "record"). The "books" or "scrolls" (NIV) and "parchments" that Paul requests Timothy to bring (2 Tim 4:13) indicate some of the material used by the apostle. We should note that parchment is tanned leather and that the Greek word used here is borrowed from the Latin *membrana* (English, membrane). The reference to "paper" (Greek *chartos*, Latin *charta*, from which we get *chart* and *charter*) in 2 John 12 should be understood as a sheet of papyrus. Our English word *paper* is derived from this ancient writing material, papyrus.

■ **The Codex.** This is a leaf-form of a book. The Latin *caudex* or *codex* originally meant the trunk of a tree and subsequently a block of wood split into a number of tablets or leaves. In earlier times, wooden tablets would have been bound together to make a "book." But with the development of new materials, sheets of papyrus or parchment were stacked on top of each other and folded down the middle in a manner resembling our modern books. Such folded sheets were called "quires" (from the Latin word *quaternio*, "a set of four") because the earliest codices contained four sheets.

Studies in early book production and publication have shown that Christians were the first to use the codex form for writing and transmitting their literature.[15] Several reasons are given why this format was adopted.

First, a codex could contain much more material than a roll. At some point this enabled larger sections of the New Testament, like the Gospels, the Pauline letters and the Catholic Letters, to be collected and bound together. Harry Gamble argues rather convincingly that the codex form was the most likely "medium" for the earliest collection of Paul's letters.[16] On parchment, the entire Old and New Testaments could form a single codex, as with Codex Sinaiticus and Codex Vaticanus from the fourth century.

Second, it was more economical because it accommodated writing on both sides of the sheet.[17]

Third, it was more convenient to use. Readers no longer had to go through the cumbersome procedure of rolling and unrolling scrolls.

Fourth, in the case of the New Testament, it enabled Christians to find Scripture references more easily for their study and teaching. The functionality of the codex accounted for its popularity, so that by the fourth century the parchment codex became the accepted and almost exclusive form for New Testament manuscripts.

Finally, there may be an apologetic motive. Bruce Metzger cites with approval a suggestion by Peter Katz that Gentile Christians changed from the roll-form to the codex-form "as part of a deliberate attempt to differentiate the usage of the Church from that of the synagogue, which was accustomed to transmit the Old Testament on scrolls."[18] At any rate, the codex form became a distinctive characteristic of Christian literature.

It is not unreasonable to suggest that the apostle Paul was the first Christian writer to use the codex form. Karl Donfried argues that the Greek word *skēnopoios*, commonly translated as "tent-maker," should be expanded to include "leather-worker." As a leather-worker, Paul may have experimented in the production of parchment notebooks. The *membrana* of 2 Timothy 4:13 ("when you come, bring the cloak that I left with Carpus at Troas, also the books, and above all the parchments [*membrana*]") could be collections, in codex form, of reference texts from the Old Testament, Paul's recorded notes on the traditions he received from early Christian communities, and early drafts of his letters, which, according to a theory mentioned earlier, he may have begun to collect.[19]

4. Writing New Testament Manuscripts

When we open up a nicely typeset copy of a Greek New Testament today, we may get the impression that this is the way the script looked to Christians in the first century. Nothing could be further from the truth. There were a large number of changes in the production of manuscripts from the first century to the age of printing, many coinciding with the development of the Greek alphabet. Basically, there are two main styles of handwriting important to the making of the New Testament.

■ **Uncial.** The type of Greek used for literary purposes was written in large square-type letters much like our own capital letters today. This style, known as "uncial" or "majuscule," was used from the third century B.C. to the tenth century A.D. Uncial, from the Latin *uncial*, means the twelfth part of anything, such as twelve inches to a foot. In the case of this script it appears that scribes divided a line into approximately twelve letters (it does not mean that the letters themselves were an inch high). Uncial letters were written as *scriptio continua*, meaning a "continuous script" with no spaces between the words or sentences.

Table 6.4. Greek Uncial Script

Greek Uncial Script (from codex Sinaiticus, 4th cent.)
(actual width of each column about 2¼ in.)

Col. a, Matt. xiii. 5–10, αλλα δε επεσεν ε|πι τα πετρωδη ο|που ουκ ειχεν γην | πολλην και ευθε|ως εξανετιλεν δι|α το μη εχιν βαθος | γης ηλιου δε ανα|τιλαντος εκαυμα|τισθη και δια το | μη εχειν ριζαν ε|ξηρανθη | αλλα δε επεσεν ε|πι τας ακανθας | και ανεβησαν αι | ακανθαι και επνι|ξαν αυτα | αλλα δε επεσεν ε|πι την γην την κα|λην και εδιδου | καρπον ο μεν ε|κατον ο δε εξηκον|τα ο δε λ̄ ο εχων | ωτα [insert ακουειν from the left-hand margin] ακουετω | και προσελθοντες ‖ col. b, Matt. xiii. 14–16 και αναπληρου|ται αυτοις η προ|φητια ησαϊου η | λεγουσα ακοη | ακουσετε και ου | μη συνητε και | βλε-ποντες βλε|ψητε και ου μη ϊ|δητε επαχυνθη | γαρ η καρδια του | λαου τουτου και | τοις ωσιν αυτων | βαρεως ηκουσαν | και τους οφθαλ|μους αυτων εκαμ|μυσαν μηποτε | ιδωσιν τοις ο|φθαλμοις και τοις | ωσιν [αυτων between the lines] ακουσωσιν | και τη καρδια συνω|σιν και επιστρε|ψωσιν και ιασομε | αυτους | ϋμων δε μακαρι. The Eusebian canon numerals stand between the columns $\left(\dfrac{\overline{ρλδ}}{\epsilon} = \dfrac{134}{5}\right)$.

One can appreciate that this made it difficult to read and translate, especially if scribes were not careful in the formation of letters or if the quality of ink and writing material was poor. The English phrase "GODISNOWHERE" is frequently used to illustrate the difficulty of this script. Some readers may divide the sentence to read "GOD IS NOWHERE"; others, "GOD IS NOW HERE." A somewhat amusing example is found in Greenlee: "ISAWABUNDANCEONTHETABLE." Is it "I SAW ABUNDANCE ON THE TABLE" or "I SAW A BUN DANCE ON THE TABLE"?[20] Reading aloud helped to avoid errors that may have occurred when reading by sight.

Nonliterary materials, such as personal letters, deeds and receipts, were written in a "cursive" (i.e., "running") style. This is a modification of the uncial script in that the capital letters were rounded off considerably and joined, much as our longhand writing is today. Paul's letters, especially those addressed to individuals (Philemon, Timothy, Titus) would have been written in this script because they would not have been considered formal literary products. Later, when they were copied as "literary works," the uncial literary script was used (see the printing on Codex Sinaiticus and note that this is not the type of script used by Paul).

The uncial manuscripts are by far the most valuable for reconstructing the New Testament text, because a significant number of them are early and contain most of the Old and New Testaments. The ability to include so much material was made possible by the change from papyrus to parchment and from the roll to the codex form.

As with the papyri, uncial manuscripts have been numbered and codified for our use. Some of the more than 299 currently cataloged are listed in the introduction of the *GNT*[4]. Six of the oldest and most important are listed in table 6.5. Not obvious in this table is that uncials such as ℵ, A, B and C contain either all or significant portions of the Old Testament and certain books now designated as the "Apocrypha."

Students need to consult the more specialized works of Metzger and of Kurt and Barbara Aland on the content and value of these manuscripts for New Testament study. The history behind the discovery and purchase of Codex Sinaiticus ℵ, for example, is filled with much the same intrigue and suspense as a modern novel. Beyond that, its journey in 1933 from the St. Catherine Monastery on Mount Sinai to its place in the British Museum is a marvelous story of God's providence.[21]

■ **Minuscule.** Sometime between the eighth and ninth century the uncial script was replaced by another cursive script called minuscle (from Latin *minusculus*, "rather small"). As a smaller book-hand script it enabled scribes to write more rapidly and compactly, thus saving both time and materials. This

Table 6.5. Significant Uncial Manuscripts

Manuscript	Contents *	Location and Name	Date
ℵ01	eapr[22]	London: Sinaiticus	IV
A02	eapr	London: Alexandrinus	V
B03	eap	Rome: Vaticanus	IV
C04	eapr	Paris: Ephraemi Rescriptus	V
D05	ea	Cambridge: Bezae Cantabrigiensis	V
D06	p	Paris: Claromontanus	VI

* e = Gospels; a = Apostolos (Acts and the Catholic letters); p = Paul's Letters;
  r = Revelation

facilitated the reproduction of manuscripts, making it possible for more and more people to possess copies of the Scriptures. Numerically, minuscule manuscripts of the New Testament outnumber the uncial manuscripts about ten to one.[23] These manuscripts vary in size from a few pages to the entire New Testament and, along with the papyri and uncials, are crucial data in textual studies.

Table 6.6. Greek Minuscule Script

Greek Minuscule Script (from lectionary 303, 12th or 13th cent.)
(actual width of each column about 3¼ in.)

Col. a, Luke xxiv. 31–33, καὶ αὐτὸς ἄφαντος | ἐγένετο ἀπ' αὐτῶν· | καὶ εἶπον πρὸς ἀλλήλους· οὐχὶ ἡ καρ|δία ἡμῶν καιομέ|νη ἦν ἐν ἡμῖν. ὡς ἐ|λάλει ἡμῖν ἐν τῇ ὁ|δῷ καὶ ὡς διήνοιγεν | ἡμῖν τὰς γραφάς; | καὶ ἀναστάντες αὐ|τῇ τῇ ὥρᾳ ὑπέστρε|ψαν εἰς ἱ[ερουσα]-λήμ· καὶ | εὗρον συνηθροισμέ|νους τοὺς ἕνδεκα || col. b, John i. 35–38, Τῷ καιρῷ ἐκείνῳ· | εἱστήκει ὁ ἰωάννης | καὶ ἐκ τῶν μαθη|τῶν αὐτοῦ δύο· καὶ | ἐμβλέψας τῷ ἱ[ησο]ῦ πε|ριπατοῦντι· λέγει· | ἴδε ὁ ἀμνὸς τοῦ θ[εο]ῦ· | καὶ ἤκουσαν αὐτοῦ | οἱ δύο μαθηταὶ λα|λοῦντος. καὶ ἠκο|λούθησαν τῷ ἱ[ησο]ῦ· | στραφεὶς ὁ ἱ[ησοῦ]ς καὶ θε|ασάμενος αὐτοὺς | ἀκολουθοῦντας.

■ **Abbreviations/Contractions.** In order to save both time and space, scribes developed a system of abbreviations for the sacred names (*nomina* *sacra*) in the New Testament. The process involved using either the first and last or the first two and the last two letters of a word/name and placing a line over the two letters to indicate that it was a contraction. Some of the more common in a group of fifteen words are found in table 6.7.

Table 6.7. Scribal Contractions

English	Greek	Contraction
God	θεός	$\overline{\text{θC}}$[24]
Christ	Χριστός	$\overline{\text{XC}}$
Lord	κύριος	$\overline{\text{KC}}$
Jesus	'Ιησοῦς	$\overline{\text{IC}}$
Son	υἱός	$\overline{\text{YC}}$
Spirit	πνεῦμα	$\overline{\text{ΠNA}}$
Jerusalem	'Ιερουσαλήμ	$\overline{\text{IΛHM}}$

Variations of this practice have carried over into some of our liturgical and literary traditions today (see table 6.8).

Table 6.8. Christian symbols

The Greek word for fish (ἰχθύς—*ichthys*) was used by Christians to identify themselves as believers because the letters stand for Jesus ('Ιησοῦς—*Iēsous*) Christ (Χριστός—*Christos*) God's (θεοῦ—*theou*) Son (υἱός—*hyios*) Savior (σωτήρ—*sōtēr*). Also common are "ihs" (IHC), which uses the first three Greek letters for Jesus ('Ιησοῦς), the "Chi Rho" (XP) from the first two letters of Christ (Χριστός), and INRI from the Latin *Iesus Nazarenus Rex Iudaeorum* ("Jesus of Nazareth, King of the Jews").

■ **Aids for Readers.** In the development of the Greek language and manuscript traditions, a number of aids were developed to facilitate the individual's reading, pronouncing and studying a literary work. Metzger notes that "according to tradition it was Aristophanes of Byzantium (c. 257-180 B.C.), . . . head of the Alexandrian Library, who devised the several accent and breathing marks in order to help increasing numbers of foreigners learn how to pronounce Greek."[25]

The punctuation marks that we take for granted in our current Greek or English texts (comma, period, question and interrogation marks) are seldom found before the eighth century, and then not universally in all manuscripts. Section or chapter divisions to the manuscripts of the New Testament were drawn up independently by different scribes and editors. These "headings" (Greek *kephalē*, "head") may exist as early as the second century, although the oldest system is in Codex Vaticanus in the fourth century. This codex divides Matthew into 170 sections, Mark into 62, Luke into 152 and John into 80. The Pauline epistles are numbered continuously "as though the Epistles were regarded as comprising one book."[26] Codex Alexandrinus (fifth century) has a different number of sections. Yet another scribe, notes D. Ewert, "divided the Book of Revelation into twenty-four sections, because of the twenty-four elders before God's throne (Rev. 4:4)."[27] Headings, or *titloi*, gave a summary of the contents of a section.

These "headings" and "titles" are not unlike the chapter divisions in our present-day Bibles. Chapter divisions were introduced into the Latin Bible by Stephen Langton, archbishop of Canterbury, at the beginning of the thirteenth century while he was a lecturer at the University of Paris.[28] Verses were not added until 1551. "The current verse division in the New Testament is due to Robert Stephanus [Estienne], who in 1551 published at Geneva a Greek and Latin edition of the New Testament with the text of the chapters divided into separate verses. The first Bible in English to contain verse numbers was the Geneva Version, translated by William Whittingham and others in 1560."[29]

There was a tendency for scribes to improve upon and embellish the text with prologues, colophons (inscriptions at the end), glosses (explanations put into the margins or between the lines), expansive titles, ornamental headings and pictures (of Jesus as well as illustrations of the text). Musical notes, known as "numes," were added to many Byzantine manuscripts (ninth to twelfth centuries) to aid in the liturgies of church services where chanting was required.[30] Other significant "aids" were inserted into the New Testament manuscripts where portions of Scripture were selected to be read aloud during worship services. These "lectionary" readings were marked with αρχ (from ἀρχη—*archē*), "beginning," and τελ (from τέλος—*telos*), "end."

■ **The Authors of the Text.** When we look at the New Testament it is natural to assume that the headings or titles we see in the text for the Gospels and some of the epistles accurately reflect the original author of the work. In most versions, the Gospels appear as "The Gospel According to" Matthew, Mark, Luke, and John respectively (most editions of the NIV just list the name of the author).

The same holds true with the "Letter of James," "The First Letter of Peter," "The Second Letter of Peter," "The First Letter of John," "The Second Letter of John," "The Third Letter of John," "The Letter of Jude" and "The Revelation to John." Letters which were written to churches and individuals use the preposition *to*, hence "The Letter of Paul to the Romans," "to the Galatians," "to Philemon" and so on. We need to remember, however, that some books were originally anonymous—that is, with no name attached. Our current authorial headings reflect traditions which developed in the early church. Some of these are questioned today through continued study of internal and external evidence.

Naturally, there was a "first," or "original," manuscript (autograph) of each New Testament book. An anonymous person, for example, wrote a Gospel about the life and teaching of Jesus somewhere between A.D. 65 and 70. Later, it was attributed to an individual named Mark. Paul, the great missionary to the Gentiles, penned a number of different letters to local churches during his lifetime. But we do not have the autographs of these Gospels or letters. The best uncial manuscripts that make up our current New Testament and from which we have our English translations only go back to the fourth and fifth centuries A.D.[31]

■ **The Copiers of the Text.** The autographs fulfilled their intended purpose once they had been penned and sent to their original destination. Mark's Gospel served to instruct the Roman church (assuming this was its intended destination) about his understanding of the life and teaching of Jesus. Paul's letters to local churches were specifically written to those congregations. As such, they too accomplished their original purpose. But somewhere during the early history of the church additional copies were made from these original autographs, and these, in turn, became the possession of other individuals and churches (see parts three and four). Gradually there was a demand for more and more copies of the New Testament books. Since the autographs were not regarded as sacred, they may have been misplaced, destroyed or simply worn out from constant use.

At first, it is likely that some manuscripts were copied by individual Christians for personal and devotional reasons. However, with the spread of Christianity throughout the Roman Empire, something more along the line of mass production was needed. Other congregations desired access to the material that was gradually being recognized as authoritative in Christian worship and instruction. The copying of these ancient manuscripts was a slow and tedious process. Furthermore, the lack of any controls or standards at this early stage meant, according to Metzger, that "the speed of production sometimes outran accuracy of execution."[32]

This situation improved when Christianity became the official religion of the Empire under Constantine in the fourth century. The copying of New Testament manuscripts became more of a commercial venture in the setting of a scriptorium, where well-equipped scribes would copy the material as it was slowly read aloud.[33] Although this method produced its share of errors through faulty hearing, inattentiveness and so on, it did speed up the process of duplicating manuscripts. Correctors were hired to check for mistakes and thus minimize the number of unintentional errors that crept into the text.

Later, during the Byzantine period, copies of manuscripts were produced by monks working separately in the cells of their monastery. While this eliminated some of the transcriptional errors that resulted from dictation in the scriptorium, even the most careful and reverent monks were not immune from the mental and physical rigors of the job. Metzger has discovered a number of interesting comments in the colophons (notes at the end of a manuscript) of nonbiblical manuscripts that reveal what every scribe, including the monks, must have experienced:

> "He who does not know how to write supposes it to be no labour; but though only three fingers write, the whole body labours." A traditional formula appearing at the close of many manuscripts describes the physiological effects of prolonged labour at copying: "Writing bows one's back, thrusts the ribs into one's stomach, and fosters a general debility of the body." In an Armenian manuscript of the Gospels a colophon complains that a heavy snowstorm was raging outside and that the scribe's ink froze, his hand became numb, and the pen fell from his fingers! It is not surprising that a frequently recurring colophon in manuscripts of many kinds is the following comparison: "As travelers rejoice to see their home country, so also is the end of a book to those who toil [in writing]." Other manuscripts close with an expression of gratitude: "The end of the book; thanks be to God!" (*Text of the New Testament*, pp. 17-18)

To minimize the number of errors, monks were subject to certain rules and standards. They were expected, for example, to concentrate on their work and to keep their parchments neat and clean. Penalties were imposed for other transgressions.[34] Professional scribes were paid a fee for their work. The amount was determined by the number of lines or rows (Greek *stichoi*) in the manuscript, the standard measurement for ancient literary works.[35] A significant number of our New Testament manuscripts total the stichoi at the end.[36]

5. Transmitting the New Testament

Soon after the autographs were written they began their long and exciting journey of transmission. At first, a second copy—or perhaps several copies—

was made from the original manuscript. Shortly after, copies were made from the copies, and so on, so that in a very short time there were many copies in circulation (see table 6.9).

Table 6.9. Autograph and Copies

AUTOGRAPH

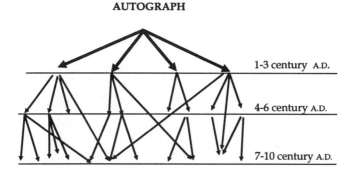

1-3 century A.D.

4-6 century A.D.

7-10 century A.D.

By the second century a similar process developed in the church, with the creation of lectionaries for private and public worship and the use of the New Testament texts by the church fathers in preaching and writing. The trajectories that were set in motion, which in some respects continue today, are sketched in table 6.10.

■ **Lectionaries** (from the Latin *lector*, a reader). By definition, lectionaries are manuscripts containing selections of biblical material arranged as lessons for the church year. Some lectionaries were intended for daily worship services, probably for use in monasteries, while others provided a carefully developed system for the entire church year. A lectionary would be called an "Evangelion" if it came from the Gospels, an "Apostolos" if it came from the Acts or the Letters, or an "Apostoloevangelion" when it included readings from all parts of the New Testament. In principal and format a lectionary was not unlike the material used in the liturgy of mainline denominations today. Currently, 2,280 of these lectionary manuscripts are cataloged.[37]

There is no scholarly consensus on the antiquity of New Testament lectionaries. Although the majority of those that are extant date from the tenth to thirteenth centuries, a few are earlier. This leads experts such as Aland and Metzger to suppose that the lectionary system had its origin around the fourth century A.D.38

■ **Versions.** Although some of the sayings of Jesus in our Gospels may have circulated in the Aramaic language, we are quite certain that all the books in the New Testament originally were written in Greek, because Greek was the

Table 6.10. The the Transmission of the New Testament

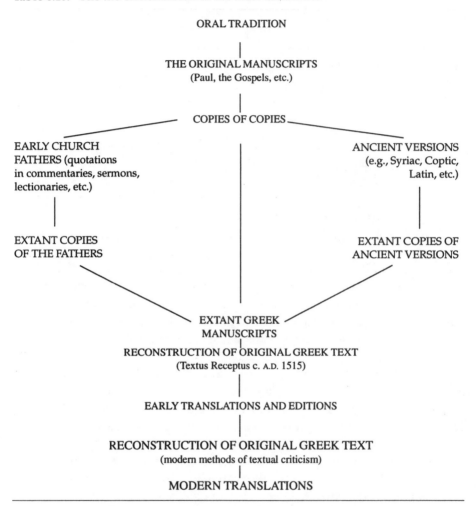

ORAL TRADITION

|

THE ORIGINAL MANUSCRIPTS
(Paul, the Gospels, etc.)

|

COPIES OF COPIES

EARLY CHURCH
FATHERS (quotations
in commentaries, sermons,
lectionaries, etc.)

ANCIENT VERSIONS
(e.g., Syriac, Coptic,
Latin, etc.)

EXTANT COPIES
OF THE FATHERS

EXTANT COPIES OF
ANCIENT VERSIONS

EXTANT GREEK
MANUSCRIPTS

RECONSTRUCTION OF ORIGINAL GREEK TEXT
(Textus Receptus c. A.D. 1515)

|

EARLY TRANSLATIONS AND EDITIONS

|

RECONSTRUCTION OF ORIGINAL GREEK TEXT
(modern methods of textual criticism)

|

MODERN TRANSLATIONS

literary and commercial language of the day. The Greek used by the New
Testament writers is known as the *koinē*, the common Greek, or the language of daily conversation. Even then, one finds within the New Testament a variety of styles—from the rather "Jewish Greek" of Revelation to
the polished literary Greek of Hebrews. The early church fathers also wrote
in the Greek language.

The early believers already possessed a Greek translation of the Hebrew
Old Testament, known as the Septuagint (LXX). This translation, as noted
earlier, was produced to enable Greek-speaking Jews (the Hellenists) to understand the Old Testament and to present God's revelation to people in their

culture. Now, in the second century, the same thing was about to happen with the Greek language. Christianity was a missionary religion (Mt 28:16-20; Acts 1:8) and as such carried its message to people of other cultures and languages. Translations of the New Testament had to be made if the message of the Gospel was to be understood; and such translations were well under way toward the end of the second century.

By approximately A.D. 200, Latin began replacing Greek in the Roman Empire. A significant number of church fathers began using Latin in their writings even though they were fluent in Greek. Aland records the following observation about the writings of Hippolytus (c. A.D. 170-236), an early bishop of Rome: "Although his writings, which were in Greek, represented the most brilliant literary achievement of any Roman bishop of the first four centuries, they fell into immediate oblivion because they evidently found no readership."[39] He also observes that "the church in Italy, not to mention Africa, Gaul, and the other provinces of the West, was a Latin church by the mid-third century if not earlier."[40] Christians in other regions likewise required copies of the New Testament in their regional languages for study, worship and evangelism. This consequently led to early versions in Syriac, Coptic, Gothic, Armenian and Ethiopic.[41]

As valuable and necessary as these versions were for the spread of Christianity, there are several limitations that must be noted. First, translations were not always made with the greatest care or expertise. Metzger records a significant complaint that Augustine raised about early translators: "No sooner did anyone gain possession of a Greek manuscript, and imagine himself to have any facility in both languages (however slight that may be) than he made himself bold to translate it" (*De doctrina Christiana* 2.11.16).[42] One can be certain that many questionable translations—and copies of translations—were made by early Christians. Even when corrections were made at a later time, they probably were made from subsequent translations rather than an earlier one.

Second, there is a deficiency in all translations because of the nature of language. Just as the Greek language of the LXX could not express all of the linguistic and conceptual nuances of the Hebrew, neither could other languages always capture and express the richness and precision of the Greek. Metzger, for example, notes that "Latin has no definite article; Syriac cannot distinguish between the Greek aorist and perfect tenses; Coptic lacks the passive voice and must use a circumlocution. In some cases, therefore, the testimony of these versions is ambiguous."[43]

Two examples from the vast literature on versions will illustrate their significance for the text of the New Testament. The first has to do with the spread of Christianity to Syria that, according to the book of Acts, began in Antioch shortly after Pentecost ("and it was in Antioch that the disciples were first called 'Christians' " [11:26]; note also the significance of Antioch as Paul's missionary headquarters in 14:26 and its role in the Jerusalem Council, 15:1-35).

Syria was a vast country whose territory spread from the shores of the Mediterranean Sea to Mesopotamia. Antioch, the third largest city of the Roman Empire, was composed of a mixture of Hellenic (Greek), Jewish and native Syrians. The Syriac language is closely related to the Aramaic.

The early Christians in Syria, particularly in Antioch, would have used the Greek Old and New Testaments. But as the gospel reached out into the rural areas where only Syriac was spoken, the need to translate the Greek into the language of the people became obvious. Unfortunately, historians have been unable to determine the date and form of the earliest Syriac versions.

Some scholars speculate that there was an old Syriac version of the Gospels by the latter part of the second century; others believe that Tatian's *Diatessaron* was the earliest. This significant "Harmony of the Four Gospels" is dated around A.D. 180 and maintained its popularity in some circles until the fifth century. It is not known whether the *Diatessaron* was compiled originally in Greek or in Syriac.

The multiplicity of Syrian texts led to a standard version in the fourth to fifth centuries known as the Peshitta (meaning "simple," "clear," as in "current language"). According to Aland and Aland, "The Peshitta version . . . is the most widely attested and most consistently transmitted of the Syriac New Testament versions. The Syriac church still preserves it and holds it in reverence in this form today."[44]

Latin versions arose for the same reasons as the other versions—the desire for people to have the Bible in their vernacular language. This may have arisen first within the context of worship, where the service would have included a reading of Scripture in Greek and then another reading in the local language, much as the Aramaic Targums supplemented Hebrew in the synagogue. As Latin gradually replaced Greek, it was not long before it became the only language used.

Text critics believe that the earliest translations were made from the Greek to the Old Latin, or Italia, before the end of the second century A.D. in such religious centers as Carthage in North Africa as well as Italy, Gaul and Spain. By the fourth century there were many manuscripts in Old Latin. This caused Jerome to lament that "there are almost as many different translations as there are manuscripts."[45] Yet, in spite of all these Old Latin manuscripts, not one of them contained the entire New Testament.

The mixture and corruption of all these Latin manuscripts had a chaotic effect upon their quality. This sad state of affairs prompted Pope Damasis, around A.D. 382, to commission Jerome (officially, Sophronius Eusebius Hieronymus) to make a revision of the Latin Bible to correct the variant readings and produce a standard version. This version became known as the Vulgate (from the Latin *vulgatis,* "common") and since has become the "official" Bible of the Roman Catholic Church. Currently, there are between eight and ten thousand manuscript copies of the Latin Vulgate.[46]

■ **The Greek Text.** We can begin our discussion of the transmission of the Greek text by using the Gospel of Mark as an example. If we accept the theory of its Roman origin, then we can safely assume that the church in Rome possessed the original manuscript. However, Rome was a large city and may have had a number of house churches, each probably desiring a copy of this wonderful new story of Jesus called a "Gospel." Thus it is not improbable that very shortly after its original composition, several copies of Mark's Gospel were made for these churches. In time, Christians from other areas of the Empire heard that the Roman church possessed this manuscript and either asked for a copy to be made or sent a copyist to Rome. By the second century, therefore, copies of Mark's Gospel would have found their way to such important Christian centers as Antioch, Jerusalem, Caesarea, Alexandria and Ephesus.

Although modes of transportation in the first century appear primitive when compared with our age, we must not forget that the Roman Empire had developed a wonderful system of roads. Trade and commerce, military campaigns, postal service, personal travel and the communication of ideas between countries surrounding the Mediterranean region were extensive. This also allowed for the speedy dissemination of literary works, including New Testament manuscripts. Eldon J. Epp's study on the transfer of official and private letters in the Greco-Roman world has validated this claim. According to Epp, "Letters could travel some 800 miles in two months; or some 350 miles in thirty-six days; or 125 miles in three weeks; or some 400 miles in fourteen days; or 150 miles in four, six, or seven days; or fifteen miles in the same day."[47]

Similar scenarios of manuscript transmission were repeated in other Christian centers as well. When the church in Alexandria, for example, received a copy of Mark, scribes would make additional copies from the one they possessed and not from the original that Mark had written in Rome. The same procedure would have been followed with the other Gospels and with Paul's epistles. The original epistle to the Romans was copied over and over so that in time most of the churches would have had a copy of this epistle for themselves (see earlier discussion of the collection of the Gospels and epistles).

At this early stage, copies were made privately with little supervision or control. Professional scribes and scriptoria (copying centers) emerged after A.D. 200.

During this time a number of "local texts" developed in the great centers of Christianity surrounding the Mediterranean Sea: Rome and Carthage in the west, Alexandria in Egypt, and Caesarea, Antioch and Byzantium in the east.

Basically, the manuscripts that circulated within a specific geographical area took on similar characteristics and thus developed a "text-type" all their own which differed somewhat from text-types in other areas. But this does not imply that all the local texts were exactly the same! Textual critics have shown that even within a certain geographical area, texts could vary considerably. Nevertheless, it is common to refer to certain "text-types" such as the Alexandrian, the Byzantine, the Caesarean and the Western.[48]

The existence of these ecclesiastical centers enables one to appreciate the magnitude of scholarly activity taking place in the postapostolic age. Early church fathers like Clement of Rome (c. 64-96?), Irenaeus (c. 130-200), Origen (c. 184-235), Eusebius (c. 260-340) and Athanasius (c. 296-373) were important church leaders (often bishops) and theologians. The Catechetical School of Alexandria had a great influence on the study and production of New Testament manuscripts and the development of Christian theology under the leadership of Clement and Origen. Later, a bishop of this city named Athanasius (c. 296-373) was instrumental in establishing the parameters of the New Testament canon. We saw earlier that his "Festal Letter" in A.D. 367 listed the twenty-seven books that now constitute the canon of the New Testament.

Caesarea, likewise, played a strategic role in the development of the New Testament textual tradition. Origen took refuge in this city after he was exiled from Alexandria. There he established a famous exegetical school where he devoted himself to his literary work and preaching. Eusebius, the famous bishop of Caesarea and early church historian, was trained in the tradition of Origen. Aland and Aland note that "the Caesarea of Eusebius at the beginning of the fourth century was undoubtedly an important center of manuscript production—significantly, it was here that Emperor Constantine turned for manuscripts to supply the churches in his newly established capital of Constantinople."[49]

Antioch in Syria continued to be a significant center of literary and theological activity as well. Tradition credits one of its theologians, Lucian (died A.D. 312), with the origin of the "Koinē" text—a text which eventually became the "Byzantine Imperial text." It was in Antioch that the early form of the New Testament text "was polished stylistically, edited ecclesiastically, and expanded devotionally."[50]

Table 6.11. A Map of Textual Traditions

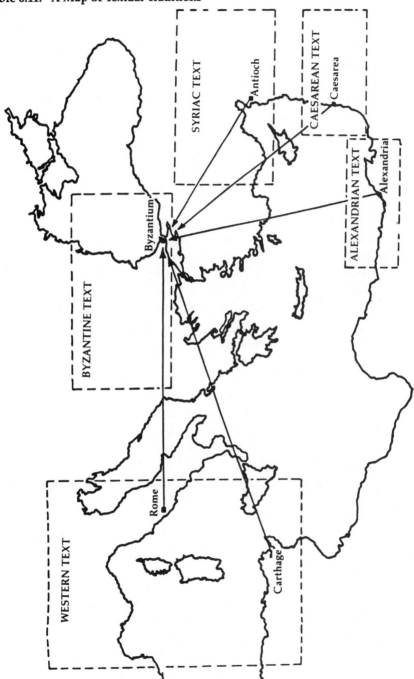

The process of transmission became more complicated when local texts in one area began to mix with local texts from other areas. A scribe from Alexandria, for example, would obtain a manuscript from Rome and compare it with the one that he was using. A different scribe from Byzantium (another name for Constantinople, now Istanbul) might do the same with a manuscript from Carthage, and so on, each in turn editing, revising and producing what is called a "mixed text." This state of affairs meant that by the fourth century the Christian church had a myriad of texts, some closely resembling each other but others containing significant differences and characteristics.

The development from original to local to mixed text was stalled during the intense persecutions of the church under the Roman Emperors Decius (A.D. 249-251), Valerian (A.D. 253-260) and Diocletian (A.D. 284-305). Under Diocletian, for example, a systematic attempt was launched to persecute the Christian church by destroying manuscripts, church buildings and ecclesiastical offices. Eusebius vividly describes the public burning of sacred Scriptures and the persecution of martyrs in Alexandria (HE 8.2-9).[51]

When Christianity was introduced as the official state religion under Emperor Constantine in the fourth century, new churches were established throughout the Empire. Now church officials were free to have manuscripts copied professionally and to compare traditions from other centers. Constantine commissioned fifty new copies of the Bible to be made for the churches in Constantinople. A number of scholars identify Codex Vaticanus as one of these, although evidence for this is inconclusive.

After Constantinople (Byzantium) became the religious center of the Eastern (Greek-speaking) church, manuscripts from other areas made their way to this religious center and were compared with the ones there. All this textual work eventually resulted in a "standardized" text. This was a very significant development in textual studies, because by the eighth century the "Byzantine" text became "the prevailing ecclesiastical form of the New Testament throughout the Greek-speaking world, and eventually constituted the basis of the Textus Receptus."[52] *Textus Receptus* means the "received text"—that is, the one edited by Erasmus which became the basis for the King James Version of 1611.

The process that I have been describing is illustrated beautifully by Aland and Aland:

> As copies multiplied their circulation became steadily wider, like the ripples from a pebble cast into a pond. This means that from the writing of a document to its use in all the churches of a single diocese or throughout the whole Church, a certain amount of time must have elapsed. Meanwhile every copy made from another copy repeated the same pattern of expan-

sion, like another pebble cast into the pond making a new series of ripples. These rippling circles would intersect. Two manuscripts in a single place (each with its own range of textual peculiarities, depending on its distance from the original text) would influence each other, producing a textual mixture and starting a new pattern of ripples—a process which would be repeated continually. Finally, to continue the metaphor, the pool becomes so filled with overlapping circles that it is practically impossible to distinguish their sources and their mutual relationships. This is precisely the situation the textual critic finds when attempting to analyze the history of the New Testament text.[53]

This quotation from Aland may give a reader the impression that the text of the New Testament is hopelessly confusing and that any resemblance of these later manuscripts to the original autographs is purely coincidental. Although the following pages will show that this is not the case, we must realize that the text of the New Testament was a "living text" in that it developed freely, especially during the first two centuries. Changes during the third and fourth centuries occurred mainly because of the process of scribal transmission. The discipline known as "textual criticism" is a positive and necessary attempt to understand this process of development (transmission) and to discover the original text. It involves a thorough analysis of the documents and procedures that have been discussed above.

As we proceed we will look closely at a number of differences between the KJV and more current English versions like the NRSV and the NIV. It is important to understand that the KJV is based upon the textual work of Erasmus of Rotterdam (1469-1536). When this great scholar was asked to produce a Greek text for publication, he hastily visited a few libraries and, for his first edition in 1516, consulted several Greek manuscripts, none of which was earlier than the twelfth century or contained the entire New Testament.

Although Erasmus's text ultimately went through five editions (1516, 1519, 1522, 1527, 1535), it was the third edition of 1522 that became the "received text" (Textus Receptus) and is the edition upon which the KJV of 1611 was based. This was a somewhat improved version of the first but still utilized only manuscripts from the tenth to twelfth centuries. "Subsequent editions," laments Metzger, "though making a number of alterations in Erasmus' text, essentially reproduced this debased form of the Greek Testament."[54]

Judgments made about the quality of the Greek text behind the KJV (also known as the Byzantium text) do not imply that it cannot be the "Word of God." Nevertheless, the discoveries of older and superior manuscripts such as Alexandrinus, Sinaiticus and Vaticanus have shown that the Byzantine text is an "inferior" text, meaning that it simply does not represent the text closest to the autographs.[55]

Some students of the New Testament approach the text with preconceived ideas of how it came into being. Certain theories of inspiration, dictation and inerrancy have led individuals to believe that the New Testament was lowered down from heaven on a golden string, "like the modern sanitary products that boast that they are 'untouched by human hands.' "[56] It is not uncommon to meet Christians who think that God told Luke, for example, to take a pen and some papyrus, find a desk and then sit down and write at the dictation of some heavenly voice. It just did not happen that way!

What God did, however, was to subject his written Word to the same historical process as he did with his incarnate Word, Jesus. The Bible is both a divine and human entity: divine in its inspiration and preservation, human in the sense of God's subjecting it to the historical process and entrusting it to the church. In this way, writes George E. Ladd, *"the Bible is the Word of God given in the words of men in history."*[57]

Textual criticism is not a pejorative term or an evil enterprise. *Criticize* (Greek *krinō*) means to "judge," "decide," "determine" or "consider." By definition, textual criticism is a study which seeks to reconstruct the original text from existing texts because the autographs are not available. The fact is that very few autographs survive for any ancient work. For example, the works of Plato (d. 347 B.C.) survive mostly in Byzantine manuscripts of the Middle Ages, the earliest of which dates to A.D. 895, more than twelve hundred years after his death.[58] The same is true of such ancient authors as Livy, Tacitus, Herodotus and Thucydides, where only small portions of their works survive in late manuscripts.

Those who engage in textual criticism are motivated by the desire to provide the most reliable text possible under the circumstances of available manuscripts and universally accepted principles of scholarship. The marvel—or should one say miracle—in all of this is that after twenty centuries of textual studies we possess a text that has to be amazingly close in wording to the original manuscripts. The information in the next section is an attempt to confirm this observation.

PART VII

TEXTUAL VARIANTS & THE PRACTICE OF TEXTUAL CRITICISM

Readers of any recent English version of the New Testament (such as the NRSV or NIV) may be unaware of the long process of textual studies that led to that particular translation. We rightly assume that what we are reading is the true "Word of God" and thus reliable for faith and practice. Occasionally, however, there are passages in our English text that have footnotes saying something like "Some early manuscripts omit" (or "add") certain words, phrases or passages (see comments below on the Lord's Prayer, Mt 6:13; a few other examples include Mt 6:25; Mk 3:14; 9:29; 16:8; Lk 8:43; Jn 3:13; 7:53—8:11; Acts 8:36; Eph 1:1; Col 1:14; 1 Jn 5:7-8). Basically, this means that the editors of that particular English version are aware that the Greek text has a variant reading at that place which they wish to reflect in the translation. What the readers of the English text do not see are the thousands of other variants in the Greek New Testament which the GNT^4 and the twenty-seventh edition of Nestlé-Aland (NA^{27}) record (see sample page of Col 1, p. 148).

In the previous chapter we discussed the process of writing and transmitting the New Testament and noted *how* it was possible for copiers of the text to make mistakes. Here I want to continue that discussion but focus specifically on the *nature* and *significance* of some variants. What are we to make of those additional notes in our New Testament? What is the nature and significance of these variants in the text? How do New Testament text critics determine which variant is original? How does all of this affect our belief in the New Testament as God's inspired and authoritative Word?

Here we will take a brief look at the principles and practice of New Testament textual criticism and see how this discipline enables us to understand and appreciate the text of the New Testament more adequately. The Greek forms of most words are retained for their illustrative and comparative value. Students without any knowledge of the Greek language are encouraged to compare the shape and placement of letters and words and not worry about their meaning.[1]

1. Unintentional Variations

Unintentional errors account for about 95 percent of the variants that are found in the New Testament. This simply means that the copyists made natural mistakes when they were copying from one manuscript to another. The fact that they were copying the New Testament did not exempt them from the frailties of their humanity, primitive writing materials, difficult script and uncomfortable settings for their work. Many mistakes were of the same type that we would make today were it not for the benefit of printing presses, photocopiers and computers. But when the human factor is involved, it is amazing how many errors occur. This realization caused Bruce Metzger to observe that a significant number of unintentional errors were committed "by well-meaning but sometimes stupid or sleepy scribes."[2]

■ **Errors of Sight.** *Confusing letters similar in appearance.* Letters in the uncial script particularly prone to such changes were

Ε Θ Ο C
Π Γ Ι Τ
Α Λ Δ
Η Ν

When one adds carelessness, poor writing conditions, inferior quality of papyrus and so on, one can easily see how mistakes were made. This appears to be the case with the variant in 2 Peter 2:13 ("reveling in their dissipation [love feasts] while they feast with you"):

ΑΓΑΠΑΙC ("love feasts")
ΑΠΑΤΑΙC ("dissipation")

Faulty division of words within a sentence. A good illustration is in 1 Timothy 3:16 ("without any doubt, the mystery of our religion is great"), where the *scriptio continua* made it difficult for scribes to divide the following phrase:

ΟΜΟΛΟΓΟΥΜΕΝΩΣΜΕΓΑ

ομολογουμενωσμεγα

Some manuscripts read:

ὁμολογοῦμεν ὡς μέγα ("we acknowledge how great")

Others: ὁμολογουμένως μέγα ("confessedly great")

Haplography: the omission of letters, words and/or sentences. At 1 Thessalonians 2:7 ("But we were gentle [babes] among you") there are two variants:

ἤπιοι ("we were gentle")

νήπιοι ("we were babes")

The omission of the ν is understandable.[3]

Another common error of omission was *parablepsis,* meaning "looking by the side." This occurred when sentences ended with similar words *(homoioteleuton)* and the scribe's eye skipped to a similar word farther down the manuscript, thus omitting part of the text. In some manuscripts the entire whole of Matthew 12:47 is missing because the copyist's eye accidentally skipped from the last word of verse 46 (λαλῆσαι) to the same last word in verse 47. What he was copying may have looked like this:

12:46 . . . ζητοῦντες αὐτῷ λαλῆσαι

12:47 . . . .

. . . . λαλῆσαι

12:48 . . . ὁ δὲ . . .[4]

Dittography ("twice written"): the repetition of words and/or sentences. This occurs, for example, in some Greek manuscripts at Acts 19:34 and 27:37. In Mark 12:27 the word *God* (θεός) is repeated twice.

Metathesis: changing the order of letters within a word or a word within a sentence. Such is the case in Mark 14:65, where one can find ἔλαβον *(elabon)* and ἔβαλον *(ebalon).*

■ **Errors of Hearing.** Many vowels and words were pronounced alike even though they were spelled differently and had different meanings—a phenomenon similar to our English homonyms (their—there; hare—hair; night—knight, etc.). Errors due to this, known as *itacisms,* were common among scribes who pronounced words to themselves as they were transcribing or those making copies from dictation in a scriptorium.

Many vowels and diphthongs (combinations of vowels such as αι, ου, οι, ει, ευ, etc.) lost their distinctive sounds and were pronounced alike. One significant variant is at Romans 5:1. Should it read, "Therefore, since we are justified through faith, we have [ἔχομεν—*echomen*] peace with God," or, "Therefore, since we are justified through faith, let us have [ἔχωμεν—*echōmen*] peace with God"?

The difference here is in the pronunciation of the Greek omega, that is, whether it was heard as a short *o* (omicron) or long *ō* (omega).

It was also common to confuse the sound of certain Greek pronouns:

ἡμεῖς *(hēmeis)* and ὑμεῖς *(hymeis)*

ἡμῖν *(hēmin)* and ὑμῖν *(hymin)*

ἡμᾶς *(hēmas)* and ὑμᾶς *(hymas)*

Notice the variant reading in the NIV at 1 John 1:4. Did John say, "We write this to make our [ἡμῶν–*hēmōn*] joy complete," or "We write this to make *your* [ὑμῶν–*hymōn*] joy complete"?

■ **Errors of Writing.** Although most unintentional errors may be the result of what the copyists saw, or thought they saw, others are the result of what they wrote. Luke 2:14 may be such an example. This familiar angelic annunciation reads quite differently in the KJV and in the newer versions such as the NIV and NRSV (see table 7.1).

Table 7.1. Luke 2:14

KJV	NRSV
Glory to God in the highest and on earth peace, good will toward men.	Glory to God in the highest heaven, and on earth peace among those whom he favors.

The difference in Greek between "good will toward men" (εὐδοκία–*eudokia*) and "among those whom he favors" (εὐδοκίας–*eudokias*) apart from the inclusive language of the NRSV, is the final ς. Which word did Luke write? If it was εὐδοκίας, was the omission of ς simply an accident of writing?[5]

■ **Errors of Judgment.** Variants often resulted from careless scribes who either did not care or were incapable of discerning some rather obvious problems. At times the marginal glosses and corrections on a manuscript were inserted into the text itself; on other occasions synonyms were substituted for the original word; or a scribe may have mistakenly copied a more familiar word for one less common. A classic example of one of these errors occurs in Luke 6:42: "First take the log out of your own eye, and then you will see clearly to take the speck out of your neighbor's eye." Instead of κάρφος—*karphos* ("log") —one scribe wrote καρπός—*karpos* ("fruit"). On this point Metzger makes a classic observation: "Other errors originated, not because of the exercise of faulty judgement, but from the lack of judgement altogether. Only heedlessness to a degree that passes comprehension can account for some of the absurdities perpetrated by witless scribes."[6]

Readers who are able to consult the recommended books on textual criticism for more detail and examples will not find it difficult to conclude that these unintentional errors are rather insignificant variants in the text. Because the reasons for these variants are quite obvious, the experts are able to show how they found their way into certain manuscripts and kept on being perpetuated until someone made the proper corrections.

2. Intentional Variations

Intentional variations are deliberate and conscious attempts to alter the text at certain places. Metzger, whose discussion of this subject is invaluable, writes: "Odd though it may seem, scribes who thought were more dangerous than those who wished merely to be faithful in copying what lay before them."[7] He also refers to Jerome's lament about those copyists who "write down not what they find but what they think is the meaning; and while they attempt to rectify the errors of others, they merely expose their own."[8] Some of the more common changes include the following.

■ **Revising Grammar and Spelling.** It is not unusual for a language to undergo certain linguistic and grammatical changes throughout the centuries. Thus scribes from a different era, or even geographical area, often corrected something that was unfamiliar to them, that was no longer in use or that lacked clarity.[9] Kurt and Barbara Aland comment, "Not only does the text tend to grow, it becomes more *stylistically polished,* conformed to the rules of Greek grammar."[10]

■ **Harmonizing Similar Passages.** Many scribes were very familiar with Scripture and over the years memorized large portions of it. When it came to copying parallel passages from the Gospels, or similar-sounding phrases from Paul's letters, there was a *deliberate* tendency to make all the readings the same. Hence in Luke 11:4 someone added the phrase "but rescue us from the evil one" because it is found in the parallel passage in Matthew 6:13. Another manuscript shows an attempt to harmonize the accounts of Paul's conversion in Acts 9:5-6 and 26:14-15. The addition of "through his blood" in some manuscripts at Colossians 1:14 came through comparison and harmonization with Ephesians 1:7. On other occasions some scribes would attempt to complete a quotation from the Old Testament that a different manuscript had quoted only partially.

Slightly different from harmonization is what Metzger calls "addition of natural complements and similar adjuncts." Here the tendency was to add words or phrases to "amplify" or "round off" passages. For example, "many a copyist found it hard to let 'the chief priests' pass without adding 'the scribes' (e.g. Matt. xxvi.3), or 'scribes' without 'Pharisees' (e.g. Matt. xxvii.41)."[11]

■ **Eliminating Apparent Discrepancies and Difficulties.** One example used to illustrate this change is Mark 1:2-3, which reads: "As it is written in the prophet Isaiah: 'See, I am sending my messenger ahead of you, who will prepare your way; the voice of one crying out in the wilderness: 'Prepare the way of the Lord, make his paths straight.' " That the first part of this composite quotation comes from Malachi 3:1 and not Isaiah led some copyist to drop the name Isaiah altogether and simply write "in the prophets" (note how the NIV attributes 1:2 to Mal 3:1; cf. also Mt 27:9, which comes from Zech 11:12-13 and not Isaiah). A geographical change is reflected in John 1:28, where the KJV follows a manuscript tradition that uses "Bethabara" instead of. Bethany (NRSV, NIV).

Revelation 1:5 has a variant with λύσαντι–*lusanti* (from λύω, "to loose," "free") and λούσαντι–*lousanti* (from λούω, "to wash," "bathe"). Should the text read "Unto him that loved us, and washed [λούσαντι] us from our sins in his own blood" (KJV) or "freed [λύσαντι] us" (NIV, RSV, NRSV)? Since the best manuscripts read "freed," one can only conclude that "washed" may either have come from a similar expression in 7:14 ("washed their robes and made them white in the blood of the Lamb") or from baptismal imagery, or that it was an error of faulty hearing by a scribe unable to distinguish between the sound of υ and ου.

■ **Conflating the Text.** Scribes who were confronted with two or more different readings on a certain passage could either choose one of several variants or combine several into one reading. This appears to have happened in Luke 24:53 ("and they were continually in the temple blessing God"), where one manuscript reads "blessing"(εὐλογοῦντες—*eulogountes*) and another "praising" (αἰνοῦντες—*ainountes*) God. An examination of the critical apparatus in the Greek text shows that some manuscripts prefer "blessing" (as RSV, NRSV), and some "praising" (as NIV), while others conflate the two to produce "praising and blessing" (as KJV) or "blessing and praising." Acts 20:28 is another passage which shows how the readings "church of God" and "church of the Lord" were conflated to read "the church of the Lord and God."

■ **Adapting Different Liturgical Traditions.** Believers who are familiar with the Lord's Prayer in either private or public worship inevitably conclude the prayer with "For yours is the kingdom and the power and the glory for ever. Amen." Yet this phrase is not in the best Greek manuscripts, and it appears it is not something that our Lord said (note that it is not quoted in the NIV or NRSV, even though it is in the KJV). The question then is why and by whom this phrase was added to the prayer our Lord taught his disciples. Metzger provides the most definitive response when he writes that "an ascription, usually in a threefold form, was composed (perhaps on the basis of 1 Chr 29.11-13) in order to adapt the Prayer for liturgical use in the early church."[12]

A similar change, although not necessarily liturgical, relates to the practice of exorcism in the early church. Mark 9:29 records that Jesus said, "This kind [of evil spirit] can come out only through prayer." The footnote in the NRSV and NIV records "prayer and fasting," probably indicating that for some scribes fasting was as important a component for exorcism as was prayer. The growing importance of fasting in the early church may account for similar interpolations (insertions) in Acts 10:30 and 1 Corinthians 7:5.

Acts 8:37 is another significant variant that fits into this category. After Philip meets the Ethiopian eunuch and clarifies the Scripture to him, the eunuch requests water baptism: "What is to prevent me from being baptized?" (v. 36). The NIV and NRSV note a variant which is recorded in a number of manuscripts and followed by the KJV as verse 37: "And Philip said, If thou believest with all thine heart, thou mayest. And he answered and said, I believe that Jesus Christ is the Son of God." As useful as such a confession may be, or as much as it may have belonged to some early baptismal liturgies, it does not belong in the text. It undoubtedly was inserted—perhaps first in the margin and later brought into the text—by a scribe whose knowledge of the practice of baptism included such a confession of faith.

■ **Making Theological or Doctrinal Changes.** Metzger points out that basically there are two types of doctrinal changes: "those which involve the elimination or alteration of what was regarded as doctrinally unacceptable or inconvenient, and those which introduce into the Scriptures 'proof' for a favorite theological tenet or practice."[13] The footnote at Mark 1:1 ("The beginning of the good news of Jesus Christ, the Son of God") indicates that some manuscripts do not have "the Son of God." Was the phrase omitted accidentally, or was it a deliberate attempt to expand the title of Jesus at this place? For John 1:13, the NRSV reads "who were born, not of blood or of the will of the flesh or of the will of man, but of God." The "who were" accurately translates the Greek plural "who" or "those who" (οἱ). The manuscripts that change the plural οἱ to the singular ὅς ("he who") probably reflect a desire to insert the virgin birth into John's Gospel. The NIV seeks to alleviate any misunderstanding by using "children born."

Matthew 1:25 refers to Mary, who "gave birth to a son." The KJV, on the other hand, follows a manuscript tradition that substitutes "firstborn son." One cannot be sure whether there is some doctrinal motivation here or whether it was an attempt to harmonize this passage with Luke 2:7, which uses "firstborn" (Greek *prōtotokos*). Another example is Mark 13:32, where some manuscripts do not have "nor the Son": "But about that day or hour no one knows, neither the angels in heaven, nor the Son, but only the Father." Did a scribe intentionally omit "nor the Son" because it appeared to compromise the divine omniscience of Jesus regarding the "last days"?

Doctrinal changes are most likely intended in the additions made to Romans 8:1 and 1 Corinthians 6:20. The NIV on Romans 8:1 simply reads, "Therefore, there is now no condemnation for those who are in Christ Jesus." However, the footnote shows a manuscript tradition that added, "who do not live according to the sinful nature but according to the Spirit." And to Paul's statement "Therefore honor God with your body" (1 Cor 6:20 NIV), some scribes added "and in your spirit, which are God's" (as KJV), in order to teach that we should glorify God with our spirit as well as our body (unfortunately, the NRSV omits any reference to this variant).

The classic example in this category is the so-called *comma Johanneum* of 1 John 5:6-8. It is important to note that the modern versions such as the NIV and NRSV omit the familiar verse 7 of the KJV entirely (see table 7.2).

Table 7.2. 1 John 5:7

KJV	NRSV
(6) This is he that came by water and blood, even Jesus Christ; not by water only, but by water and blood. And it is the Spirit that beareth witness, because the Spirit is truth. (7) For there are three that bear record in heaven, the Father, the Word, and the Holy Ghost: and these three are one. (8) And there are three that bear witness in earth, the Spirit, and the water, and the blood: and these three agree in one.	(6) This is the one who came by water and blood, Jesus Christ, not with the water only but with the water and the blood. And the Spirit is the one that testifies, for the Spirit is the truth. (7) There are three that testify: (8) the Spirit and the water and the blood, and these three agree.

Scholars unanimously agree that the statement in verse 7 does not occur in any Greek manuscripts before the sixteenth century.[14] It can be found in a few earlier Latin manuscripts but obviously is an attempt to insert the doctrine of the Trinity into this particular text. Metzger comments, "The *Comma* probably originated as a piece of allegorical exegesis of the witness and may have been written as a marginal gloss in a Latin manuscript of I Jn, whence it was taken into the text of the Old Latin Bible during the fifth century."[15]

The intentional changes that we have seen—and the others that are part of the Greek text—should not lead us to despair of the reliability of the New Testament text.[16] That these variants are present cannot be denied; but their significance needs to be evaluated in light of other considerations.

First, most copyists were careful and accurate. Metzger reminds us that they were not "altogether willful and capricious in transmitting ancient copies of the New Testament."[17]

Second, most scribes were copyists and not theologians; they were not evaluating the text theologically nor always thinking deeply about what they were copying. Otherwise there might have been more changes to the text.

Third, as noted by J. Harold Greenlee, "Intentional doctrinal changes which have received any appreciable mss. support have almost invariably been changes in the direction of orthodoxy or stronger doctrinal emphasis. Movement toward a doctrinally weaker text is more likely to be an unintentional change."[18] This truth is further corroborated by the fact that changes made at one place in the text did not call for a wholesale corruption throughout the entire New Testament. There was, for example, no systematic conspiracy to remove references to the blood of Jesus from the text or to insert the doctrine of the Trinity wherever it may have been possible.

This point should not be taken to discount the serious impact that heresies had upon the early church. Heretics were both able and willing to change the text or to twist its meaning. Metzger refers to several church fathers who "accused the heretics of corrupting the Scriptures in order to have support for their special views . . . and that Tatian's Harmony of the Gospels contains several textual alterations which lent support to ascetic or encratite views."[19] Marcion, we saw earlier, altered the Gospel of Luke to omit any references to the Jewish background of Jesus.

The church fathers were unable to appeal to the autographs for the "original reading" because they obviously had been lost at an early period in the life of the church. A helpful comment in this regard is made by Greenlee:

> Marcion and others like him were not scribes, however; they were teachers. They did not advance their views by copying manuscripts incorrectly, even though they may have made changes in their own New Testaments. They depended instead upon teaching and publicizing their doctrines. Scribes, on the other hand, were not engaged in studying the text but simply in copying it.[20]

Finally, the doctrinal variants add up to a very small percentage of all the intentional changes. Again, it bears repeating that *no significant doctrine of the New Testament hinges on a variant.* One can safely—but cautiously—affirm that we have a text which at all significant points gives us what the authors wrote. "The student of the N.T.," cautions Greenlee, "must beware of wanting his text to be more orthodox or doctrinally stronger than in the inspired original."[21]

In most cases, textual agreement between manuscripts of the Greek New Testament is closer than the verbal agreement of most English versions of the New Testament. One can note this by comparing the KJV with the NRSV and the NIV. The Living Bible contains a number of significant variations and interpretations from the Greek and standard English texts. Yet no one would say that it is not "the Bible." At the same time, however, we must require that all versions, translations and paraphrases remain true to the text of the best manuscripts that we possess today.

3. Evaluating the Evidence

It is one thing to have all the manuscripts available to see which ones support a certain reading of the text. Basically, this is an objective experience and does not require much specialized training in Greek or in textual criticism. The *practice* of textual criticism, on the other hand, is a different matter because it requires considerable knowledge, skill and ingenuity. "To teach another how to become a text critic," writes Metzger, "is like teaching another how to become a poet. The fundamental principles and criteria can be set forth and certain processes can be described, but the appropriate application of these in individual cases rests upon the student's own sagacity and insight."[22]

The history of the science of textual criticism is a long and complex one. Metzger takes the readers of his *The Text of the New Testament* through the beginning stages in the second century to the twentieth century. Even though knowledge of this material is essential for understanding the complexity of the task and appreciating the standard principles that govern the work of the text critic, a complete discussion goes beyond the scope of this book. Thus we will look closely at only those items that contribute most to our understanding of the making of the New Testament.

One could take any of the examples mentioned above under the unintentional or intentional changes and ask the following question: How, on the basis of the available evidence, do we decide which reading is the original? Obviously, only one reading can make that claim. Fortunately, text critics have developed a system of principles or "criteria" that guide them through their search in determining the probable wording of the original text. Fundamental to all the criteria is what Michael Holmes calls "the overarching guideline": "the variant most likely to be original is the one which best accounts for the existence of others."[23]

The following outline is an adaptation of Metzger's discussion of the criteria used to evaluate textual variants:[24]

External Evidence

1. The date (age) of the manuscript witness
2. The type of text which the manuscript embodies—that is, Alexandrian, Western, etc.
3. The geographical distribution of the witnesses
4. The genealogical relationship of texts

Internal Evidence

1. Transcriptional probabilities based upon considerations of ancient writing and scribal habits

    a. Generally, the more difficult reading—that is, difficult to the scribe—is to be preferred

    b. Generally, the shorter reading is to be preferred except where unintentional or intentional motives may have been at work

    c. Generally, passages which remain in "verbal dissidence" with each other are preferred to those where harmonization may have occurred

    d. Generally, passages are preferred which have not been subject to grammatical and linguistic changes

2. Intrinsic probabilities, based upon considerations of what the original authors most likely wrote

    a. Their style, vocabulary and usage elsewhere in the New Testament

    b. The immediate context of a passage

    c. The application of accepted theories of New Testament research regarding the origin and transmission of the New Testament documents[25]

To illustrate, observe the section of Colossians 1 *(GNT⁴)* in table 7.3. The solid line about halfway down the page divides the text from the "critical apparatus" that contains the variants for the first five verses. While the NIV lists one variant at 1:2 ("Some manuscripts *Father and the Lord Jesus Christ*"), the Greek text recognizes other variants and so lists them with the supporting manuscript evidence. Verse 2 includes the following variations:

    1. "our"

    2. "our Father and Lord Jesus Christ"

    3. "our Father and our Lord Jesus Christ"

    4. "our Father and Jesus Christ our Lord"

It is both natural and legitimate for us to wonder what Paul actually wrote and when and by whom these variants arose. Which reading truly is the Word of God? Can they all be? Does it really matter? What does this do to our claim as Christians that the New Testament is God's infallible and inspired Word of God?

Text critics are trained to interpret the manuscript evidence and to make intelligent decisions on which reading is likely to be original. In this case they ended the statement at "grace to you and peace from God our Father," believing that the additional phrase "and our Lord Jesus Christ" is unwarranted even though it can be found in a number of good manuscripts (the NRSV omits the footnote). Bruce Metzger concludes that if the phrase had been in the original, there would have been no reason to omit it. It was, therefore, probably "added by copyists who assimilated the text to Pauline usage."[26] The KJV is the only English version to include it. Although Colossians 1:2 is but

Table 7.3. A Page from a Modern Greek New Testament

ΠΡΟΣ ΚΟΛΟΣΣΑΕΙΣ

Salutation

1 Παῦλος ἀπόστολος Χριστοῦ Ἰησοῦ διὰ θελήματος θεοῦ καὶ Τιμόθεος ὁ ἀδελφός[a] **2** τοῖς ἐν Κολοσσαῖς ἁγίοις καὶ πιστοῖς ἀδελφοῖς ἐν Χριστῷ,[b] χάρις ὑμῖν καὶ εἰρήνη ἀπὸ θεοῦ πατρὸς ἡμῶν[1].[c]

Paul Thanks God for the Colossians

3 Εὐχαριστοῦμεν τῷ θεῷ πατρί[2] τοῦ κυρίου ἡμῶν Ἰησοῦ Χριστοῦ[d] πάντοτε[e] περὶ ὑμῶν προσευχόμενοι, **4** ἀκούσαντες τὴν πίστιν ὑμῶν ἐν Χριστῷ Ἰησοῦ καὶ τὴν ἀγάπην ἣν ἔχετε εἰς πάντας τοὺς ἁγίους **5** διὰ τὴν ἐλπίδα τὴν ἀποκειμένην ὑμῖν ἐν τοῖς οὐρανοῖς, ἣν προηκούσατε ἐν τῷ λόγῳ τῆς ἀληθείας τοῦ εὐαγγελίου **6** τοῦ παρόντος εἰς ὑμᾶς, καθὼς καὶ ἐν παντὶ τῷ κόσμῳ ἐστὶν καρποφορούμενον καὶ αὐξανόμενον καθὼς καὶ ἐν ὑμῖν, ἀφ' ἧς ἡμέρας ἠκούσατε καὶ ἐπέγνωτε τὴν χάριν

---

[1] **2** {A} ἡμῶν B D K L Ψ 33 81 1175 1739 1852 1881 *l* 156 *l* 170 *l* 617 *l* 751 *l* 883 *l* 1021 *l* 1298 *l* 1356 *l* 1365 *l* 1439 *l* 1443 *l* 1977 it[ar. d. mon*] vg[ww. st] syr[p. pal] cop[sa] arm[mss] geo[1] slav Origen[lat] Chrysostom Theodore[lat]; Ambrosiaster Pelagius ‖ ἡμῶν καὶ κυρίου Ἰησοῦ Χριστοῦ (*see* Rm 1.7 *etc.*) ℵ A C F G I 075 6 104 256 263 365 424 436 459 (1241[vid] *but* ὑμῶν) 1319 1573 1912 1962 2127 2200 2464 *Byz Lect* it[(b). f. g. monᶜ] vg[cl] (cop[bo]) arm[mss] (eth) geo[2] ‖ ἡμῶν καὶ Ἰησοῦ Χριστοῦ τοῦ κυρίου ἡμῶν P (0150 vg[mss] Χριστοῦ Ἰησοῦ) vg[mss] (syr[h with *])

[2] **3** {C} θεῷ πατρί 𝔓[61vid] B C* (D* F G τῷ πατρί) 1739 it[b. d. g. mon. o] vg[mss] cop[sa. bo] eth slav[mss] (Chrysostom) Theodore[lat]; Ambrosiaster Augustine ‖ θεῷ καὶ πατρί ℵ A C² D² I Ψ 075 0150 6 33 81 104 256 263 365 424 436 459 1175 1319 1573 1852 1881 1912 1962 2127 2200 2464 *Byz* [K L P] *Lect* it[ar. f] vg arm geo slav[mss] Pelagius

---

[a]**1** P: RSV TEV FC NIV NRSV [b]**2** P: RSV TEV NIV Lu REB ‖ [c] P: TR WH (AD) NA M Seg REB [d]**3** C: TR Seg VP TOB NJB ‖ [e] C: RSV TEV FC NIV Lu (REB) NRSV

---

1 Παῦλος ... θεοῦ 1 Cor 1.1; Eph 1.1   **3** Eph 1.16; 1 Th 1.2   **4** Eph 1.15   **5** τὴν ἐλπίδα ... οὐρανοῖς 1 Pe 1.4 τῷ ... εὐαγγελίου Eph 1.13   **6** καθὼς ... κόσμῳ 1 Tm 3.16 ἐστὶν ... αὐξανόμενον Ro 1.13

one of many examples that could be used, the verse serves to illustrate how carefully scholars proceed in analyzing the text and the manuscript evidence.

The work of textual criticism is never complete, because each year more papyri are being discovered, translated and evaluated. Recent textual work led to the revision, completion and publication of the NA^{27} and the GNT^4 in 1993. And even though the NRSV was just completed in 1990 after thirteen years of editorial work, a committee is already at work on the next revision. Who knows what lies beneath the sands of some arid country bordering the Mediterranean? The Dead Sea Scrolls that were discovered in 1947 contained manuscripts of the Old Testament that were one thousand years older than those previously known. Dare we hope for something equally exciting in New Testament manuscripts?

APPENDIX I

CANON OF THE OLD TESTAMENT

HEBREW BIBLE (24)	ENGLISH BIBLE (39) (Protestant)	ENGLISH BIBLE (46) (Catholic)
TORAH (5)	LAW (5)	LAW (5)
Genesis	Genesis	Genesis
Exodus	Exodus	Exodus
Leviticus	Leviticus	Leviticus
Numbers	Numbers	Numbers
Deuteronomy	Deuteronomy	Deuteronomy
PROPHETS (8)	HISTORY (12)	HISTORY (14)
Former Prophets (4)	Joshua	Josue (Joshua)*
Joshua	Judges	Judges
Judges	Ruth	Ruth
1—2 Samuel	1 Samuel	1 Kings (1 Samuel)
1—2 Kings	2 Samuel	2 Kings (2 Samuel)
Latter Prophets	1 Kings	3 Kings (1 Kings)
Isaiah	2 Kings	4 Kings (2 Kings)
Jeremiah	1 Chronicles	1 Paralipomenon (1 Chron)
Ezekiel	2 Chronicles	2 Paralipomenon (2 Chron)
The Twelve	Ezra	Esdras-Nehemias (Ezra, Neh)
Hosea	Nehemiah	Tobias (Tobit)
Joel	Esther	Judith

---

* Recent editions of the Catholic Bible and some recent Roman Catholic writers have conformed to the names as used in the RSV.

HEBREW BIBLE (24)	ENGLISH BIBLE (39) (Protestant)	ENGLISH BIBLE (46) (Catholic)
Amos	POETRY (5)	Esther
Obadiah	Job	
Jonah	Psalms	POETICAL & WISDOM (7)
Micah	Proverbs	Job
Nahum	Ecclesiastes	Psalms
Habakkuk	Song of Solomon	Proverbs
Zephaniah		Ecclesiastes
Haggai	MAJOR PROPHETS (5)	Canticle of Canticles
Zechariah	Isaiah	Wisdom of Solomon
Malachi	Jeremiah	Ecclesiasticus (Sirach)
	Lamentations	
WRITINGS (11)	Ezekiel	PROPHETICAL
'Emeth (Truth) (3)	Daniel	LITERATURE (20)
Psalms		Isaias (Isaiah)
Proverbs	MINOR PROPHETS (12)	Jeremias (Jeremiah)
Job	Hosea	Lamentations
Megilloth (Scrolls) (5)	Joel	Baruch
Song of Solomon	Amos	Ezechiel (Ezekiel)
Ruth	Obadiah	Daniel
Lamentations	Jonah	Osee (Hosea)
Ecclesiastes	Micah	Joel
Esther	Nahum	Amos
Daniel	Habakkuk	Abdias (Obadiah)
Ezra-Nehemiah	Zephaniah	Jonas (Jonah)
1—2 Chronicles	Haggai	Micheas (Micah)
	Zechariah	Nahum
	Malachi	Habacuc (Habakkuk)
		Sophonias (Zephaniah)
		Aggeus (Haggai)
		Zecharias (Zechariah)
		Malachias (Malachi)
		1 Machabees (1 Maccabees)
		2 Machabees (2 Maccabees)

APPENDIX II

SIGNIFICANT LEADERS OF THE EARLY CHURCH
(arranged alphabetically)

Athanasius: c. A.D. 296-373
Augustine: c. A.D. 354-430
Barnabas: c. A.D. 70-130+
Clement of Alexandria: c. A.D. 150-215
Clement of Rome: fl. c. A.D. 80s-90s
Cyprian: c. A.D. 200-258
Eusebius: c. A.D. 264-340
Hippolytus: c. A.D. 165/170-236
Ignatius: c. A.D 50-107
Irenaeus: c. A.D. 130/150-202
Jerome: c. A.D. 340-420
Justin: c. A.D. 100-163
Marcion: c. A.D. 100-165
Origen: c. A.D. 185-254
Papias: c. A.D. 70-160
Polycarp: c. A.D. 69-155
Tatian: c. A.D. 110-180
Tertullian: c. A.D. 160-220

APPENDIX III

EARLY CANONICAL LISTS OF THE NEW TESTAMENT

MARCION	MURATORIAN CANON	P⁴⁶
Lk (Marcion's own edition)	(beginning pages missing)	(only 86/104 leaves)
Gal	Lk	Rom
1 Cor	Jn	Heb
2 Cor	Acts	1 Cor
Rom	1 Cor	2 Cor
1 Thess	2 Cor	Eph
2 Thess	Eph	Gal
Eph (=Laodicea)	Phil	Phil
Col	Col	Col
Phil	Gal	1 Thess (7 leaves missing)
Philem	1 Thess	? 2 Thess
	2 Thess	? Philem
	Rom	
	Philem	
	Tit	
	1 Tim	
	2 Tim	
	Jude	
	1-2 Jn	
	Apocalypse of John	
	Apocalypse of Peter	
	Wisdom of Solomon	
	Shepherd of Hermas	

APPENDIX IV

LATER CANONICAL LISTS OF THE NEW TESTAMENT

EUSEBIUS	ATHANASIUS	COUNCIL OF CARTHAGE
(c. A.D. 323)	(A.D. 367)	(A.D. 397)
Acknowledged	Gospels (4)	Gospels (4)
Gospels (4)	Acts	Acts
Acts		
Paul (14, incl. Heb)	**Catholic Epistles**	**Paul's Epistles**
1 Jn	Jas	(13)
1 Pet	1 Pet	
Rev (?)	2 Pet	Heb
	1 Jn	1 Pet
Disputed	2 Jn	2 Pet
Jas	3 Jn	1 Jn
Jude	Jude	2 Jn
2 Pet		3 Jn
2 Jn	**Paul's Epistles**	Jas
3 Jn	(14)	Jude
		Rev
Spurious	Rev	
Shepherd of Hermas		
Didache		
Barnabas		
Acts of Paul		
Apocalypse of Peter		

APPENDIX V

EARLY MANUSCRIPTS CONTAINING THE NEW TESTAMENT

SINAITICUS	VATICANUS	ALEXANDRINUS	CLAROMONTANUS
(IV century)	(IV century)	(V century)	(VI century)
Mt	Mt	Mt 25:6-2—8:20	Mt
Mk	Mk	Mk	Jn
Lk	Lk	Lk	Mk
Jn	Jn	Jn (6:50—8:52	Lk
Rom	Acts	missing)	Rom
1 Cor	Jas	Acts	1 Cor
2 Cor	1 Pet	Jas	2 Cor
Gal	2 Pet	1 Pet	Gal
Eph	1 Jn	2 Pet	Eph
Phil	2 Jn	1 Jn	1 Tim
Col	3 Jn	2 Jn	2 Tim
1 Thess	Jude	3 Jn	Tit
2 Thess	Rom	Jude	Col
Heb	1 Cor	Rom	Philem
1 Tim	2 Cor	1 Cor	1 Pet
2 Tim	Gal	2 Cor (4:13—12:6	2 Pet
Tit	Eph	missing)	Jas
Philem	Phil	Gal	1 Jn
Acts	Col	Eph	2 Jn
Jas	1 Thess	Phil	3 Jn
1 Pet	2 Thess	Col	Jude
2 Pet	Heb (1:1—9:14)	1 Thess	*Barnabas*
1 Jn	(ending lost)	2 Thess	Rev
2 Jn		Heb	Acts
3 Jn		1 Tim	*Shepherd of*
Jude		2 Tim	*Hermas*
Rev		Tit	*Acts of Paul*
Barnabas		Philem	*Apocalypse*
Shepherd of		Rev	*of Peter*
Hermas		*1 Clement*	
		2 Clement (1:2—12:5)	

GLOSSARY*

Agrapha—A Greek term (*hagrapha*, "unwritten") referring to sayings of Jesus that are not recorded in the canonical Gospels. The saying found in Acts 20:35, for example, "remembering the words of the Lord Jesus, for he himself said: 'It is more blessed to give than to receive,' " is not found in the Gospels.

Alexandrinus (A)—A fifth-century uncial manuscript containing the Gospels, Acts, Paul's letters and Revelation.

Amanuensis—From the Latin "by hand," thus a term for a scribe or secretary, who would usually write from dictation.

Anonymous—Name of author not stated within the literary work itself.

Apocalypse—From the Greek *apokalypsis*, "revelation," another name for the Revelation of John in the New Testament.

Apocalyptic—A literary genre (form) dealing with the "end times," often using symbolic and dramatic language and imagery.

Apocrypha/Apocryphal—Originally a term meaning "the hidden things," but now commonly used to designate books which are not included in the Protestant canon of Scripture (see appendix I). The Apocryphal books that were included in the LXX and now also form part of the Roman Catholic Bible usually are referred to as the Old Testament Apocrypha. The New Testament Apocrypha consists of the extracanonical Christian writings.

Apologist—One who defends the faith either personally or in writing.

Apostolic Fathers—Leaders of the early church during the late first and early second century whose written works were valued by Christians but did not become part of the canon.

Apophthegm—A technical term, meaning "utterance" or "pronouncement," used by Rudolf Bultmann in his development of form criticism.

Aramaic—A Semitic language spoken in Palestine and beyond during the time of Jesus.

---

* Items in this glossary were selected for their significance to the material under discussion. In some cases, students may wish to consult other dictionaries and encyclopedias. An excellent source for biblical material is Richard N. Soulen's *Handbook of Biblical Criticism*, 2d ed. (Atlanta: John Knox, 1981).

Augustinian Hypothesis—The opinion of Augustine that the current canonical order of the Gospels is the actual chronological order in which they were composed. This view was later modified by J. J. Griesbach's hypothesis that Mark was the latest Gospel to be composed.

Autograph—A reference to the original manuscript of an author's work. Since we do not possess any original manuscripts of the Bible, scholars must work with later copies.

B.C.E./C.E.—"Before the Common Era" and "The Common Era," respectively. Terms that mean the same as B.C. and A.D., respectively, but without Christian or theological implications.

Bezae (D)—A sixth-century uncial manuscript containing the Gospels, Acts and Paul's letters.

Bible—From the Latin *biblia*, the name given to Holy Scripture which contains the Old and New Testaments. Originally the term comes from *biblos*, the center of the papyrus plant which was used to create writing material. The written product was then referred to as a *biblos*. Chrysostom, bishop of Constantinople from A.D. 397 to 407, is credited with being the first person to use the plural, *ta biblia* (books), as a designation of the Old and New Testaments.

Bibliolatry—A negative term sometimes used of the attitude of regarding or "worshiping" the Bible as a book in itself to the point of obscuring its message or its divine author.

Canon—From the Greek *kanōn*, "rule," "norm" or "standard," now designating those books of the Bible which have become the church's accepted and authoritative guide for faith and practice.

Captivity Epistles—The letters of Paul which he is thought to have written from prison (commonly considered to be Ephesians, Philippians, Colossians, Philemon, 1 Timothy, 2 Timothy and Titus).

Catalog of Virtues or Vices—List of vices or virtues commonly used in Stoic philosophy and found in various sections of the New Testament (e.g., Gal 5:19-21, 22-23).

Catechesis/Catechetical—From the Greek *katēcheō*, "to instruct," usually in the form of oral exhortations to new Christians.

Catholic Letters—Also known as the General Letters or General Epistles. From "universal," thus designating those letters in the New Testament which were not written to specific congregations (James, 1 and 2 Peter, 1, 2 and 3 John and Jude).

C.E.—*see* B.C.E./C.E.

Codex—Ancient manuscripts of either papyrus or vellum that were put into book form rather than a scroll.

Collate—A technical term in textual criticism to describe the process by which text critics compare manuscripts in order to reconstruct the original text.

Colophon—A paragraph or subscript added to an ancient book, often giving the title and information about the author and place of composition.

Comma Johanneum—The passage in 1 John 5:7-8 which Erasmus inserted into his Greek text and subsequently was included in the KJV. The passage is not found in the earliest manuscripts.

Conflation—In textual criticism, the fusion of two or more passages into a single or composite one.

Constantine—Also known as Constantine the Great, Roman emperor 306-337, whose conversion to Christianity facilitated the spread of the church and Christian ideals throughout the Empire.

Corpus—A collection of letters, such as "the Pauline Corpus" or "the Johannine Corpus."

Council of Carthage—The Third Council of Carthage in A.D. 397 appears to have been the first council to officially endorse the twenty-seven books which make up the New Testament canon.

Council of Trent—An important council of the Roman Catholic Church held in 1545-1563, at which, among other things, the Latin Vulgate was declared to be the official Bible of the church.

Covenant—Greek *diathēkē*, a binding agreement, will or testament.

Critical Apparatus—Those critical footnotes in the Hebrew or Greek text which show textual variations in manuscripts.

Criticism—From the Greek *krinō*, to judge, discriminate, decide. Not to be considered as a negative term in New Testament studies.

Dead Sea Scrolls—Manuscripts and fragments of the Old Testament and other Jewish literature discovered in caves near the Dead Sea, generally dating from 250 B.C. to A.D. 68.

Deutero-Pauline—Written by a "second" or "another" Paul. Commonly used to refer to letters attributed to Paul but which he may not have written himself.

Diaspora—The dispersion or spread of the Jewish people beyond the borders of Palestine, particularly in the Hellenistic world.

Diatessaron—Tatian's harmony of the Gospels (literally, through the four— i.e., the four Gospels), which was used extensively in the Syrian churches for several centuries.

Diatribe—A Greek form of rhetoric popularized by Cynic and Stoic philosophers and occasionally used by Paul.

Didache—Teaching, from the Greek *didachē*. The *Didache*, or *Teaching of the Twelve Apostles*, is an early second-century manual of church instruction.

Dittography—A term used in textual criticism meaning "written twice," a scribal error of repeating a word or phrase.

Docetism—An early Christian heresy which denied the reality of the humanity of Jesus. First John may be an example of early Christian attempts to combat this heresy.

Early Catholicism—A technical term in New Testament studies indicating the early institutionalization of the church in areas such as leadership and sacramentalism.

Eastern Church—A term generally applied to the geographical area of the church which bordered the eastern part of the Mediterranean Sea from Constantinople to Alexandria in Egypt.

Ebionite—An early Jewish-Christian sect which continued to emphasize the observance of the Mosaic law while minimizing the doctrine of the person of Christ.

Ecclesiastical History—The most significant and extensive writing of Eusebius (c. A.D. 264-340), bishop of Caesarea.

Ecclesiology—From the Greek *ekklēsia*, "church," meaning the doctrine of the church.

Eisegesis—The practice of reading into or bringing to a text the meaning which one desires to find (the opposite of *exegesis*, bringing meaning out of the text).

Episcopacy—From the Greek *episkopos*, a system of leadership by which the church is governed by bishops.

Epistle—Basically another word for letter. The distinction between "epistle" (enduring, artistic) and "letter" (momentary, situational) made by A. Deissmann is no longer accepted by scholars.

Erasmus—A distinguished Dutch scholar and humanist who produced the first Greek edition of the New Testament in 1516.

Eschatology—From the Greek *eschaton*, hence the doctrine of the last things.

Essenes—A Jewish ascetic sect that existed c. 200 B.C. to A.D. 100 in Palestine and that may be associated with the Qumran community near the Dead Sea and the Dead Sea Scrolls.

Eucharist—Another term for the Lord's Supper, from the Greek *eucharisteō*, to give thanks.

Evangelist—Broadly used for anyone who proclaims the good news of the gospel; technically, a term in Gospel studies used to designate the writers of the Gospels.

Exegesis—From the Greek *exēgeomai*, to "draw out" of the biblical text what the author initially intended to say.

Family—In textual criticism, an identifiable group of manuscripts with common characteristics.

Form Criticism—A study of the early forms in which the oral material of the

Gospels circulated before they were written down.

Gemara—From the Hebrew *gāmar*, to complete, i.e., to complete knowledge that has been learned. The Mishnah and the gemara together constitute the Talmud (from *lāmad*, study; *limmad*, to teach, to instruct).

Genre—From the French word for style, kind; thus it is used of classifications of literature such as Gospels, letters and biographies.

Gloss—In textual criticism, comments or interpretations which scribes often made in the margins while copying manuscripts but which later were incorporated into the text itself.

Gnosticism—From Greek *ginōskō*, to know. An early Christian heresy which stressed privately revealed knowledge above that which is generally available to everyone through the Scriptures.

Gospel—Greek *euangelion*, good news. Later designated as a book which tells the good news of the life and teaching of Jesus.

Griesbach Hypothesis—The theory of J. J. Griesbach (1745-1812) that Matthew was the earliest Gospel and that it was used by Mark and Luke (cf. Augustinian Hypothesis).

Haggadah—Edifying material that is intended to enhance the Torah with stories, parables, legends, etc., by describing what life lived according to the law is like.

Halakah—To go, walk; thus rules of conduct handed down by the rabbis in the Torah.

Hapax Legomenon—A Greek term meaning "said only once." A certain word, for example, may only be used once in all of Paul's letters.

Haplography—A scribal error in copying manuscripts in which a word, syllable or line is accidentally omitted because of similar adjacent material.

Harmonization—In textual criticism, the tendency to want the wordings of texts to agree, i.e., to be in harmony with one another. There has been a strong desire in some circles to harmonize accounts in the Gospels.

Hasidim—From the Hebrew *ḥesed*, the pious, righteous, orthodox: individuals within Judaism during the intertestamental period who disagreed with extreme forms of Hellenism. This small group of religious conservatives may have been the forerunners of the Pharisees.

Haustafeln—A German term referring to the household rules or tables in the New Testament which deal with domestic relationships within the home and church (e.g., Col 3:18—4:1; Eph 5:21—6:9).

Hellenism—Admiration for and adoption of Greek ideas, culture and religion.

Hellenists—Greek-speaking Jews, often from the Diaspora, whose ideas sometimes conflicted with those of the Hebrew or Aramaic Jews of Palestine (cf. Acts 6:1-7).

Hermeneutics—The science or theory of explaining and interpreting a text.

Heterodox—Opinions or doctrines not judged orthodox.

Homily—In church circles, a type of abbreviated sermon.

Homoioteleuton—From the Greek meaning "similar ending"; in textual transmission, similar endings to lines or words often resulted in scribal errors of omission.

Hortatory—Marked by the giving of advice or exhortation.

Inerrancy—The belief that the Bible is without error in anything about which it speaks when properly interpreted and understood.

Interpolation—In textual criticism, material that was inserted into the original text either unintentionally or intentionally by scribes or copyists.

Ipsissima Verba—From the Latin meaning "the very words." Used in Gospel studies to distinguish between the very words of Jesus *(ipsissima verba Jesu)* and words which may have been attributed to Jesus by the early church and/or Evangelists.

Itacism—In textual criticism, the term used when words and vowels were pronounced alike but had different meanings (e.g., the English *their* and *there*).

Jamnia (or Jabneh)—A town on the coast slightly northwest of Jerusalem which became an important rabbinical center after the fall of Jerusalem in A.D. 70 and where some think the books of the Old Testament were canonized c. A.D. 90.

Josephus—A Jewish historian and apologist c. A.D. 38-110 who wrote a number of significant works, such as *The Jewish War* and *Jewish Antiquities.*

Judaizers—Jewish Christians who opposed a law-free gospel for the Gentiles as presented by Paul. The Judaizers' opposition to Paul is reflected, for example, in Acts 15:1-35, Galatians 2 and Philippians 3.

Kephalaia—In textual criticism, the sections into which early manuscripts of the New Testament books were divided.

Kerygma—From the Greek *kērygma,* meaning preaching or proclamation.

Koinē—The common Greek, i.e., the Greek of daily conversation and the form or type of Greek language used by the writers of the New Testament.

L—In source criticism "L" designates material peculiar, or unique, to Luke.

Lectionary—An early Christian book containing Scripture selections from the New Testament for use in worship and/or private devotion. Lectionaries are useful evidence for scholars seeking to reconstruct the early Greek text.

Letter—Another term for epistle, a form, or genre, of writing.

Liturgical—Pertaining to worship and/or the components of worship services of the church.

Logia—From the Greek for "words," or "sayings," used in connection with words of Jesus or supposed collections of sayings of Jesus which antedate the Gospels.

M—In source criticism "M" designates material peculiar or unique to Matthew.

Masoretic Text—The most common or received text of the Hebrew Old Testament, with vowel points and punctuation introduced by the Masoretes (Jewish grammarians) between the seventh and tenth centuries A.D.

Midrash—From the Hebrew, to search out, with the aim of exegeting and interpretating a portion of Scripture. The word refers to a method of rabbinic interpretation and to a form of interpretation such as interpretive paraphrases of Exodus or Leviticus.

Minuscule—In textual studies, the term given to the small cursive or "running" letters that were used quite extensively by the time of the ninth and tenth centuries A.D.

Mishnah—From the Hebrew, to repeat, to learn, now designating a collection of authoritative rabbinical materials assembled by the third century A.D.

Muratorian Canon/Fragment—A partial codex of the New Testament containing a list of twenty books. It was discovered by L. A. Muratori in 1740 and is dated between A.D. 200 and 400.

Nag Hammadi—An ancient town in Upper Egypt where an important collection of Gnostic and other writings dating from the fourth century was discovered in 1945-1946.

Neutral Text—In textual criticism, the name given to the so-called Alexandrian Text by F. J. A. Hort in 1882 because he considered it to be the purest representative of the New Testament manuscripts.

Nomina Sacra—In textual criticism, the term used for "sacred names" such as God, Jesus, Christ, Son, etc. These were frequently abbreviated in New Testament manuscripts.

Novum Testamentum—The Latin title for the New Testament.

Oral Tradition—Traditions that were passed on orally before they were written down in permanent form. The term is used for the period between Jesus' exaltation and the writing of the first Gospel, approximately A.D. 33-70.

Orthodox—Doctrines and views in conformity with established beliefs.

Ostraca—In antiquity, broken pieces of pottery that were used as writing material.

Oxyrhynchus Papyri—A cache of ancient papyrus fragments that was discovered at Oxyrhynchus in Upper Egypt between 1897 and 1907 and that includes material dating from the second century B.C. to the seventh century A.D.

P^{46}—One of the earliest papyrus manuscripts (c. A.D. 200) of the letters of Paul.

Paleography—The study of ancient inscriptions and writings.

Palimpsest—A manuscript which has been erased, scraped and used again for writing.

Papyrus—A plant growing in the delta area of the Nile in Egypt that was used as writing material from the fourth century B.C. to the seventh century A.D.

Parablepsis—In textual criticism, "a looking by the side," i.e., a scribe would either skip or repeat similar words or phrases.

Paradigm—A model or pattern.

Paraenesis—A technical term in New Testament studies for moral exhortation and admonition.

Parchment—Also called vellum; the skins of cattle and other animals used as writing material as early as the second century B.C.

Parousia—A term used in the New Testament (Greek *parousia*) to refer to the coming of Christ at the end of history.

Pastoral Epistles—A technical term referring to the letters of 1 and 2 Timothy and Titus because of their pastoral nature.

Pauline *homologoumena*—The seven undisputed letters attributed to Paul (Romans, 1 and 2 Corinthians, Galatians, Philippians, 1 Thessalonians, Philemon).

Pericope—A short section or unit of text such as a miracle story or parable.

Peshitta—The common Bible of the Syrian church since the fourth and fifth centuries A.D.

Philo of Alexandria (c. 20 B.C.-A.D. 45)—A Hellenistic Jewish scholar who sought to interpret the Old Testament by utilizing Greek philosophy and allegorical exegesis.

Pliny—A Roman governor of Bithynia in the second century A.D.

Pneumatology—From the Greek *pneuma*, spirit or wind; hence pneumatology is the study of the Holy Spirit.

Protoevangelium—From the Greek, the first or the earliest form of the gospel.

Pseudepigrapha—From the Greek, false writings, or works falsely written in the name of another person or attributed to a different author. Works of this kind are included in "The Pseudepigrapha."

Q Source—From the German *Quelle*, meaning "source," and referring to material not found in Mark but common to both Matthew and Luke.

Qumran—The location of a settlement of Jewish Essenes in the wilderness near the Dead Sea where the Dead Sea Scrolls were discovered.

Rabbi—A Hebrew word for teacher or master.

Rabbinic—A term used to refer to the schools and ideas of rabbis that produced such literary works as the Talmud.

Recto—The front side of a sheet of papyrus.

Redaction Criticism—From the German *Redaktionsgeschichte,* a method of New Testament study, particularly of the Gospels, which understands the Evangelists to have been independent theologians and seeks to understand their selection, arrangement and interpretation of Gospel material as a disclosure of their theological concerns.

Redactor—Someone who shapes, arranges and edits oral and literary material into a final composition.

Scriptio continua—Continuous script which has no spacing between the words, as in uncial manuscripts such as Sinaiticus.

Scroll, Roll—The product of pasting papyrus sheets side by side to form a continuous sheet which could be rolled up to form a scroll.

Septuagint (LXX)—A Greek translation of the Hebrew Old Testament made in Alexandria at different stages around 285 B.C.

Sinaiticus (א)—A fourth-century uncial manuscript containing the Gospels, Acts, Paul's letters and Revelation.

Sitz im Leben—From the German meaning "situation in life." The term is used in Gospel studies to refer both to the setting in which a saying of Jesus was originally spoken (*Sitz im Leben Jesu*) and to the setting in which a saying was used by the early church (*Sitz im Leben Kirche*).

Source Criticism—A method of studying the New Testament, particularly the Gospels, which considers the literary sources that might have been used by the Evangelists.

Stichometry—A list in which the number of lines (*stichoi*) of a book is given to indicate the length of the writing.

Synoptic—A "seeing together," especially used in comparing the Gospels of Matthew, Mark and Luke, hence the term Synoptic Gospels.

Synoptic Problem—Questions that arise from comparing the Synoptic Gospels for their similarities and differences and attempting to explain them.

Talmud—From the Hebrew, study or instruction. Basically a comprehensive term to designate the material in the Mishnah and Gemara. There is a Babylonian as well as a Jerusalem Talmud.

Targum—Aramaic translations of the Hebrew Scriptures which were read in synagogues for people whose main language was Aramaic.

Terminus a quo—Latin term to indicate the date after, or "from which," an event has taken place.

Terminus ad quem— Latin term to indicate the date before, or "until which," an event has taken place.

Testament—From the Latin *testamentum,* often used to translate the Hebrew and Greek words for covenant. Since the time of Tertullian it has been used to designate the two main divisions of Scripture: the Old and New Testaments.

Textus Receptus—Latin for "received text," the name given to Erasmus's Greek text of 1535 upon which the KJV of 1611 is based.

Torah—In a limited sense, a term referring to the Law, the Pentateuch (first five books of the Old Testament), but more broadly it is used of the entire Old Testament.

Uncial—Capital or large Greek letters, characteristic of manuscripts written on parchment from the third to tenth centuries A.D.

Urevangelium—A German term meaning "Primitive Gospel." Some scholars posit a hypothetical primitive Gospel which preceded our written canonical Gospels.

Variant—In textual criticism this term indicates a particular difference or variation found in manuscripts.

Vaticanus (B)—An early uncial of the New Testament from the fourth century A.D. containing the Gospels, Acts and Paul's letters.

Verbal Inspiration—The belief that every word of Scripture is inspired by God. In some extreme forms this implies a mechanical or dictational process, thus eliminating the human element in writing and copying.

Verso—The reverse or back side of a sheet of papyrus.

Vulgate—The Latin version of the Bible produced by Jerome in the fourth century A.D. and ratified by the Council of Trent in 1546 as the official Scripture for the Roman Catholic Church.

Western Church—A term generally applied to the geographical area of the church which bordered the western side of the Mediterranean Sea from Rome westward, including Carthage in North Africa.

Notes

Part I: The Literary World of the New Testament

[1]See James B. Pritchard, *Ancient Near Eastern Texts Relating to the Old Testament* (Princeton, N.J.: Princeton University Press, 1955). An abbreviated version of this text is available by James B. Pritchard, ed., *The Ancient Near East*, vol. 1, *An Anthology of Texts and Pictures* (Princeton, N.J.: Princeton University Press, 1958).

[2]Some scholars have concluded that Daniel was written as late as the second century B.C. For a helpful discussion on the date of Daniel see W. S. LaSor, D. A. Hubbard and F. W. Bush, eds., *Old Testament Survey* (Grand Rapids, Mich.: Eerdmans, 1982), pp. 662-68.

[3]Edgar J. Goodspeed, *Christianity Goes to Press* (New York: Macmillan, 1940), p. 27.

[4]Ibid., p. 32.

[5]See Adolf Deissmann, *Light from the Ancient East* (1927; reprint, Grand Rapids, Mich.: Baker, 1978).

[6]Goodspeed, *Christianity Goes to Press*, p. 34.

[7]See "The Burning of Sacred Books" in Lee M. McDonald, *The Formation of the Christian Biblical Canon* (Nashville: Abingdon, 1988), pp. 106-10; and J. A. Fitzmyer, "Did Jesus Speak Greek?" *Biblical Archaeology Review* 18, no. 5 (1992): 58-63, 76-77.

[8]See pp. 68-69.

[9]A commonly used term for the Hebrew Old Testament today is "Tanak," a Hebrew acronym derived from the initial letters of the names of these three divisions: *Tôrâh* (Law); *Nᵉbî'îm* (Prophets); *Kᵉtûbîm* (Writings or Hagiographa).

[10]This theory has lost favor in recent years primarily because of lack of evidence. It seems that the process of forming the canon was much too complex to be attributed to a single generation of scholars whose authority was at best dubious. See D. E. Aune, "On the Origins of the 'Council of Javneh' Myth," *JBL* 110, no. 3 (1991): 491-93; Shaye J. D. Cohen, *From the Maccabees to the Mishnah* (Philadelphia: Westminster, 1989), pp. 228-29.

[11]For some important studies on these issues, consult Roger Beckwith, *The Old Testament Canon of the New Testament Church and Its Background in Early Judaism* (Grand Rapids, Mich.: Eerdmans, 1983); Roger Beckwith, "A Modern Theory of the Old Testament Canon," *VT* 41, no. 4 (1991): 385-95; G. L. Robinson, "The Canon of the Old Testament," in *ISBE*, 1:591-601; McDonald, *Formation*, p. 53; David Kraemer, "The Formation of Rabbinic Canon: Authority and Boundaries," *JBL* 110, no. 4 (1991): 613-30. Cf. "Canon of the Old Testament," from LaSor, Hubbard and Bush, *Survey*, app. 1, pp. 24-25.

[12]Helpful resources on the LXX include A. J. Saldarini, "Septuagint," in *Harper's Bible Dictionary*, ed. Paul J. Achtemeier (San Francisco: Harper, 1985), p. 925; M. K. H. Peters, "Septuagint," in *ABD*, 5:1093-104; S. K. Soderlund, "Septuagint," in *ISBE*, 4:400-409; J. W. Wevers, "Septuagint," in *IDB*, 4:273-78; M. Müller, "The Septuagint as the Bible of the New Testament Church: Some Reflections," *Scandinavian Journal of Old Testament* 7, no. 2 (1993): 194-207.

[13]For some minor variations on the appearance of these books in the Roman Catholic, Greek Orthodox, Russian Orthodox and Coptic Scriptures, see the table in Craig A. Evans, *Noncanonical Writings and New Testament Interpretation* (Peabody, Mass.: Hendrickson, 1992), p. 189.

[14]See appendix I.

[15]Bruce M. Metzger, *An Introduction to the Apocrypha* (Oxford: Oxford University Press, 1957), pp. 151-73; Evans, *Noncanonical Writings*, app. 2 and app. 3, pp. 190-224.

[16]James H. Charlesworth, *The Old Testament Pseudepigrapha*, 2 vols. (New York: Doubleday, 1983), 1:xxv. Charlesworth's two volumes on the Old Testament pseudepigrapha is an essential resource for any serious student of this literature. They include fifty-two documents and represent the most current and complete collection ever assembled. Books that qualify as pseudepigraphal, according to Charlesworth, have the following characteristics: (1) they must be Jewish or Christian; (2) they often are attributed to idealized figures in Israel's past; (3) they customarily claim to contain God's word or message; (4) they frequently build upon ideas and narratives present in the Old Testament; and (5) they were composed during the period 200 B.C. to A.D. 200 (or, if composed later, they apparently preserve, albeit in an edited form, Jewish traditions that date from that period). See also K. Koch, "Pseudonymous Writing," in *IDBSup*, pp. 712-14.

[17]Adapted from Charlesworth, *Pseudepigrapha*, and Evans, *Noncanonical Writings*.

[18]Although the identity of the Qumran community is still debated in some circles, there is a large consensus that the Qumran community represents some form of the Essene movement.

[19]For a good translation of the scrolls see F. G. Martinez, *The Dead Sea Scrolls Translated* (Leiden: E. J. Brill, 1992); Geza Vermes, *The Dead Sea Scrolls in English*, rev. ed. (New York: Penguin Books, 1988). For secondary sources see J. J. Collins, "Dead Sea Scrolls," in *ABD*, 2:85-101, and bibliography by Jerome Murphy-O'Connor, "Qumran and the New Testament," in *NTMI*, pp. 55-71.

[20]A current and extensive monograph is by David E. Aune, *The New Testament in Its Literary Environment* (Philadelphia: Westminster, 1989).

[21]Ibid., p. 200.

[22]Stanley Stowers, *Letter Writing in Greco-Roman Antiquity* (Philadelphia: Westminster, 1986), pp. 41-175.

[23]Ibid., p. 15.

Part II: The Gospels

[1]For a brief discussion and assessment of Jesus in non-Christian literature and the apocryphal Gospels, see C. A. Evans, "Jesus in Non-Christian Sources," in *DJG*, pp. 364-68, and C. L. Blomberg, "Gospels (Apocryphal)," in *DJG*, pp. 286-97.

[2]For further discussion, see Rainer Riesner, "Teacher," in *DJG*, pp. 807-11.

[3]See B. D. Chilton, "Rabbinic Traditions and Writings," in *DJG*, pp. 651-60; Shaye J. D.

Cohen, "The Emergence of Rabbinic Judaism," in *From the Maccabees to the Mishnah* (Philadelphia: Westminster, 1987), pp. 214-31; J. A. Overman and W. S. Green, "Judaism (Judaism in the Greco-Roman Period)," in *ABD*, 2:1037-54; S. D. Fraade, "Judaism (Palestinian Judaism)," in *ABD*, 2:1054-61.

[4]Some helpful studies on these and related issues include Klyne Snodgrass, "The Use of the Old Testament in the New," in *NTCI*, pp. 409-34; E. Earle Ellis, *The Old Testament in Early Christianity* (Tübingen: J. C. B. Mohr, 1991); E. Earle Ellis, "How the New Testament Uses the Old," in *NTI*, pp. 199-219; Craig A. Evans, "The Function of the Old Testament in the New," in *Introducing New Testament Interpretation*, ed. Scot McKnight (Grand Rapids, Mich.: Baker, 1989), pp. 163-93; A. J. Saldarini, "Judaism and the New Testament," in *NTMI*, pp. 27-54; J. Neusner, *What Is Midrash?* (Minneapolis: Augsburg/Fortress, 1987).

[5]Aramaic is a Semitic language closely related to Hebrew. It was common as early as 2000 B.C. and became the universal language of the ancient Near East during the time of the Assyrians, Babylonians and Persians. The Israelites probably would have spoken Aramaic during their captivity in Babylon and in Palestine upon their return. Ezra 4:7 refers to a letter that "was written in Aramaic and translated," and the footnote in the NRSV comments: "Heb adds *in Aramaic*, indicating that 4:8—6:18 is in Aramaic. Another interpretation is *The letter was written in the Aramaic script and set forth in the Aramaic language.*" Nehemiah 8:8 states: "So they read from the book, from the law of God, with interpretation. They gave the sense, so that the people understood the reading."

[6]Although the Targumim originally were oral renderings of the Hebrew Bible, written copies of most books eventually appeared. Some Aramaic fragments of Leviticus and Job were found in the Qumran caves. Most extant Targums, however, were written much later and may not have been put into final form until the Middle Ages. As such, they have limited value for illuminating Judaism during the time of Jesus.

[7]See Stanley E. Porter, "Did Jesus Ever Teach in Greek?" *Tyndale Bulletin* 44, no. 2 (1993): 199-235. Cf. also Philip E. Hughes, "The Languages Spoken by Jesus," in *NDNTS*, pp. 127-43; Saldarini, "Judaism and the New Testament," pp. 39-40; M. O. Wise, "Languages of Palestine," in *DJG*, pp. 434-44.

[8]Rainer Riesner's book "Jesus as Teacher" (*Jesu als Lehrer* [Tübingen: J. C. B. Mohr, 1988]) deals with the transmission of texts in Jewish life in homes, elementary schools and synagogues; see also H. Wansbrough, ed., *Jesus and the Oral Gospel Tradition*, JSNT Supplement Series 64 (Sheffield, U.K.: JSOT Press, 1991); P. J. J. Botha, "Greco-Roman Literacy as Setting for New Testament Writings," *Neotestamentica* 26, no. 1 (1992): 195-215.

[9]Riesner, "Teacher," p. 810.

[10]E. P. Sanders and Margaret Davies, *Studying the Synoptic Gospels* (Philadelphia: Trinity Press International, 1989), p. 145. Their entire section on "creativity and oral tradition" (pp. 138-45) is illuminating.

[11]Two recent studies challenge the traditional approach to the Synoptic Gospels. Eta Linnemann, in *Is There a Synoptic Problem?* (Grand Rapids, Mich.: Baker, 1992), questions the literary dependence of the Synoptics, while John Wenham, *Redating Matthew, Mark and Luke: A Fresh Assault on the Synoptic Problem* (Downers Grove, Ill.: InterVarsity Press, 1992), argues for a high degree of verbal independence for each Gospel, the priority of Matthew, and the composition of the Synoptics before A.D. 55.

[12]Cf. his *The Apostolic Preaching and Its Developments* (London: Hodder & Stoughton, 1963), especially pp. 21-24; also Robert Mounce, *The Essential Nature of New Testament Preaching* (Grand Rapids, Mich.: Eerdmans, 1960).

[13]See James D. G. Dunn, *Unity and Diversity in the New Testament*, 2d ed. (Philadelphia: Trinity Press, 1990).

[14]Detailed discussion and bibliographies on the history of form criticism are available in most standard introductions to the New Testament. Helpful summaries of form criticism include C. L. Blomberg, "Form Criticism," in *DJG*, pp. 243-50; Darrell L. Bock, "Form Criticism," in *NTCI*, pp. 175-96; Howard C. Kee, "Synoptic Studies," in *NTMI*, pp. 245-69; Edgar V. McKnight, "Form and Redaction Criticism," in *NTMI*, pp. 149-74; Stephen Travis, "Form Criticism," in *NTI*, pp. 153-64. A good annotated bibliography is in Edgar V. McKnight, *What Is Form Criticism?* (Philadelphia: Fortress, 1969).

[15]Travis, "Form Criticism," p. 153.

[16]Ibid., p. 154.

[17]The idea of an early self-contained passion narrative is receiving new support by a number of current scholars. For discussion, see J. B. Green, "Passion Narrative," in *DJG*, pp. 601-4.

[18]*The Birth of the New Testament*, 3d ed. (San Francisco: Harper, 1982), p. 71.

[19]The best synopsis is by Kurt Aland, *Synopsis of the Four Gospels*, 7th ed. (Stuttgart: German Bible Society, 1984).

[20]*A Study of Early Christianity* (New York: Macmillan, 1973), pp. 166-67. R. T. France provides a helpful analysis of how form and redaction criticism work together in exegesis. See his study of the healing of the centurion's servant (Mt 8:5-13) in "Exegesis in Practice: Two Samples," in *NTI*, pp. 252-64. For further discussion of this process see under "Redaction Criticism."

[21]*The Formation of the Gospel Tradition* (London: Macmillan, 1933), p. 41.

[22]*The Living Word* (Philadelphia: Fortress, 1987), p. 34. There is no scholarly unanimity on the historical trustworthiness of the Gospel tradition. The most recent challenge to their trustworthiness is found in *The Five Gospels: The Search for the Authentic Words of Jesus*, ed. Robert W. Funk and Roy W. Hoover (New York: Macmillan, 1993). This volume reflects the opinions of a small minority of New Testament scholars working together for six years on a project known as the Jesus Seminar. Some early critiques of their work include D. A. Carson, "Five Gospels, No Christ," *Christianity Today*, April 24, 1994, pp. 30-33; Richard Hays, "The Corrected Jesus," *First Things* 43 (May 1994): 43-48.

[23]Bock, "Form Criticism," pp. 181-86. Blomberg's classification includes (1) individual logia, or sayings, (2) pronouncement stories, (3) parables, (4) speeches, (5) miracle stories, (6) other historical narratives (Blomberg, "Form Criticism," pp. 243-44).

[24]Bock, "Form Criticism," p. 184.

[25]See James D. G. Dunn, "Demythologizing—The Problem of Myth in the New Testament," in *NTI*, pp. 285-301; James D. G. Dunn, "Myth," in *DJG*, pp. 566-69.

[26]William Barclay, *The Making of the Bible* (Nashville: Abingdon, 1961), p. 50; also E. J. Goodspeed, *Christianity Goes to Press* (New York: Macmillan, 1940); Stanley K. Stowers, "Education, Art and Professional Letter Writing," in *Letter Writing in Greco-Roman Antiquity* (Philadelphia: Westminster, 1986), pp. 32-35.

[27]W. Kelber, "Oral Tradition," in *ABD*, 5:30. See also Paul J. Achtemeier, *"Omne verbum*

sonat: The New Testament and the Oral Environment of Late Western Antiquity," *JBL* 109, no. 1 (1990): 3-27. A response by Frank D. Gilliard, "More Silent Reading in Antiquity: *Non omne verbum sonabat,*" *JBL* 112, no. 4 (1993): 689-96, modifies Achtemeier's thesis with examples that show silent reading also was common during the first and second centuries of the Christian era. We must not assume that all the people in Palestine, apart from the scribes and Pharisees, were illiterate. The statement in Acts 4:13 that Peter and John were "uneducated and ordinary men" expresses the disdainful attitude of the Jewish authorities toward a new challenge to their authority. The disciples, like many others, including slaves, observes C. F. D. Moule, "need not have been without a good verbal [aural] education" (*The Birth of the New Testament,* 3d rev. ed. [San Francisco: Harper, 1981], p. 208).

[28]Stephen Neill and Tom Wright, *The Interpretation of the New Testament 1861-1986,* rev. ed. (Oxford: Oxford University Press, 1988), p. 294. Hence the Evangelists may have felt more urgency to put the oral traditions into writing.

[29]W. D. Davies, *Invitation to the New Testament* (London: Darton, Longman & Todd, 1967), p. 83.

[30]W. J. Ong, *Orality and Literacy: The Technologizing of the Word* (London: Methuen, 1982), 40. For other references, see Achtemeier, "Omne Verbum Sonat," especially pp. 3-9. Achtemeier also takes issue with Werner Kelber's *The Oral and the Written Gospel* (Philadelphia: Fortress, 1983), by commenting, "One ought to avoid a too-hasty application of the change from the oral medium to the written medium to the time the NT was written" (p. 27, n. 156). W. A. Graham discusses the significant oral roles of written sacred texts in the history of religion in his *Beyond the Written Word: Oral Aspects of Scripture in the History of Religion* (Cambridge: Cambridge University Press, 1987); cf. James D. G. Dunn, *The Living Word* (Philadelphia: Fortress, 1987), pp. 32-33.

[31]Moule, *Birth of the New Testament,* p. 13.

[32]Students exposed to courses in New Testament introduction will realize that there is no scholarly consensus about the priority of Mark nor its date and place of composition. For an excellent survey and evaluation of current ideas and literature see the essay by Scot McKnight, "Source Criticism," in *NTCI,* pp. 137-71; also S. L. Johnson, *The Griesbach Hypothesis and Redaction Criticism,* SBLMS 41 (Atlanta: Scholars Press, 1991).

[33]Scot McKnight employs the terms "the phenomenon of wording," "the phenomenon of content" and "the phenomenon of order" to describe the Synoptic problem ("Source Criticism," p. 139). These phenomena become most apparent when one consults a synopsis of the Gospels or Gospel parallels. For a helpful color chart see A. Barr, *A Diagram of Synoptic Relationships* (Edinburgh: T & T Clark, 1957). For additional material see Robert Stein, *The Synoptic Problem: An Introduction* (Grand Rapids, Mich.: Baker, 1987); Robert Stein, "Synoptic Problem," in *DJG,* pp. 784-92; C. M. Tuckett, "Synoptic Problem," in *ABD,* 6:263-70; Bo Reicke, *The Roots of the Synoptic Gospels* (Philadelphia: Fortress, 1986).

[34]Along with the standard introductions to the New Testament, cf. the articles, all called "Source Criticism," by McKnight in *NTCI,* pp. 137-72; David Wenham in *NTI,* pp. 139-52, and D.-A. Koch in *ABD,* 6:165-71.

[35]To be distinguished from the "Two-Gospel Hypothesis," which goes back to J. J. Griesbach and claims the priority of Matthew and Luke (D. Dungan, "Two-Gospel Hypothesis," in *ABD,* 6:671-79).

[36]Cf. W. G. Kümmel, *Introduction to the New Testament*, rev. ed. (Nashville: Abingdon, 1973), pp. 63-64. Also Moule, *Birth of the New Testament*, p. 105, n. 2: "As for the origin of the symbol Q, it is usually assumed to stand for 'Quelle,' German for 'source,' and this, though it has been questioned, seems now to be decisively vindicated."

[37]The Q hypothesis continues to be debated by contemporary scholars. Helpful discussions can be found in Burton Mack, *The Lost Gospel: The Book of Q and Christian Origins* (San Francisco: Harper, 1992); Ralph P. Martin, *New Testament Foundations*, rev. ed. (Grand Rapids, Mich.: Eerdmans, 1985), 1:143-51; C. M. Tuckett, " 'Q' (Gospel Source)," in *ABD*, 5:567-72. For further bibliographies consult McKnight, "Source Criticism," p. 166, nn. 24-29, and p. 170, nn. 52-53, as well as G. N. Stanton, "Q," in *DJG*, pp. 644-50. Although scholars vary somewhat on the content of Q, a useful chart is available in H. Wayne House, *Chronological and Background Charts of the New Testament* (Grand Rapids, Mich.: Zondervan, 1981), p. 90.

[38]Stanton, "Q," p. 650.

[39]For Streeter's reconstruction see his *The Four Gospels* (London: Macmillan, 1961), pp. 26-27. Current and helpful discussions on this material are available by K. Giles, " 'L' Tradition," in *DJG*, pp. 431-32, and F. W. Burnett, " 'M' Tradition," in *DJG*, pp. 511-12.

[40]This is a modified version of one suggested by John H. Reumann in his *Jesus in the Church's Gospel* (Philadelphia: Fortress, 1968).

[41]R. Stein, "What Is Redaktionsgeschichte?" *JBL* 83, no. 1 (1969): 46. For other descriptions of this discipline see any introductions to the New Testament, as well as Stephen Smalley, "Redaction Criticism," in *NTI*, pp. 181-95; G. R. Osborne, "Redaction Criticism," in *NTCI*, pp. 199-224; and G. R. Osborne, "Redaction Criticism," in *DJG*, pp. 662-69. All these essays have current and extensive bibliographies.

[42]Robert A. Guelich, "The Gospels: Portraits of Jesus and His Ministry," *JETS* 24, no. 3 (1981): 117-25.

[43]Osborne, "Redaction Criticism," pp. 199-224.

[44]W. Barnes Tatum, *In Quest of Jesus* (Atlanta: John Knox, 1982), p. 55. These rather simplistic comments on the purpose of the Gospels are intended to be illustrative only. N. T. Wright has a more expansive but creative way of presenting the Gospels as "stories" of Jesus, as a climax to Israel's story (*The New Testament and the People of God* [Minneapolis: Fortress, 1992], pp. 371-417). By consulting specialized monographs, commentaries and articles, one quickly realizes that there are many proposals and complexities on the theme, purpose, structure and so on of each Gospel.

[45]Osborne, "Redaction Criticism," p. 216. The appreciation of the Evangelists as theologians has led to a plethora of books and articles. Apart from those mentioned in the bibliographies of the sources already cited, others worth noting include Ralph P. Martin, *Mark: Evangelist and Theologian* (Grand Rapids, Mich.: Zondervan, 1973); I. Howard Marshall, *Luke: Historian and Theologian* (Grand Rapids, Mich.: Zondervan, 1971); David E. Aune, "The Gospels: Biography or Theology?" *BibRev* 6, no. 1 (1990): 14-21; Stephen Smalley, *John: Evangelist and Interpreter* (Grand Rapids, Mich.: Zondervan, 1978). One should not overlook the significance of communities in the formation of the tradition either. Cf. Krister Stendahl, *The School of St. Matthew*, 2d ed. (Philadelphia: Fortress, 1968); Alan Culpepper, *The Johannine School: An Evaluation of the Johannine-School Hypothesis Based on an Investigation of the Nature of Ancient Schools*, SBLDS 26 (Missoula, Mont.: Scholars Press, 1975).

[46]G. N. Stanton, *The Gospels and Jesus* (Oxford: Oxford University Press, 1991), pp. 102-3.

[47]Raymond Brown, *The Gospel According to John*, Anchor Bible 29 (New York: Doubleday, 1966), pp. xxxiv-xxxix; cf. also Brown's *The Community of the Beloved Disciple* (New York: Paulist, 1979); Helmut Koester, "The Johannine Circle," in his *Introduction to the New Testament* (Philadelphia: Fortress, 1980), 2:178-98; Rudolf Bultmann, *The Gospel of John* (Oxford: Blackwell, 1971); E. Haenchen, *A Commentary on the Gospel of John*, 2 vols., Hermeneia (Philadelphia: Fortress, 1984).

[48]Gerhard Friedrich, "εὐαγγέλλιον," in *TDNT*, 2:735.

[49]Relevant literature includes David E. Aune, *The New Testament in Its Literary Environment* (Philadelphia: Westminster, 1989); David E. Aune, ed., *Greco-Roman Literature and the New Testament: Selected Forms and Genres*, SBL Sources for Biblical Study 21 (Atlanta: Scholars Press, 1988); Aune, "Gospels: Biography or Theology?" pp. 14-21; Richard A. Burridge, *What Are the Gospels? A Comparison with Greco-Roman Biography*, SNTSMS 70 (Cambridge: Cambridge University Press, 1992); Albrecht Dihle, "The Gospels and Greek Biography," in *The Gospel and the Gospels*, ed. Peter Stuhlmacher (Grand Rapids, Mich.: Eerdmans, 1991), pp. 361-86; Robert A. Guelich, "The Gospel Genre," in *The Gospel and the Gospels*, ed. Peter Stuhlmacher (Grand Rapids, Mich.: Eerdmans, 1991), pp. 173-208; Robert Gundry, "Recent Investigations into the Literary Genre 'Gospel,' " in *NDNTS*, pp. 97-114; Larry Hurtado, "Gospel (Genre)," in *DJG*, pp. 276-82; Helmut Koester, "From the Kerygma-Gospel to Written Gospels," *NTS* 35 (1989): 361-81; Helmut Koester, "The Term 'Gospel,' " in *The Gospel and the Gospels*, ed. Peter Stuhlmacher (Grand Rapids, Mich.: Eerdmans, 1991), pp. 1-48; Charles H. Talbert, *What Is a Gospel? The Genre of the Canonical Gospels* (Philadelphia: Fortress, 1977); E. P. Sanders and Margaret Davies, "Genre and Purposes" and "The Genre of the First Gospel," in *Studying the Synoptic Gospels*, pp. 25-47, 252-98; Clyde Votaw, *The Gospels and Contemporary Biographies in the Greco-Roman World* (1915; reprint, Philadelphia: Fortress, 1970).

[50]Hurtado, "Gospel (Genre)," p. 279.

[51]See Guelich, "Gospel Genre," pp. 202-3.

[52]Martin, *New Testament Foundations*, 1:23.

[53]Craig L. Blomberg, "The Diversity of Literary Genres in the New Testament," in *NTCI*, p. 511.

[54]The issue of "understanding" the Gospels—and all biblical literature—goes beyond the scope of this study into the realm of interpretation. My purpose has been to consider *how* we got the text rather that to consider its meaning. Interested readers are encouraged to consult commentaries and/or specialized monographs on exegetical methods, exegesis and interpretation. Dictionary articles from the sources I have been using *(ABD, DJG, IDB, ISBE)* will introduce the reader to current trends in biblical studies such as historical, sociological, literary, rhetorical, narrative, reader-response and canonical criticism.

[55]Barclay, *Making of the Bible*, p. 75. See also Oscar Cullmann, "The Plurality of the Gospels as a Theological Problem in Antiquity," in *The Early Church* (Philadelphia: Westminster, 1956), pp. 37-54; Harry Gamble, "Canon," in *ABD*, 1:854-55.

[56]Some useful sources beyond those already mentioned include Kümmel, "The Formation of the Canon," in *Introduction to the New Testament*, pp. 475-510; W. Schneemelcher, "On the History of the New Testament Canon," in *New Testament Apocrypha*, rev. ed. (Louisville, Ky.: Westminster/John Knox, 1990); Charles B. Puskas, "Appendix A: The Formation of the New Testament Canon," in *An Introduction to the New Testament*

(Peabody, Mass.: Hendrickson, 1989), pp. 253-67; T. Donner, "Some Thoughts on the History of the New Testament Canon," *Themelios* 7, no. 3 (1982): 23-27. For a list of significant early church leaders see appendix II in this book.

[57]Helmut Koester, *Ancient Christian Gospels* (Philadelphia: Trinity Press, 1990), p. 33.

[58]F. F. Bruce, "New Light on the Origins of the New Testament Canon," in *NDNTS*, p. 8; also Harry Gamble, "The Canon of the New Testament," in *NTMI*, pp. 208-9.

[59]Bruce M. Metzger, *The Early Versions of the New Testament* (Oxford: Oxford University Press, 1977): Tatian probably "worked from four separate manuscripts, one for each of the Gospels, and, as he wove together phrases, now from this Gospel and now that, he would no doubt cross out those phrases in the manuscripts from which he was copying. Otherwise it is difficult to understand how he was able to combine so successfully phrases from four documents into a remarkable cento which reminds one of delicate filigree work" (pp. 11-12).

[60]Ibid., pp. 12-13.

[61]Harry Gamble, *The New Testament Canon* (Philadelphia: Fortress, 1985), pp. 30-31.

[62]Bruce M. Metzger, *The Canon of the New Testament: Its Origin, Development and Significance* (Oxford: University Press, 1987), pp. 115-16. Regarding extracanonical material in Tatian, Metzger notes, "On the whole, however, the amount of extra-canonical material that seems to have been present in Tatian's Diatessaron hardly justifies the opinion of some scholars that Tatian made extensive use of a fifth, apocryphal Gospel when he compiled his Harmony" (*Early Versions*, p. 36). Also see F. W. Beare, "Canon of the New Testament," in *IDB*, p. 527. Bruce cautions, "Let no one be taken in by the argument that Tatian would never have dared to deal so freely with documents recognized as canonical; in our day this very exercise has been undertaken not once but repeatedly by people who firmly believed not only in the canonicity of the four gospels but in their verbal inspiration" ("New Light," p. 9).

[63]Metzger, *Canon of the New Testament*, p. 154: "The Great Church by the time of Irenaeus had ceased to recognize any but the four Gospels, or rather as he puts it, one single gospel in four forms τὸ εὐαγγέλιον τετράμορφον [*to euangelion tetramorphon*]). . . . Thus for Irenaeus the Gospel canon is closed and its text is holy." H. Conzelmann and A. Lindemann, *Interpreting the New Testament* (Peabody, Mass.: Hendrickson, 1988), p. 6: "By the time of Irenaeus (c. A.D. 200), however, the paralleling of Matthew, Mark, Luke, and John was firmly established while their precise order remained fluid." F. F. Bruce confirms this opinion in *The Canon of Scripture* (Downers Grove, Ill.: InterVarsity Press, 1988), p. 175: "But the general impression given by his words is that the fourfold pattern of the gospel was by this time no innovation but so widely accepted that he can stress its cosmic appropriateness as though it were one of the facts of nature."

[64]Raymond Collins, *Introduction to the New Testament* (Garden City, N.Y.: Doubleday, 1983), p. 23; cf. also Metzger, *Canon of the New Testament*, pp. 301-4.

[65]For the text see Metzger, *Canon of the New Testament*, pp. 305-6. This translation is the best and most helpful one available because it includes numerals that indicate the lines of the original text and expansions enclosed in square brackets.

[66]Gamble, *New Testament Canon*, pp. 33-34.

[67]Beare, "Canon of the New Testament," p. 527; cf. also Metzger, *Canon of the New Testament*, p. 195; F. F. Bruce, "Some Thoughts on the Beginning of the New Testament Canon," *BJRL* 65 (1983): 50. The value of the Muratorian Canon depends upon an

early—that is, late-second-century—date (see part three for further discussion).
[68]Bruce, *Canon of Scripture,* p. 189.
[69]Ibid., p. 123.
[70]Cf. Metzger's cautious analysis of Gospel sayings in Ignatius (*Philadelphians* 8.2) and Polycarp (*Philippians* 6.3) in his *Canon of the New Testament,* pp. 48-49 and 62-63 respectively: he finds no evidence that these authors referred to the Gospels or epistles as "Scripture."
[71]Gamble, "Canon of the New Testament," p. 212, and *New Testament Canon,* p. 30; Lee M. McDonald, *The Formation of the Christian Biblical Canon* (Nashville: Abingdon, 1988), p. 84.

Part III: The Pauline Literature
[1]This would date his conversion to about A.D. 34-35. In addition to standard introductions to the New Testament, there are several significant works on the chronology of Paul, such as those by Robert Jewett, *A Chronology of Paul's Life* (Philadelphia: Fortress, 1979), and G. Lüdemann, *Paul, Apostle to the Gentiles: Studies in Chronology* (Philadelphia: Fortress, 1984).
[2]For a current evaluation of these statements, see Hans-Martin Schenke, "Four Problems in the Life of Paul Reconsidered," in *The Future of Christianity: Essays in Honor of Helmut Koester,* ed. Birger A. Pearson (Minneapolis: Fortress, 1991), pp. 319-28.
[3]Adolf Deissmann, *Light from the Ancient East* (1927; reprint, Grand Rapids, Mich.: Baker, 1978).
[4]W. Doty, *Letters in Primitive Christianity* (Philadelphia: Fortress, 1973), 26. On Deissmann, cf. E. Randolph Richards, "The 'Literary or Non-literary' (Deissmann) Debate: The Problem of Classifying the Letters of Paul," in *The Secretary in the Letters of Paul* (Tübingen: J. C. B. Mohr, 1991), app. G, pp. 211-16.
[5]Stanley K. Stowers, *Letter Writing in Greco-Roman Antiquity* (Philadelphia: Westminster, 1986); David E. Aune, *The New Testament in Its Literary Environment* (Philadelphia: Westminster, 1989); and Doty, *Letters*; also note the following: N. A. Dahl, "Letter," in *IDBSup,* pp. 538-41; J. S. Lown, "Epistle," in *ISBE,* 2:122-25; T. O'Brien, "Letters, Letter Forms," in *DPL,* pp. 550-53; Stanley K. Stowers, "Letters (Greek and Latin Letters)," in *ABD,* 3:290-93; John L. White, *Light from Ancient Letters* (Philadelphia: Fortress, 1986); John L. White, "Saint Paul and the Apostolic Letter Tradition," *CBQ* 45, no. 3 (1983): 433-44.
[6]Aune, *New Testament in Its Literary Environment,* p. 204.
[7]See Stanley K. Stowers, *The Diatribe and Paul's Letter to the Romans* (Chico, Calif.: Scholars, 1981).
[8]For example, A. Cameron, *Christianity and the Rhetoric of Empire: The Development of Christian Discourse,* Sather Classical Lectures 55 (Berkeley: University of California Press, 1991); Robert Jewett, *The Thessalonian Correspondence: Pauline Rhetoric and Millenarian Piety* (Philadelphia: Fortress, 1986); G. A. Kennedy, *The Art of Rhetoric in the Roman World* (Princeton, N.J.: Princeton University Press, 1972); Burton L. Mack, *Rhetoric and the New Testament* (Minneapolis: Fortress, 1990); A. J. Malherbe, " 'Seneca' on Paul as Letter Writer," in *The Future of Early Christianity,* ed. Birger Pearson (Minneapolis: Fortress, 1991), pp. 414-21; J. Smit, "The Genre of I Corinthians 13 in the Light of Classical Rhetoric," *NovT* 33, no. 3 (1991): 193-216; D. F. Watson, "The New Testament and Greco-Roman Rhetoric: A Bibliographical Update," *JETS* 33, no.

4 (1990): 513-24; D. F. Watson, ed., *Persuasive Artistry: Studies in New Testament Rhetoric in Honor of George A. Kennedy*, JSNT Supplement Series 50 (Sheffield, U.K.: JSOT Press, 1991).

[9]The parameters of "rhetorical criticism" exceed the purpose of this study. Readers are encouraged to consult the following: B. Fiore, "Rhetoric and Rhetorical Criticism (NT Rhetoric and Rhetorical Criticism)," in *ABD*, 5:715-19; G. W. Hansen, "Rhetorical Criticism," in *DPL*, pp. 822-26; R. Majercik, "Rhetoric and Rhetorical Criticism (Rhetoric and Oratory in the Greco-Roman World)," in *ABD*, 5:710-12; D. F. Watson, "Rhetorical Criticism," in *DJG*, pp. 698-701; The bibliographies in these brief articles will provide students with a deeper appreciation of the scope of research. Many critics follow the principles established by George A. Kennedy in his *New Testament Interpretation Through Rhetorical Criticism* (Chapel Hill: University of North Carolina Press, 1984).

[10]Credit for these insights belongs to Raymond F. Collins in his *The Birth of the New Testament* (New York: Crossroads, 1993).

[11]Quoted from Stowers, *Letter Writing*, 62-63. For other examples cf. C. K. Barrett, *New Testament Background: Selected Documents*, rev. ed. (San Francisco: Harper, 1989).

[12]The long-established views of Paul Schubert in his *Form and Function of the Pauline Thanksgivings* (Berlin: Töpelmann, 1939) have recently been challenged by Peter Arzt, "The 'Epistolary Introductory Thanksgiving' in the Papyri and in Paul," *NovT* 36, no. 1 (1994): 29-46.

[13]For lists of vices and virtues see Galatians 5:19-23; Ephesians 5:3-5; Colossians 3:5-15. Household rules *(Haustafeln)* are given in Ephesians 5:21—6:9; Colossians 3:18—4:1; Titus 2:1-10. There also are other moral exhortations such as one finds in Romans 12:9-13. For "words of the Lord" in Paul cf. Calvin Roetzel, *The Letters of Paul*, 3d ed. (Louisville, Ky.: Westminster/John Knox, 1991), pp. 76-79. My purpose does not permit the full development of the above material. Excellent resources are available in George E. Cannon, *The Use of Traditional Materials in Colossians* (Macon, Ga.: Mercer, 1983); A. M. Hunter, *Paul and His Predecessors* (Philadelphia: Westminster, 1961); Eduard Lohse, *The Formation of the New Testament* (Nashville: Abingdon, 1972); Ralph P. Martin, *New Testament Foundations*, rev. ed. (Grand Rapids, Mich.: Eerdmans, 1985), 2:248-75; Ralph P. Martin, *Worship in the Early Church* (Grand Rapids, Mich.: Eerdmans, 1974); Roetzel, *Letters of Paul*, pp. 72-82; E. Schweizer, "Traditional Ethical Patterns in the Pauline and Post-Pauline Letters and Their Development [Lists of Vices and House-Tables]," in *Text and Interpretation: Studies in the New Testament Presented to Matthew Black*, ed. E. Best and R. M. Wilson (Cambridge: Cambridge University Press, 1979), pp. 195-200. Richards uses the term "preformed material" or "preformed traditions" (*Secretary in the Letters of Paul*, pp. 158-59).

[14]Roetzel, *Letters of Paul*, p. 73.

[15]W. Schmithals, *Paul and the Gnostics* (Nashville: Abingdon, 1972), pp. 253-54.

[16]For further discussions see G. L. Bahnsen, "Autographs, Amanuenses and Restricted Inspiration," *EvQ* 45 (1973): 100-110; Gordon J. Bahr, "Paul and Letter Writing in the First Century," *CBQ* 28 (1966): 465-77; Gordon J. Bahr, "The Subscriptions in the Pauline Letters," *JBL* 87 (1968): 27-41; P. J. J. Botha, "Letter Writing and Oral Communication in Antiquity: Suggested Implications for the Interpretation of Paul's Letter to the Galatians," *Scriptura* 42 (1992): 17-34; Richard N. Longenecker, "Ancient Amanuenses and the Pauline Epistles," in *NDNTS*, pp. 281-97; J. Murphy-O'Connor,

"Paul the Letter-Writer," *Revue biblique* 100, no. 1 (1993): 151-53; Richards, *Secretary in the Letters of Paul*; E. Iliff Robson, "Composition and Dictation in New Testament Books," *JTS* 18 (1917): 288-301.

[17]See Richards's extensive study, *Secretary in the Letters of Paul*, especially pp. 23-67.

[18]Ibid., p. 201.

[19]For a general description of this hypothesis see Arthur G. Patzia, "The Deutero-Pauline Hypothesis," *EvQ* 52, no. 1 (1980): 27-42. Support for this approach includes Kurt Aland, "The Problem of Anonymity and Pseudonymity in Christian Literature of the First Two Centuries," in his *The Authority and Integrity of the New Testament* (London: SPCK, 1965), pp. 1-13; Richard Bauckham, "Pseudo-Apostolic Letters," *JBL* 107 (1988): 469-94; Raymond F. Collins, *Letters That Paul Did Not Write* (Wilmington, Del.: Glazier, 1988); L. R. Donelson, *Pseudepigraphy and Ethical Argument in the Pastoral Epistles*, Hermeneutische Untersuchungen zur Theologie 22 (Tübingen: J. C. B. Mohr/Paul Siebeck, 1986); J. C. Fenton, "Pseudonymity in the New Testament," *Theology* 58 (1955): 51-56; David Meade, *Pseudonymity and Canon* (Grand Rapids, Mich.: Eerdmans, 1986); Bruce M. Metzger, "Literary Forgeries and Canonical Pseudepigrapha," *JBL* 91 (1972): 3-24; M. Rist, "Pseudepigraphy and the Early Christians," in *Studies in New Testament and Early Christian Literature*, ed. David E. Aune (Leiden, Netherlands: Brill, 1972), pp. 3-24.

[20]For arguments supporting these views see F. F. Bruce, *The Canon of Scripture* (Downers Grove, Ill.: InterVarsity Press, 1988), p. 261; D. A. Carson, Douglas J. Moo and Leon Morris, *An Introduction to the New Testament* (Grand Rapids, Mich.: Zondervan, 1992), pp. 367-71; E. Earle Ellis, "Pseudonymity and Canonicity of New Testament Documents," in *Worship, Theology and Ministry in the Early Church* (Sheffield, U.K.: JSOT Press, 1992), pp. 212-24; C. Gempf, "Pseudonymity and the New Testament," *Themelios* 17, no. 2 (1992): 8-10; Donald Guthrie, "Epistolary Pseudepigraphy," in his *New Testament Introduction*, rev. ed. (Downers Grove, Ill.: InterVarsity Press, 1990), pp. 1011-28; Thomas D. Lea, "The Early Christian View of Pseudepigraphic Writings," *JETS* 27 (1984): 65-75; Thomas D. Lea, "Pseudonymity in the New Testament," in *NTCI*, pp. 535-59.

[21]On P[46] see following discussion.

[22]See most commentaries for this type of reconstruction as well as N. A. Dahl, "The Particularity of the Pauline Epistles as a Problem in the Ancient Church," in *Neotestamentica et Patristica: Eine Freundesgabe Herrn Prof. Dr. Oscar Cullmann zu seinem 60 Geburtstag*, NovTSup 6 (Leiden, Netherlands: Brill, 1962), pp. 261-71; Robert Jewett, "The Redaction of 1 Corinthians and the Trajectory of the Pauline School," *JAAR* 46 (1978): 398-444; J. Murphy-O'Connor, "Co-authorship in the Corinthian Correspondence," *Revue biblique* 100, no. 4 (1993): 562-79.

[23]The most extensive study devoted to this issue of Romans is by Harry Gamble, *The Textual History of the Letter to the Romans* (Grand Rapids, Mich.: Eerdmans, 1977). For a current discussion see Norman R. Petersen, "On the Ending(s) to Paul's Letter to Rome," in *The Future of Early Christianity* (Minneapolis: Fortress, 1991), pp. 337-47.

[24]Cf. most commentaries; also David E. Garland, "The Composition and Unity of Philippians: Some Neglected Literary Factors," *NovT* 27 (1985): 141-73.

[25]See Arthur G. Patzia, *Ephesians, Colossians, Philemon* (Peabody, Mass.: Hendrickson, 1991), pp. 145-46; A. T. Lincoln, *Ephesians* (Waco, Tex.: Word, 1991), pp. 1-4.

[26]Victor Paul Furnish, "Pauline Studies," in *NTMI*, p. 325. For further study, cf. M. C.

Parsons, "Appendices in the New Testament," *Themelios* 17, no. 2 (1992): 11-13; W. O. Walker, "Text-Critical Evidence for Interpolations in the Letters of Paul," *CBQ* 50, no. 4 (1988): 622-63; W. O. Walker, "The Burden of Proof in Identifying Interpolations in the Pauline Letters," *NTS* 33, no. 4 (1987): 610-18.

[27]R. M. Grant suggests that Clement knew 1 Corinthians, Romans, Galatians, Philippians and Ephesians and "perhaps has a definite allusion to Hebrews" (*The Formation of the New Testament*, [London: Hutchinson, 1965], pp. 81-83). Martin believes that "at best" Clement knew only four of Paul's letters (*New Testament Foundations*, 2:277).

[28]Cf. C. L. Mitton, *The Formation of the Pauline Corpus of Letters* (London: Epworth, 1955).

[29]Cf. 1 Thessalonians 5:27. Thus M. Luther Stirewalt, "Paul's Evaluation of Letter Writing," in *Search the Scriptures*, ed. J. M. Myers (Leiden, Netherlands: Brill, 1969), p. 189: "Paul was surrounded by a large number of people through whom he remained in contact with the churches. There were men like Titus, trusted ambassadors, special representatives, full time ministers; there were men of less prominence like Tychicus and Tertius, perhaps limited in time or talents, whose services Paul used. There were also visitors from the congregations, devoted to the work, who on returning home could easily deliver a letter. Such men were Onesimus of Colossae, Epaphroditus of Philippi, Stephanas and Fortunatus and Achaicus of Corinth."

[30]L. Mowry, "The Early Circulation of Paul's Letters," *JBL* 63 (1944): 73-86; Jack Finegan, "The Original Form of the Pauline Collections," *HTR* 49 (1956): 85-104; L. Hartman, "On Reading Others' Letters," *HTR* 79, nos. 1-3 (1986): 137-46; also G. Zuntz, *The Text of the Epistles: A Disquisition upon the Corpus Paulinum* (London: Oxford University Press), pp. 278-79; David Trobisch, *Die Entstehung der Paulusbriefesammlung* (Göttingen, Germany: Vandenhoeck & Ruprecht, 1989); C. F. D. Moule, *The Birth of the New Testament*, 3d rev. ed. (San Francisco: Harper, 1981), p. 263.

[31]So David Trobisch, *Paul's Letter Collection* (Minneapolis: Fortress, 1994).

[32]See part four for similar possibilities of a Johannine School and Petrine Circle.

[33]Patzia, "Deutero-Pauline Hypothesis"; H.-M. Schenke, "Das Weiterwirken des Paulus und die Pflege seines Erbs durch die Paulusschule," *NTS* 21 (1975): 505-18.

[34]Bruce, *Canon of Scripture*, pp. 129-30.

[35]E. J. Goodspeed was professor of New Testament at the University of Chicago for about forty years. The following summary is drawn from two of his main works: *The Formation of the New Testament*, 2d ed. (Chicago: University of Chicago Press, 1927), and *Christianity Goes to Press* (New York: Macmillan, 1940).

[36]So named by Guthrie, *New Testament Introduction*, p. 647.

[37]Zuntz, *Text of the Epistles*, p. 276.

[38]Richards, *Secretary in the Letters of Paul*, p. 191.

[39]E. Earle Ellis, "Pastoral Letters," in *DPL*, p. 660. Richards's book is a revision of a Ph.D. dissertation written under Ellis's supervision at Southwestern Baptist Theological Seminary in Fort Worth, Texas.

[40]Trobisch, *Entstehung der Paulusbriefsammlung*.

[41]Trobisch, *Paul's Letter Collection*.

[42]Bruce, *Canon of Scripture*, p. 130; Theodor Zahn, according to Bruce M. Metzger, *The Canon of the New Testament: Its Origin, Development and Significance* (Oxford: University Press, 1987), p. 23; F. W. Beare, "Canon of the New Testament," in *IDB*, 1:520-32.

[43]Zuntz, *Text of the Epistles*, p. 14.

[44]Harry Gamble, "The Pauline Corpus and the Early Christian Book," in *Paul and the*

Legacies of Paul, ed. William S. Babcock (Dallas: Southern Methodist University Press, 1990), pp. 265-80.

[45]Ibid., pp. 273-74.

[46]Cf. John J. Clabeaux, *A Lost Edition of the Letters of Paul: A Reassessment of the Text of the Pauline Corpus Attested by Marcion*, CBQMS 21 (Washington, D.C.: Catholic Biblical Association of America, 1989); J. Knox, *Marcion and the New Testament* (Chicago: University of Chicago Press, 1942), especially "The Pauline Corpus," pp. 39-76.

[47]Bruce M. Metzger, *Manuscripts of the Greek Bible* (Oxford: Oxford University Press, 1981), p. 64.

[48]Both Bruce (*Canon of Scripture*, p. 130) and Metzger (*Canon of the New Testament*, p. 259) confidently affirm that Paul's letters circulated only *as a collection* from the beginning of the second century. This means that with the possible exception of Clement of Rome, all subsequent collectors, including Marcion, worked from an early *corpus Paulinum*. Harry Gamble dismisses the idea of a single archetypal corpus prior to the second century as "untenable" ("The Redaction of the Pauline Letters and the Formation of the Pauline Corpus," *JBL* 94 [1975]: 415; "The Canon of the New Testament," in *NTMI*, p. 208), and Kurt Aland calls the idea a "fantasy of wishful thinking" (from Metzger, *Canon of the New Testament*, pp. 260-61, quoting a German article by Aland, "Die Entstehung des Corpus Paulinum"). For detailed discussion of a primitive "archetype" of the Pauline corpus and P^{46} see Zuntz, *Text of the Epistles*, especially pp. 14-23.

[49]For text and translation cf. Metzger, *Canon of the New Testament*, pp. 305-7.

[50]A. C. Sundberg, "Canon Muratori: A Fourth Century List," *HTR* 66 (1973): 1-41. See similar positions in H. von Campenhausen, *The Formation of the Christian Bible* (Philadelphia: Fortress, 1972), and Lee M. McDonald, *The Formation of the Christian Biblical Canon* (Nashville: Abingdon, 1988).

[51]Bruce, *Canon of Scripture*, p. 158, n. 2.

[52]Metzger, *Canon of the New Testament*, p. 191.

[53]E. Ferguson, "Canon Muratori: Date and Provenance," *Studia Patristica* 18 (1982): 677-83.

[54]Metzger, *Canon of the New Testament*, p. 194.

[55]McDonald, *Formation of the Christian Biblical Canon*, p. 139.

[56]Cf. lines 73-80 from Metzger's translation, *Canon of the New Testament*, p. 307.

[57]Bruce, *Canon of Scripture*, p. 220; cf. C. Anderson, "The Epistle to the Hebrews and the Pauline Letter Corpus," *HTR* 59 (1966): 429-38.

Part IV: Other New Testament Literature

[1]Students should consult the standard introductions to the New Testament for the critical questions relating to authorship, date, purpose, etc.

[2]David E. Aune, *The New Testament in Its Literary Environment* (Philadelphia: Westminster, 1989), p. 77.

[3]New appreciation for the historical reliability and accuracy of Luke's writings has been evident in many publications by F. F. Bruce. See also Colin J. Hemer, *The Book of Acts in the Setting of Hellenistic History* (Tübingen: J. C. B. Mohr, 1989); Bruce W. Winter and Andrew D. Clarke, eds., *The Book of Acts in Its First Century Setting*, vol. 1 (Grand Rapids, Mich.: Eerdmans, 1993).

[4]Scholars continue to evaluate Luke as historian, theologian and literary critic in

numerous commentaries, monographs, and journal and dictionary articles. In fact, a bibliography of studies on Luke-Acts during the last fifteen years would fill in a sizable book. For brief introductory and survey purposes I recommend I. H. Marshall, *The Acts of the Apostles* (Sheffield, U.K.: Sheffield Academic Press, 1992); M. A. Powell, *What Are They Saying About Acts?* (Mahwah, N.J.: Paulist, 1991); Charles H. Talbert, "Luke-Acts," in *NTMI*, pp. 297-320.

[5]Aune, *New Testament in Its Literary Environment*, p. 124. For a detailed discussion of Luke's sources, see Hemer, *Book of Acts in the Setting*, pp. 308-64.

[6]Other possibilities include (1) that Luke just decided to publish Acts at that point in history, c. A.D. 62; (2) that the readers already knew about Paul's fate; (3) that Luke intended to write a third volume; (4) that Luke was more interested in Paul's mission than in his personal fate; and (5) that Luke did not want to publicize Paul's release from prison in case it might jeopardize his future missionary activity.

[7]W. G. Kümmel, for example, uses the heading "The Letter to the Hebrews and the Catholic Letters" in his *Introduction to the New Testament*, rev. ed. (Nashville: Abingdon, 1973), p. 387. By necessity, my discussion of these particular letters will focus on their literary genre, theories of composition and canonicity rather than the historical-critical issues. Where questions of date, authorship, purpose, etc., arise, readers are advised to consult reputable introductions to the New Testament and/or serious commentaries on each book (a comparison of Kümmel with Donald Guthrie or with D. A. Carson, Douglas Moo and Leon Morris often will reveal opposite positions on certain issues). Hebrews will be discussed separately, and 1, 2 and 3 John will form part of a section on Johannine literature rather than under the rubric of "Catholic Letters."

[8]Harry Gamble, "The Canon of the New Testament," in *NTMI*, p. 212.

[9]Cf. Jeffrey S. Siker, "The Canonical Status of the Catholic Epistles in the Syriac New Testament," *JTS* 38 (1987): 311-40.

[10]See introductions to the New Testament for questions relating to how this "uneducated and ordinary" man (Acts 4:13) could produce such a literary masterpiece. For the most part commentators consider 1 Peter a pseudonymous writing, perhaps written by a Petrine disciple toward the close of the first century A.D.

[11]Peter Davids, however, finds the above theories more intriguing than convincing. For him, "I Peter is formally simply a Christian letter from a leader to distant churches, just as Paul's letters were, although Peter does not appear to have founded or even necessarily visited the churches in question." (See *The First Epistle of Peter* [Grand Rapids, Mich.: Eerdmans, 1990], p. 14.)

[12]Donald Guthrie, *New Testament Introduction*, rev. ed. (Downers Grove, Ill.: InterVarsity Press, 1990), p. 805.

[13]Ibid., p. 841. Guthrie reaches this conclusion while acknowledging that the external evidence for Petrine authorship is not strongly favorable in the case of this epistle (p. 809). Petrine authorship is strongly defended by D. A. Carson, Douglas J. Moo and Leon Morris, *An Introduction to the New Testament* (Grand Rapids, Mich.: Zondervan, 1992), pp. 433-40.

[14]Richard J. Bauckham, *Jude, 2 Peter*, WBC 9 (Waco, Tex.: Word, 1983), pp. 159-62; cf. also D. Farkasfalvy, "The Ecclesial Setting of Pseudepigraphy in Second Peter and Its Role in the Formation of the Canon," *Second Century* 5, no. 1 (1985-1986): 3-29.

[15]Ralph P. Martin, *New Testament Foundations*, rev. ed. (Grand Rapids, Mich.: Eerdmans, 1985), 2:387.

[16]Ibid. Also Kümmel, *Introduction to the New Testament*, pp. 433-34.

[17]Bauckham, *Jude, 2 Peter*, pp. 14-15.

[18]Kümmel, *Introduction to the New Testament*, pp. 427-29.

[19]Martin, *New Testament Foundations*, pp. 358, 364. He notes 60 verbal imperatives in 108 verses. Kümmel (*Introduction to the New Testament*, p. 404) describes James as "a chain of individual admonitions of larger and smaller compass, of groups of sayings and short saying which more or less randomly follow one another."

[20]Peter Davids, *James*, NIBC (Peabody, Mass.: Hendrickson, 1989), p. 7.

[21]See Martin Webber's section, "The Role of James in Ecclesiastical Circles," in Ralph P. Martin, *James*, WBC 48 (Waco, Tex.: Word, 1988), pp. xlvii-lxi. Webber traces the letter from the early second to the late fourth century as well as discussing its canonical status.

[22]Ibid., p. lxi.

[23]See Aune, *New Testament in Its Literary Environment*, p. 213; Martin, *New Testament Foundations*, 2:348.

[24]Cf. a recent survey by Philip E. Hughes, "Hebrews," in *NTMI*, pp. 351-70.

[25]Aune, *New Testament in Its Literary Environment*, p. 212.

[26]Donald Hagner, *Hebrews*, NIBC (Peabody, Mass.: Hendrickson, 1990), pp. 12-13.

[27]Kümmel, *Introduction to the New Testament*, p. 393; also pp. 500-501. On differences in the development of the canon, see Bruce M. Metzger, "Development of the Canon in the East" and "Development of the Canon in the West," in *The Canon of the New Testament: Its Origin, Development and Significance* (Oxford: Oxford University Press, 1987), pp. 113-64, 209-47.

[28]Raymond Brown, *The Gospel According to John*, Anchor Bible 29-29A (New York: Doubleday, 1966, 1970), provides the most thorough documentation on traditions about John. Additional sources for understanding the composition of the Johannine literature include Raymond Brown, *The Community of the Beloved Disciple* (New York: Paulist, 1979); R. A. Culpepper, *The Johannine School: An Evaluation of the Johannine-School Hypothesis Based on an Investigation of the Nature of Ancient Schools*, SBLDS 26 (Missoula, Mont.: Scholars Press, 1975); D. Moody Smith, *John* (Philadelphia: Fortress, 1981); Helmut Koester, "The Johannine Circle," in *Introduction to the New Testament* (Philadelphia: Fortress, 1980), 2:178-98; G. Strecker, "Die Anfänge der johanneischen Schule," *NTS* 32, no. 1 (1986): 31-47.

[29]For additional comments I recommend Stephen S. Smalley, *1, 2 and 3 John*, WBC 51 (Waco, Tex.: Word, 1984); I. Howard Marshall, *The Epistles of John* (Grand Rapids, Mich.: Eerdmans, 1978).

[30]For further development of epistolary qualities, cf. Charles B. Puskas, *An Introduction to the New Testament* (Peabody, Mass.: Hendrickson, 1989), pp. 152-53; George R. Beasley-Murray, *Revelation* (Grand Rapids, Mich.: Eerdmans, 1981), pp. 12-29; Robert Wall, *Revelation*, NIBC (Peabody, Mass.: Hendrickson, 1991), pp. 12-25.

[31]Beasley-Murray, *Revelation*, p. 64; also George E. Ladd, *A Commentary on Revelation* (Grand Rapids, Mich.: Eerdmans, 1972), p. 30; R. H. Mounce, *The Book of Revelation* (Grand Rapids, Mich.: Eerdmans, 1977).

[32]Wall, *Revelation*, p. 27. Extensive summaries on the history of Revelation in the early church and its claim to canonical status are provided by Wall in *Revelation*, 25-32;

Mounce, "Circulation and Reception in the Early Church," in *Book of Revelation*, p. 36-39.

[33]These are approximate percentages based on word counts from the Greek text (corrected), *GNT*[3].

Part V: The Criteria of Canonicity

[1]For the historical development of this concept see H. W. Beyer, "κανών," in *TDNT*, 3:596-602; Bruce M. Metzger, "History of the Word Κανών," in *The Canon of the New Testament: Its Origin, Development and Significance* (Oxford: Oxford University Press, 1987), app. 1, pp. 289-93.

[2]F. W. Beare, "Canon of the New Testament," in *IDB*, 1:522. See also E. Best, "Scripture, Tradition and the Canon of the New Testament," *BJRL* 61 (1978-1979): 258-89; B. S. Childs, *The New Testament as Canon: An Introduction* (Philadelphia: Fortress, 1985).

[3]Quoted from F. F. Bruce, *The Canon of Scripture* (Downers Grove, Ill.: InterVarsity Press, 1988), p. 247.

[4]Especially James D. G. Dunn, *Unity and Diversity in the New Testament* (Philadelphia: Westminster, 1977); John Reumann, *Variety and Unity in New Testament Thought* (Oxford: Oxford University Press, 1991).

[5]Metzger, *Canon of the New Testament*, p. 287; see also J. A. Brooks, "Clement of Alexandria as a Witness to the Development of the New Testament Canon," *Second Century* 9, no. 1 (1992): 41-55.

[6]Krister Stendahl, "The Apocalypse of John and the Epistles of Paul in the Muratorian Fragment," in *Current Issues in New Testament Interpretation*, ed. W. Klassen and G. F. Snyder (New York: Harper, 1962), p. 243. Metzger attempts to clarify the interdependence between inspiration and canonicity when he writes, "Thus, while it is true that the Biblical authors were inspired by God, this does not mean that inspiration is a criterion of canonicity. A writing is not canonical because the author was inspired, but rather an author is considered to be inspired because what he has written is recognized as canonical, that is, is recognized as authoritative in the Church" (*Canon of the New Testament*, p. 257).

[7]Metzger, *Canon of the New Testament*, p. 256.

[8]Shaye J. D. Cohen poses a similar question when he discusses the special authoritative status of the Tanak, the Hebrew Scriptures: "Which is the cause and which the effect? Did the Tanak's status as the revealed or inspired word of God confer on it unusual authority, or did the Tanak's special authority engender the belief in its divinity? The answer is probably something between the two" (*From the Maccabees to the Mishnah* [Philadelphia: Westminster, 1987], p. 179). Cohen reckons that over one-half of the Hebrew canon consists of works whose authors do not claim to be inspired by God (*From the Maccabees*, p. 181). For further reading see Paul J. Achtemeier, *The Inspiration of Scripture: Problems and Proposals* (Philadelphia: Westminster, 1980); E. Kahlin, "The Inspired Community: A Glance at Canon History," *Concordia Theological Monthly* 42 (1971): 541-49; G. I. Mavrodes, "The Inspiration of Autographs," *EvQ* 41 (1969): 19-29; T. A. Hoffman, "Inspiration, Normativeness, Canonicity and the Unique Sacred Character of the Bible," *CBQ* 44, no. 3 (1982): 447-68.

[9]Metzger, *Canon of the New Testament*, p. 239. Also see Roy W. Hoover, "How the Books of the New Testament Were Chosen," *BibRev* 9, no. 2 (1993): 44-47; and the tables in appendixes III, IV and V in this book.

[10]See Metzger, "Questions Concerning the Canon Today," in *Canon of the New Testament*, pp. 267-88.

[11]Bruce, *Canon of Scripture*, p. 250.

[12]Metzger notes eight sequences differing from the canonical order (*Canon of the New Testament*, p. 296).

[13]See Scot McKnight, "Source Criticism," in *NTCI*, pp. 141-42. Further discussion can be found in D. Farkasfalvy, "The Presbyters' Witness on the Order of the Gospels as Reported by Clement of Alexandria," *CBQ* 54, no. 2 (1992): 260-70; and Bernard Orchard and Harold Riley, *The Order of the Synoptics: Why Three Gospels?* (Macon, Ga.: Mercer University Press, 1987), especially pp. 111-226.

[14]E. J. Goodspeed, *The Formation of the New Testament*, 2d ed. (Chicago: University of Chicago Press, 1927), p. 35.

[15]Bruce, *Canon of Scripture*, p. 289.

[16]Bruce M. Metzger, *The Text of the New Testament*, 2d ed. (Oxford: Oxford University Press, 1968), p. 49. In his *Canon of the New Testament* Metzger lists nine different combinations of the Gospels (pp. 296-97).

[17]H. Conzelmann and A. Lindemann, *Interpreting the New Testament* (Peabody, Mass.: Hendrickson, 1988), pp. 6-7.

[18]Bruce, *Canon of Scripture*, p. 206.

[19]William Barclay, *The Making of the Bible* (Nashville: Abingdon, 1961), p. 82. For additional comments on Acts cf. Mikeal Parsons, "Canonical Criticism," in *NTCI*, pp. 280-84.

[20]See previous discussion, part three.

[21]Using Metzger's count in *Canon of the New Testament*, p. 298.

[22]David Trobisch's idea that Ephesians is an appendix to an authorized literary unit of Romans, 1 and 2 Corinthians and Galatians which Paul personally edited and prepared for publication warrants further scrutiny. If Paul is responsible for such an "authorized recension," it is still not clear how or why Ephesians serves as an appendix to these letters (*Paul's Letter Collection* [Minneapolis: Fortress, 1994], p. 54).

[23]Metzger, *Canon of the New Testament*, pp. 295-96.

[24]For a brief but excellent history on the position of Hebrews in ancient manuscripts and lists see Bruce M. Metzger, *A Textual Commentary on the Greek New Testament* (New York: United Bible Societies, 1971), pp. 661-62. Metzger credits most of his information to an article by W. H. P. Hatch, "The Position of Hebrews in the Canon of the New Testament," *HR* 29 (1936): 135-55.

[25]Metzger, *Canon of the New Testament*, p. 295.

[26]Beare, "Canon of the New Testament," p. 529. Bruce responds to this idea as a possibility ("Some Thoughts on the Beginning of the New Testament Canon," *BJRL* 65 [1983]: 49). See also the discussion by Harry Gamble, "The Pauline Corpus and the Early Christian Book," in *Paul and the Legacies of Paul*, ed. William S. Babcock (Dallas: Southern Methodist University Press, 1990).

[27]Bruce, *Canon of Scripture*, p. 246; Metzger, *Canon of the New Testament*, p. 242, n. 27.

Part VI: Writing, Copying and Transmitting the New Testament Manuscripts

[1]Donald J. Wiseman, "Books in the Ancient Near East and in the Old Testament," *CHB*, 1:37.

[2]Cf. "Writing in Biblical Times," in J. B. Gabel and C. B. Wheeler, *The Bible as Literature:*

An Introduction (New York: Oxford University Press, 1986), app. 2, pp. 272-80; T. C. Skeat, "Early Christian Book-Production: Papyri and Manuscripts," in *CHB*, 2:54-79; André Lemaire, "Writing and Writing Materials," in *ABD*, 6:999-1008.

[3]For an English translation and commentary on these texts see J. M. Robinson's *The Nag Hammadi Library* (San Francisco: Harper & Row, 1981).

[4]This list in the *GNT*[4] follows that of Kurt Aland and Barbara Aland in *The Text of the New Testament*, 2d ed. (Grand Rapids, Mich.: Eerdmans, 1989), pp. 96-102.

[5]This *GNT*[4] column "indicates only the contents of the manuscripts which are used in this edition" (p. 6). For further descriptions see Aland and Aland, *Text of the New Testament*, pp. 96-102.

[6]See the helpful discussion in Bruce M. Metzger, *Manuscripts of the Greek Bible* (Oxford: Oxford University Press, 1981), pp. 18-19. J. Harold Greenlee calculates that "more than fifty Greek N.T. mss. of the tenth century and earlier are palimpsests" (*Introduction to New Testament Textual Criticism*, [Grand Rapids, Mich.: Eerdmans, 1954], p. 26); Bruce M. Metzger lists fifty-two of them with their numbers in *The Text of the New Testament*, 2d ed. (Oxford: Oxford University Press, 1968), p. 12, n. 1.

[7]J. Harold Greenlee, *Scribes, Scrolls and Scripture* (Grand Rapids, Mich.: Eerdmans, 1964), pp. 9-10.

[8]Jack Finegan, *Encountering New Testament Manuscripts* (Grand Rapids, Mich.: Eerdmans, 1974), p. 25.

[9]"The Grab Bag," *San Francisco Chronicle*, August 13, 1989.

[10]Metzger, *Text of the New Testament*, p. 67. The Alands calculate that a good-sized flock of fifty or sixty sheep or goats was required for an average-sized manuscript of New Testament writings (Aland and Aland, *Text of the New Testament*), p. 27.

[11]William Barclay, *The Making of the Bible* (Nashville: Abingdon, 1961), p. 50.

[12]Ibid., p. 46.

[13]See Metzger, *Manuscripts of the Greek Bible*, pp. 17-18, for interesting details.

[14]F. F. Bruce, *The Canon of Scripture* (Downers Grove, Ill.: InterVarsity Press, 1988), p. 214.

[15]Aland and Aland, *Text of the New Testament*, p. 76; Metzger, *Text of the New Testament*, pp. 6-7; E. J. Goodspeed, *Christianity Goes to Press* (New York: Macmillan, 1940), pp. 67-75; Harry Gamble, "The Pauline Corpus and the Early Christian Book," in *Paul and the Legacies of Paul*, ed. William S. Babcock (Dallas: Southern Methodist University Press, 1990); Karl Donfried, "Paul as Σκηνοποιός and the Use of the Codex in Early Christianity," in *Christus Bezeugen: Festschrift für Wolfgang Trilling zum 65 Geburtstag*, ed. Karl Kertelge, Trautgot Holtz and Claus-Peter März (Leipzig: St. Benno-Verlag, 1989), pp. 249-56.

[16]Gamble, "Pauline Corpus and the Early Christian Book," pp. 271-80. Gamble and Donfried both provide extensive bibliographies on the subject.

[17]According to Metzger, estimates suggest a 44 percent saving in the cost of papyrus when one used the codex format (*Text of the New Testament*, p. 261).

[18]Ibid., p. 6; cf. Peter Katz, "The Early Christians' Use of Codices Instead of Rolls," *JTS* 44 (1945): 63-65; and I. M. Resnick, "The Codex in Early Jewish and Christian Communities," *Journal of Religious Hisotry* 17, no. 1 (1992): 1-17.

[19]Donfried, "Paul as Σκηνοποιός," pp. 254-56.

[20]Greenlee, *Scribes, Scrolls and Scripture*, p. 63.

[21]Cf. Metzger, *Text of the New Testament*, pp. 42-46; also *The Codex Sinaiticus and the Codex*

Alexandrinus (London: British Museum, 1955), for text and illustrations; Aland and Aland, *Text of the New Testament,* pp. 103-28.

[22]Codex Sinaiticus is the only uncial manuscript containing *all* the books of the New Testament.

[23]Currently, according to Aland and Aland, there are 2,812 (*Text of the New Testament,* p. 128). For a sample, including number, contents and date, see *GNT*[4], pp. 16-18.

[24]The final sigma (C) in this uncial contraction is called a lunate sigma because of the lunate, or crescent, shape. Only later did the letter evolve into the form Σ, better known from modern printed versions of the Greek New Testament.

[25]Metzger, *Manuscripts of the Greek Bible,* p. 12.

[26]Ibid., p. 41.

[27]D. Ewert, *From Ancient Tablets to Modern Translations: A General Introduction to the Bible* (Grand Rapids, Mich.: Zondervan, 1983), 138.

[28]Metzger, *Manuscripts of the Greek Bible,* p. 41.

[29]Ibid., pp. 41-42. For other ancient systems and aids, see pp. 42-43; and Finegan, *Encountering New Testament Manuscripts,* pp. 34-35.

[30]Metzger, *Manuscripts of the Greek Bible,* pp. 43-46.

[31]The implications of this for the reconstruction and study of the New Testament will be discussed below. This does not mean that we minimize the significance of the earlier papyri, even though no single one contains the entire New Testament.

[32]Metzger, *Text of the New Testament,* p. 14.

[33]Ibid., pp. 14-15.

[34]Ibid., pp. 18-19.

[35]"From it is derived the word 'stichometry,' for the science of the measurement of books" (Finegan, *Encountering the New Testament Manuscripts,* p. 39).

[36]Cf. Metzger, *Manuscripts of the Greek Bible,* p. 39, for counts and illustrations from certain manuscripts. On the number of stichoi for the Pauline letters see David E. Aune, *The New Testament in Its Literary Environment* (Philadelphia: Westminster, 1989), pp. 204-5. Also Barclay, *Making of the Bible,* p. 46. Students interested in other literary devices used to assist readers of ancient manuscripts should read Metzger's discussion of "colometry," the arrangement of the text according to sense, thus enabling the reader to make correct inflections and proper pauses in the public reading of Scripture (*Text of the New Testament,* pp. 29-30).

[37]Aland and Aland, *Text of the New Testament,* p. 163. For a brief list of important lectionaries see *GNT*[4], pp. 21-22.

[38]Aland and Aland, *Text of the New Testament,* p. 166-67.

[39]Ibid., p. 52.

[40]Ibid., pp. 53, 68.

[41]Cf. Metzger, *Text of the New Testament,* pp. 67-86, and his appendix, pp. 269-76; also his *The Early Versions of the New Testament* (Oxford: Oxford University Press, 1977); Aland and Aland, *Text of the New Testament,* pp. 185-221; Arthur Vööbus, *Early Versions of the New Testament: Manuscript Studies* (Stockholm: Estonian Theological Society in Exile, 1954).

[42]Metzger, *Text of the New Testament,* p. 67, n. 3.

[43]Ibid., p. 68.

[44]Aland and Aland, *Text of the New Testament,* p. 190; for a thorough history of the Syriac texts cf. Metzger, *Early Versions of the New Testament,* pp. 4-98.

[45]Aland and Aland, *Text of the New Testament*, p. 183.

[46]For detailed discussion of the significance and character of Latin versions cf. Metzger, *Early Versions of the New Testament*, pp. 285-374.

[47]Eldon J. Epp, "The Significance of the Papyri for Determining the Nature of the New Testament Text in the Second Century: A Dynamic View of Textual Transmission," in *Studies in the Theory and Method of New Testament Textual Criticism*, ed. Eldon J. Epp and Gordon D. Fee (Grand Rapids, Mich.: Eerdmans, 1993), p. 287. For a more extensive treatment on this topic by Epp, see "New Testament Papyrus Manuscripts and Letter Carrying in Greco-Roman Times," in *The Future of Early Christianity*, ed. Birger Pearson (Minneapolis: Fortress, 1991), pp. 35-56.

[48]This theory of local texts was pioneered by B. H. Streeter in his *The Four Gospels: A Study of Origins* (London: Macmillan, 1961). For a brief but current discussion of "text-types" see Michael W. Holmes, "Textual Criticism," in *NTCI*, p. 128, n. 22; Metzger, *Text of the New Testament*, 287-295. Epp prefers the term "textual group" or "textual cluster" (*Studies in the Theory and Method*, p. 284).

[49]Aland and Aland, *Text of the New Testament*, p. 66; Bruce, *Canon of Scripture*, pp. 203-5. For a brief critique of the Caesarean text see Holmes, "Textual Criticism," p. 128, n. 22.

[50]Aland and Aland, *Text of the New Testament*, p. 64. For additional valuable insights on this aspect of history cf. Edgar Goodspeed, *The Formation of the New Testament*, 2d ed. (Chicago: University of Chicago Press, 1927); R. M. Grant, *The Formation of the New Testament* (London: Hutchinson, 1965); J. N. Birdsall, "The New Testament Text," *CHB*, 1:357-60.

[51]See Lee M. McDonald, "The Burning of Sacred Books," in his *The Formation of the Christian Biblical Canon* (Nashville: Abingdon, 1988), pp. 106-10.

[52]Metzger, *Text of the New Testament*, p. 170.

[53]Aland and Aland, *Text of the New Testament*, p. 70.

[54]Metzger, *Text of the New Testament*, p. 103.

[55]Many well-meaning Christians seek to defend this text on dogmatic grounds, arguing that the "Majority Text" is more theologically sound, that it alone is tied to verbal inspiration and that we should not seek to abandon something God has so wonderfully preserved all these centuries. Thus even the New King James Version of 1980 continues to follow this text. A defense of the Byzantine text can be found in the following: David Otis Fuller, *Which Bible?* 5th ed. (Grand Rapids, Mich.: Grand Rapids International, 1975); Zane Hodges, "Modern Textual Criticism and the Majority Text: A Response," *JETS* 21 (1978): 143-55; Wilbur Pickering, *The Identity of the New Testament* (Nashville: Thomas Nelson, 1977); Zane Hodges and Arthur Farstad, *Greek New Testament According to the Majority Text*, 2d ed. (Nashville: Broadman, 1982); M. A. Robinson and W. G. Pierpont, *The New Testament in the Original Greek According to the Byzantine/Majority Textform* (Atlanta: Original Word, 1991); D. B. Wallace, "Inspiration, Preservation, and New Testament Textual Criticism," *Grace Theological Journal* 12, no. 1 (1991): 21-50. Most of these contemporary scholars build upon the earlier works of F. H. A. Scrivener, J. W. Burgon and Edward Miller. Don Carson has clearly presented and convincingly destroyed the arguments of these authors in his *The King James Version Debate* (Grand Rapids, Mich.: Baker, 1979). For additional critiques, see Holmes, "Textual Criticism," p. 132, n. 55; Metzger, *Text of the New Testament*, pp. 283-84; Gordon D. Fee, "The Majority Text and the Original Text of the

New Testament," in *Studies in the Theory and Method of New Testament Textual Criticism*, ed. Eldon J. Epp and Gordon D. Fee (Grand Rapids, Mich.: Eerdmans, 1993), pp. 183-208.

[56]O. C. Edwards, *How Holy Writ Was Written* (Nashville: Abingdon, 1989), p. 13.

[57]George E. Ladd, *New Testament Criticism* (Grand Rapids, Mich.: Eerdmans, 1967), p. 12. This is a helpful book for Christians wanting to understand the nature and purpose of biblical criticism.

[58]Joseph Kelly, *Why Is There a New Testament?* (Wilmington, Del.: Michael Glazier, 1986), p. 124. For other examples of secular literature that has not survived, see F. F. Bruce, *The New Testament Documents: Are They Reliable?* (Grand Rapids, Mich.: Eerdmans, 1978), pp. 16-17.

Part VII: Textual Variants and the Practice of Textual Criticism

[1]Since this is not a textbook on textual criticism, I recommend that students who desire a deeper understanding of this discipline consult the standard monographs by such authors as Kurt and Barbara Aland, J. Harold Greenlee, Jack Finegan and Bruce M. Metzger, as well as Eldon J. Epp and Gordon D. Fee, eds., *Studies in the Theory and Method of New Testament Textual Criticism* (Grand Rapids, Mich.: Eerdmans, 1992); David Alan Black, *New Testament Textual Criticism* (Grand Rapids, Mich.: Baker, 1994); Michael W. Holmes, "Textual Criticism," in *DPL*, pp. 927-32; Michael W. Holmes, "Textual Criticism," in *NTCI*, pp. 101-34; Clayton Harrop, *History of the New Testament in Plain Language* (Waco, Tex.: Word, 1984).

[2]Bruce M. Metzger, *The Text of the New Testament*, 2d ed. (Oxford: Oxford University Press, 1968), p. 194. For more detail and illustrations I recommend pp. 186-206 in that work, and also J. Harold Greenlee, *Introduction to New Testament Textual Criticism* (Grand Rapids, Mich.: Eerdmans, 1964), pp. 63-68; P. M. Head, "Observations on Early Papyri of the Synoptic Gospels, Especially on the 'Scribal Habits,' " *Biblica* 71, no. 2 (1990): 240-47.

[3]Cf. Kurt Aland and Barbara Aland, *The Text of the New Testament*, 2d ed. (Grand Rapids, Mich.: Eerdmans, 1989), pp. 284-85.

[4]For other examples, cf. Metzger, *Text of the New Testament*, pp. 189-90.

[5]Many readers of the *Reader's Digest* enjoy the "Pardon, Your Slip Is Showing" section because of the humorous errors in writing or printing that are recorded. Two of them in the January 1992 issue were particularly amusing and illustrate how easy it is for mistakes to slip into a text. From a Sarasota, Florida, church bulletin: "Students will study Matthew 14:22-23, 'Jesus walks on Walter.'" And from a Lewiston, Idaho, church bulletin: "We need models for our 'Satan and Lace Wedding Party' " (p. 118).

[6]Metzger, *Text of the New Testament*, p. 194.

[7]Ibid., p. 195.

[8]Ibid., p. 195, n. 3. For examples of intentional changes in contemporary English fairy tales, nursery rhymes and hymnody, see Greenlee, *Introduction to New Testament Textual Criticism*, p. 68, n. 5.

[9]Even in quoting Metzger earlier it was tempting to change his spelling of *judgement* to the more familiar *judgment*. This sort of problem arises often in differences of spelling between North America and Great Britain. For example, is it *Saviour* or *Savior*?

[10]Aland and Aland, *Text of the New Testament*, p. 285.

[11]Metzger, *Text of the New Testament*, pp. 198-99. Metzger also discusses attempts to "embroider" or "adorn" the text. See also Kurt Aland, "Glosse, Interpolation, Redak-

tion und Komposition in der Sicht der neutestamentlichen Textkritik," *Studien zur Überlieferung des neuen Testaments und seines Textes,* Arbeiten zur neutestamentlichen Textforschung 2 (Berlin: de Gruyter, 1967).

[12]Bruce M. Metzger, *A Textual Commentary on the Greek New Testament* (New York: United Bible Societies, 1971), p. 17.

[13]Metzger, *Text of the New Testament,* p. 201. He also mentions how difficult it is to assess "deliberate alterations made in the interests of doctrine."

[14]For the fascinating but disturbing story of how this passage was included in Erasmus's text and hence in the Textus Receptus on which the KJV is based, see ibid., pp. 100-103.

[15]Ibid., p. 102.

[16]F. F. Bruce's *The New Testament Documents: Are They Reliable?* (Grand Rapids, Mich.: Eerdmans, 1978) is a helpful book on this issue.

[17]Metzger, *Text of the New Testament,* p. 206.

[18]Greenlee, *Introduction to New Testament Textual Criticism,* p. 68. J. N. Birdsall admits that although many variants reflect this development, "in other instances we see clear traces of the suppression of an original reading which appeared to support heterodoxy" ("The New Testament Text," *CHB,* 1:375).

[19]Metzger, *Text of the New Testament,* p. 201.

[20]J. Harold Greenlee, *Scribes, Scrolls and Scripture* (Grand Rapids, Mich.: Eerdmans), p. 71.

[21]Greenlee, *Introduction to New Testament Criticism,* p. 68.

[22]Metzger, *Text of the New Testament,* pp. 211-12.

[23]Holmes, "Textual Criticism," in *DPL,* p. 929.

[24]Metzger, *Text of the New Testament,* pp. 209-211. See also "Twelve Basic Rules of Textual Criticism" in Aland and Aland, *Text of the New Testament,* pp. 280-82, and Holmes, "Textual Criticism," in *NTCI,* pp. 99-134.

[25]A number of the criteria mentioned above appeal to other disciplines of New Testament study to complement the work of the text critic. Students who are able to familiarize themselves with such information will gain a new appreciation for the text and will be able to assist others in the search for truth. For further confirmation of this observation consult books like Gordon Fee, *New Testament Exegesis,* rev. ed. (Louisville, Ky.: Westminster/John Knox, 1993); John Hayes and Carl Holladay, *Biblical Exegesis,* rev. ed. (Atlanta: John Knox, 1987); Werner Stenger, *New Testament Exegesis* (Grand Rapids, Mich.: Eerdmans, 1993), and George E. Ladd, *New Testament Criticism* (Grand Rapids, Mich.: Eerdmans, 1967).

[26]Metzger, *Textual Commentary on the Greek New Testament,* p. 619.

Selected Bibliography

Achtemeier, Paul. *The Inspiration of Scripture: Problems and Proposals*. Philadelphia: Westminster, 1980.

_____. *"Omne verbum sonat:* The New Testament and the Oral Environment of Late Western Antiquity." *JBL* 109, no. 1 (1990): 3-27.

Aland, Kurt, and Barbara Aland. *The Problem of the New Testament Canon*. Oxford: Mowbray, 1962.

_____. *The Text of the New Testament*. 2d ed. Grand Rapids, Mich.: Eerdmans, 1989.

Aune, David E. "The Gospels: Biography or Theology?" *BibRev* 6, no. 1 (1990): 14-21.

_____. *Greco-Roman Literature and the New Testament: Selected Forms and Genres*. SBL Sources for Biblical Study 21. Atlanta: Scholars Press, 1988.

_____. *The New Testament in Its Literary Environment*. Philadelphia: Westminster, 1989.

Bahnsen, G. L. "Autographs, Amanuenses and Restricted Inspiration." *EvQ* 45 (1973): 100-110.

Bahr, Gordon J. "Paul and Letter Writing in the First Century." *CBQ* 28 (1966): 465-77.

_____. "The Subscriptions in the Pauline Letters." *JBL* 87 (1968): 27-41.

Barclay, William. *The Making of the Bible*. Nashville, Tenn.: Abingdon, 1961.

Barrett, C. K. *New Testament Background: Selected Documents*. Rev. ed. San Francisco: Harper, 1989.

Bauckham, Richard J. "Pseudo-Apostolic Letters." *JBL* 3 (1988): 469-94.

Baxter, M. *The Formation of the Christian Scriptures*. Philadelphia: Westminster, 1988.

Beare, F. W. "Canon of the New Testament." In *Interpreter's Dictionary of the Bible*, edited by George A. Buttrick, 1:520-32. Nashville, Tenn.: Abingdon, 1962.

Beasley-Murray, George R. *John*. WBC 36. Waco, Tex.: Word, 1987.

Beck, Brian E. *Reading the New Testament Today*. Atlanta: John Knox, 1978.

Beckwith, R. *The Old Testament Canon of the New Testament Church and Its Background in Early Judaism*. Grand Rapids, Mich.: Eerdmans, 1985.

Best, E. *Mark: The Gospel as Story*. Edinburgh: T & T Clark, 1983.

Birdsall, J. N. "The New Testament Text." In *The Cambridge History of the Bible*, edited by P. R. Ackroyd and C. F. Evans, 1:308-77. Cambridge: Cambridge University Press, 1970.

Black, David Alan, ed. *Scribes and Scripture: New Testament Essays in Honor of J. Harold Greenlee*. Winona Lake, Ind.: Eisenbrauns, 1991.

Bock, Darrell L. "Form Criticism." In *New Testament Criticism and Interpretation*, edited by David A. Black and David S. Dockery, pp. 174-96. Grand Rapids, Mich.: Zondervan, 1991.

Brown, Raymond E. *The Community of the Beloved Disciple*. New York: Paulist, 1979.

_____. *The Gospel According to John*. Anchor Bible 29 and 29A. New York: Doubleday, 1966, 1970.

Brown, Schuyler. *The Origins of Christianity*. Rev. ed. Oxford: Oxford University Press, 1993.

Bruce, F. F. *The Books and the Parchments*. Westwood, N.J.: Revell, 1950.

———. *The Canon of Scripture*. Downers Grove, Ill.: InterVarsity Press, 1988.

———. "New Light on the Origins of the New Testament Canon." In *New Dimensions in New Testament Study*, edited by Richard N. Longenecker and Merrill C. Tenney, pp. 3-18. Grand Rapids, Mich.: Zondervan, 1974.

———. "Some Thoughts on the Beginning of the New Testament Canon." *BJRL* 65 (1983): 37-60.

Buck, C. H. "The Early Order of the Pauline Corpus." *JBL* 68 (1949): 351-57.

Bultmann, Rudolf. *The History of the Synoptic Tradition*. Oxford: Blackwell, 1963.

Campenhausen, H. von. *The Formation of the Christian Bible*. Philadelphia: Fortress, 1972.

Cannon, George E. *The Use of Traditional Material in Colossians*. Macon, Ga.: Mercer, 1983.

Carson, D. A., Douglas J. Moo and Leon Morris. *An Introduction to the New Testament*. Grand Rapids, Mich.: Zondervan, 1992.

Charlesworth, James. *The Old Testament Pseudepigrapha*. 2 vols. New York: Doubleday, 1983.

Childs, B. S. *The New Testament as Canon: An Introduction*. Philadelphia: Fortress, 1985.

Clabeaux, John J. *A Lost Edition of the Letters of Paul: A Reassessment of the Text of the Pauline Corpus Attested by Marcion*. CBQMS 21. Washington, D.C.: Catholic Biblical Association of America, 1989.

Collins, Raymond F. *The Birth of the New Testament: The Origin and Development of the First Christian Generation*. New York: Crossroads, 1993.

———. *Introduction to the New Testament*. Garden City, N.Y.: Doubleday, 1983.

———. *Letters That Paul Did Not Write*. Wilmington, Del.: Glazier, 1988.

Conzelmann, H., and A. Lindemann. *Interpreting the New Testament*. Peabody, Mass.: Hendrickson, 1985.

Culpepper, R. Alan. *The Johannine School: An Evaluation of the Johannine-School Hypothesis Based on an Investigation of the Nature of Ancient Schools*. SBLDS 26. Missoula, Mont.: Scholars Press, 1975.

Dahl, Nils. "Acts and the Pauline Letter Corpus." In *Studies in Luke-Acts*, edited by L. Keck and J. L. Martyn, pp. 279-87. Nashville, Tenn.: Abingdon, 1966.

———. "The Particularity of the Pauline Epistles as a Problem in the Ancient Church." In *Neotestamentica et Patristica: Eine Freundesgabe Herrn Prof. Dr. Oscar Cullmann zu seinem 60. Geburtstag*, pp. 261-71. NovTSup 6. Leiden: Brill, 1962.

Davids, Peter. *The First Epistle of Peter*. New International Commentary on the New Testament. Grand Rapids, Mich.: Eerdmans, 1990.

———. *James*. NIBC. Peabody, Mass.: Hendrickson, 1989.

Dibelius, Martin. *From Tradition to Gospel*. New York: Scribners, 1934.

Dihle, Albrecht. "The Gospels and Greek Biography." In *The Gospel and the Gospels*, edited by Peter Stuhlmacher, pp. 361-85. Grand Rapids, Mich.: Eerdmans, 1991.

Dodd, C. H. *The Bible Today*. Cambridge: Cambridge University Press, 1962.

Doty, William G. *Letters in Primitive Christianity*. Philadelphia: Fortress, 1973.

Dunn, J. D. G. *The Living Word*. Philadelphia: Fortress, 1987.

———. *Unity and Diversity in the New Testament*. Philadelphia: Westminster, 1977.

Edwards, O. C. *How Holy Writ Was Written*. Nashville, Tenn.: Abingdon, 1989.

Ellis, E. Earle. "Paul and His Co-workers." *NTS* 17 (1971): 437-52.

_____. "Pseudonymity and Canonicity of New Testament Documents." In *Worship, Theology and Ministry in the Early Church*, edited by M. J. Wilkins and T. Paige, pp. 212-24. Sheffield, U.K.: JSOT Press, 1992.

Epp, Eldon J., and Gordon D. Fee. "New Testament Papyrus Manuscripts and Letter Carrying in Greco-Roman Times." In *The Future of Early Christianity*, edited by Birger Pearson, pp. 35-56. Minneapolis: Fortress, 1991.

_____, eds. *Studies in the Theory and Method of New Testament Textual Criticism.* Grand Rapids, Mich.: Eerdmans, 1993.

Evans, C. F. "The New Testament in the Making." In *Cambridge History of the Bible*, edited by P. R. Ackroyd and C. F. Evans, 1:232-84. Cambridge: Cambridge University Press, 1970.

Ewert, D. *From Ancient Tablets to Modern Translations: A General Introduction to the Bible.* Grand Rapids, Mich.: Zondervan, 1983.

Farmer, W. R. *Jesus and the Gospel: Tradition, Scripture and Canon.* Philadelphia: Fortress, 1982.

Farmer, W. R., and D. M. Farkasfalvy. *The Formation of the New Testament Canon: An Ecumenical Approach.* Edited by H. W. Attridge. New York: Paulist, 1983.

Fee, Gordon D. *The Pastoral Epistles.* NIBC. Peabody, Mass.: Hendrickson, 1988.

Fenton, J. C. "Pseudonymity in the New Testament." *Theology* 58 (1955): 51-56.

Finegan, Jack. *Encountering New Testament Manuscripts.* Grand Rapids, Mich.: Eerdmans, 1974.

_____. "The Original Form of the Pauline Collections." *HTR* 49 (1956): 85-104.

Gabel, J. B., and C. B. Wheeler. *The Bible as Literature: An Introduction.* Oxford: Oxford University Press, 1986.

Gamble, Harry. "The Canon of the New Testament." In *The New Testament and Its Modern Interpreters*, edited by Eldon J. Epp and G. W. MacRae, pp. 201-43. Atlanta: Scholars Press, 1989.

_____. *The New Testament Canon.* Philadelphia: Fortress, 1985.

_____. "The Redaction of the Pauline Letters and the Formation of the Pauline Corpus." *JBL* 94 (1975): 403-18.

Goodspeed, E. J. *Christianity Goes to Press.* New York: Macmillan, 1940.

_____. *The Formation of the New Testament.* 2d ed. Chicago: University of Chicago Press, 1927.

Graham, W. A. *Beyond the Written Word: Oral Aspects of Scripture in the History of Religion.* Cambridge: Cambridge University Press, 1987.

Grant, R. M. "The Canon of the New Testament." In *Cambridge History of the Bible*, edited by P. R. Ackroyd and C. F. Evans, 1:284-308. Cambridge: Cambridge University Press, 1970.

_____. *The Formation of the New Testament.* London: Hutchinson, 1965.

_____. "Literary Criticism and the New Testament Canon." *JSNT* 16 (1982): 24-44.

Greenlee, J. Harold. *Introduction to New Testament Textual Criticism.* Grand Rapids, Mich.: Eerdmans, 1964.

_____. *Scribes, Scrolls and Scripture.* Grand Rapids, Mich.: Eerdmans, 1985.

Guelich, Robert. "The Gospel Genre." In *The Gospel and the Gospels*, edited by Peter Stuhlmacher, pp. 173-208. Grand Rapids, Mich.: Eerdmans, 1991.

_____. "The Gospels: Portraits of Jesus and His Ministry." *JETS* 24, no. 3 (1981): 117-25.

Gundry, Robert. "Recent Investigations into the Literary Genre 'Gospel.' " In *New Dimensions in New Testament Study*, edited by Richard N. Longenecker and Merrill C. Tenney, pp. 97-114. Grand Rapids, Mich.: Zondervan, 1974.

Guthrie, Donald. *New Testament Introduction*. Rev. ed. Downers Grove, Ill: InterVarsity Press, 1990.

Harrop, C. *History of the New Testament in Plain Language*. Waco, Tex.: Word, 1984.

Hartman, L. "On Reading Others' Letters." *HTR* 79, nos. 1-3 (1986): 137-46.

Hoffman, T. A. "Inspiration, Normativeness, Canonicity and the Unique Sacred Character of the Bible." *CBQ* 44, no. 3 (1982): 447-69.

Hunter, A. M. *Paul and His Predecessors*. London: SCM Press, 1961.

Johnson, Luke T. *The Writings of the New Testament*. Philadelphia: Fortress, 1986.

Katz, P. "The Early Christian Use of Codices Instead of Rolls." *JTS* 44 (1945): 63-65.

Kelber, Werner H. *The Oral and Written Gospel*. Philadelphia: Fortress, 1983.

Kelly, J. F. *Why Is There a New Testament?* Wilmington, Del.: Glazier, 1986.

Knox, John. *Marcion and the New Testament*. Chicago: Chicago University Press, 1942.

_____. *Philemon Among the Letters of Paul*. New York: Abingdon, 1959.

Koch, K. "Pseudonymous Writing." *IDBSup*, pp. 712-14. Nashville, Tenn.: Abingdon, 1982.

Koester, Helmut. *Ancient Christian Gospels*. Philadelphia: Trinity Press, 1990.

_____. *Introduction to the New Testament*. 2 vols. Philadelphia: Fortress, 1980.

Kümmel, W. G. *Introduction to the New Testament*. Rev. ed. Nashville, Tenn.: Abingdon, 1973.

Ladd, George E. *The New Testament and Criticism*. Grand Rapids, Mich.: Eerdmans, 1967.

Lohse, E. *The Formation of the New Testament*. Nashville, Tenn.: Abingdon, 1972.

Longenecker, Richard N. "Ancient Amanuenses and the Pauline Epistles." In *New Dimensions in New Testament Studies*, edited by Richard N. Longenecker and Merrill C. Tenney, pp. 281-97. Grand Rapids, Mich.: Eerdmans, 1974.

McDonald, Lee M. *The Formation of the Christian Biblical Canon*. Nashville, Tenn.: Abingdon, 1988.

McKnight, Edgar V. *What Is Form Criticism?* Philadelphia: Fortress, 1969.

Martin, Ralph P. *New Testament Foundations*. 2 vols. Grand Rapids, Mich.: Eerdmans, 1975-1986.

Meade, David G. *Pseudonymity and Canon: An Investigation into the Relationship of Authorship and Authority in Jewish and Earliest Christian Tradition*. Tübingen: J. C. B. Mohr/Paul Siebeck, 1986.

Metzger, Bruce M. *The Canon of the New Testament: Its Origin, Development and Significance*. Oxford: Oxford University Press, 1987.

_____. *The Early Versions of the New Testament*. Oxford: Clarendon Press, 1977.

_____. *Manuscripts of the Greek Bible*. Oxford: Oxford University Press, 1981.

_____. *The Text of the New Testament*. 2d ed. Oxford: Oxford University Press, 1968.

Meye, Robert P. "Canon of the New Testament." In *International Standard Bible Encyclopedia*, edited by Geoffrey Bromiley, 1:601-6. Rev. ed. Grand Rapids, Mich.: Eerdmans, 1988.

Mitton, C. Leslie. *The Formation of the Pauline Corpus of Letters*. London: Epworth, 1955.

Moule, C. F. D. *The Birth of the New Testament*. 3d rev. ed. San Francisco: Harper, 1981.

Mowry, Lucetta. "The Early Circulation of Paul's Letters." *JBL* 63 (1944): 73-86.

Ong, W. J. *Orality and Literacy: The Technologizing of the Word*. London: Methuen, 1982.

Orchard, Bernard, and Harold Riley. *The Order of the Synoptics: Why Three Synoptic Gospels?* Macon, Ga.: Mercer University Press, 1987.

Patzia, Arthur G. "The Deutero-Pauline Hypothesis: An Attempt at Clarification." *EvQ* 52, no. 1 (1980): 27-42.

Perrin, Norman. *What Is Redaction Criticism?* Philadelphia: Fortress, 1969.

Puskas, Charles B. *An Introduction to the New Testament.* Peabody, Mass.: Hendrickson, 1989.

Richards, E. Randolph. *The Secretary in the Letters of Paul.* Tübingen: J. C. B. Mohr, 1991.

Rist, M. "Pseudepigraphy and the Early Christians." In *Studies in New Testament and Early Christian Literature,* edited by David E. Aune, pp. 3-24. Leiden: Brill, 1972.

Roberts, C. H. "Books in the Graeco-Roman World and in the New Testament." In *Cambridge History of the Bible,* edited by P. R. Ackroyd and C. F. Evans, 1:48-66. Cambridge: Cambridge University Press, 1970.

Roetzel, Calvin. *The Letters of Paul.* 3d ed. Louisville, Ky.: Westminster/John Knox, 1991.

Sanders, E. P., and Margaret Davies. *Studying the Synoptic Gospels.* Philadelphia: Trinity Press, 1989.

Sanders, J. A. *From Sacred Story to Sacred Text: Canon as Paradigm.* Philadelphia: Fortress, 1987.

Schmithals, Walter. *Paul and the Gnostics.* Nashville, Tenn.: Abingdon, 1972.

Schneemelcher, W. "On the History of the New Testament Canon." In *New Testament Apocrypha,* edited by E. Hennecke and W. Schneemelcher, 1:15-34. 2d ed. Louisville, Ky.: Westminster/John Knox, 1990.

Schubert, Paul. *The Form and Function of the Pauline Thanksgivings.* Berlin: Töpelmann, 1939.

Selby, Donald J., and James King West. *Introduction to the Bible.* New York: Macmillan, 1971.

Skeat, T. C. "Early Christian Book-Production: Papyri and Manuscripts." In *Cambridge History of the Bible,* edited by P. R. Ackroyd and C. F. Evans, 2:54-79. Cambridge: Cambridge University Press, 1969.

Stein, Robert. *The Method and Message of Jesus' Teaching.* Philadelphia: Westminster, 1978.

Stendahl, Krister. *The School of St. Matthew.* 2d ed. Philadelphia: Fortress, 1968.

Stirewalt, M. L. "Paul's Evaluation of Letter-Writing." In *Search the Scriptures,* edited by J. M. Myers, pp. 179-96. Leiden: Brill, 1969.

Stowers, Stanley K. *Letter Writing in Greco-Roman Antiquity.* Philadelphia: Westminster, 1986.

Streeter, B. H. *The Four Gospels.* London: Macmillan, 1961.

Sundberg, A. C. "Canon Muratori: A Fourth-Century List." *HTR* 66 (1973): 1-41.

Talbert, Charles H. *What Is a Gospel? The Genre of the Canonical Gospels.* Philadelphia: Fortress, 1977.

Taylor, Vincent. *The Formation of the Gospel Tradition.* London: Macmillan, 1933.

Trobisch, David. *Die Entstehung der Paulusbriefsammlung.* Göttingen, Germany: Vandenhoeck & Ruprecht, 1989.

_____. *Paul's Letter Collection.* Minneapolis: Fortress, 1994.

Twilley, L. D. *The Origin and Transmission of the New Testament.* Grand Rapids, Mich.: Eerdmans, 1957.

Votaw, Clyde. *The Gospels and Contemporary Biographies in the Greco-Roman World.* Philadelphia: Fortress, 1970.

Watson, Duane F. "The New Testament and Greco-Roman Rhetoric: A Bibliographical Update." *JETS* 33, no. 4 (1990): 513-24.

White, John L. *Form and Function of the Body of the Greek Letter.* SBLDS 2. Missoula, Mont.: Scholars Press, 1972.

_____. *Light from Ancient Letters.* Philadelphia: Fortress, 1986.

_____. "Saint Paul and the Apostolic Letter Tradition." *CBQ* 45, no. 3 (1983): 433-44.

Wright, N. T. *The New Testament and the People of God.* Minneapolis: Fortress, 1992.

Zuntz, G. *The Text of the Epistles: A Disquisition upon the Corpus Paulinum.* London: Oxford University Press, 1953.

Index of Subjects